SACRÉ BLEU

SACRÉ BLEU

FROM ZIDANE TO MBAPPÉ – A FOOTBALL JOURNEY

MATTHEW SPIRO

Biteback Publishing

First published in Great Britain in 2020 by
Biteback Publishing Ltd
Westminster Tower
3 Albert Embankment
London SE1 7SP
Copyright © Matthew Spiro 2020

ISBN 978-178590-554-4

10 9 8 7 6 5 4 3 2 1

A CIP catalogue record for this book is available from the British Library.

Set in Minion Pro

Printed and bound in Great Britain by
CPI Group (UK) Ltd, Croydon CR0 4YY

To Éva, Lucie and Alice

CONTENTS

FOREWORD BY ARSÈNE WENGER

For French people, watching the national team has been an emotional experience in recent years. The player strike at the World Cup in 2010 was a terrible low. You could say that Knysna was like our Waterloo. It was a sad period for everybody who loves French football. But it was also an opportunity to make a fresh start, and I believe we learned from it. We thought: 'This cannot be allowed to happen again. The players have to behave better.' It proved to be a good learning curve for us.

In 2018, I always thought France would win the World Cup. Why? Because physically the team was fantastic, and they had a good balance between physical power and technical ability. The longer the competition went on, the more this physical power took over. Even within the matches, the longer they lasted, the more they were able to dominate their opponent physically. It is simple, if I play against Kylian Mbappé and in the first twenty minutes he runs at me at 90 per cent, I have to go at 110 per cent to stay with him. If after an hour he goes at 100 per cent, then I can no longer stay with him!

Mbappé is of course very important. It has felt like God had sent us this boy to show us how to play – and how to behave. He typifies what French football is about. He is a boy who has received a very good education. His parents are sports people – his mother was an international handball player and his father was a football coach – and they clearly educated him well. But he also has something inside him, something he was born with. We have seen great young football players before, but when you hear Mbappé doing his first interview at eighteen, and you feel like he has been doing that his whole life, you realise he is different. This is not something that he learned. He was born to do this. Of course he has the footballing talent, but what is needed today to be a star is the ability to communicate with the rest of the world from one single interview. And he has that.

What we are currently seeing is that through immigration France has a huge opportunity. The absolute heart of the national team is made up of players from immigrant backgrounds who have been educated in the French game. I'm talking about Paul Pogba, N'Golo Kanté, Blaise Matuidi, Kylian Mbappé and Samuel Umtiti. This isn't new. Historically the successful national teams have always had strong links to immigration, from Raymond Kopa, Michel Platini and Zinédine Zidane, to Mbappé and Pogba. So of course we are lucky to have so many fine players with origins from big football countries like Senegal, Côte d'Ivoire, Mali, Cameroon, Algeria, Morocco and Tunisia.

In France, young players often learn their skills by playing football against each other in their home suburbs. I believe 60 per cent of professional players in France come from the Paris suburbs. That is incredible! I remember when I was Monaco coach, I asked Lilian Thuram to explain to me what his childhood was like. He said that after school, it was football, football and more football. He played together with people from all sorts of different backgrounds. It was tough and there were many good players. You have to be strong to survive in those conditions because there is a real competitive edge. You want to prove you are the best, and you're playing with kids who are ready to fight to show you that you're not. So the guys who come out from there, they are ready for the fight. I believe the football education they receive gives them great mental strength.

As a parent, when you educate your children you think you absolutely want to protect them from danger. But actually the best thing to do is to get them to fight against disappointment and adversity. This is the best preparation for life. Their hunger to achieve will be high and they will have developed their capacity to fight. That's not something you get taught in the best schools.

For many years, France has been good at developing young players. When I was the Arsenal manager, I knew that if I took a player from France he would be at the physical level required to perform immediately. France has been ahead of the game in this respect. The other advantage that France coach Didier Deschamps has is that French players get to play from a young age in Ligue 1. They play, then as soon as they do well they leave for other leagues. When they leave Ligue 1 they are well prepared. This then opens the door for somebody else and that's why we have so many good young players.

The big problem in England is in the category of players aged between seventeen and twenty-one. In England, they scout well and they coach well. But the integration of young players into the first team is often not successful because the competition for places is too high, the level of performance in the league is too high and the pressure put on the managers to succeed is too high. The last part of a player's education is gained in competition. In France, unlike in England, the players get the opportunity to compete.

Looking forward, I think this generation of French players has the chance to create a legacy. Usually when a team wins a World Cup, it is the end of an era. But in 2018 the France team was full of young players. It was the start of an era. When it comes to players, we are spoilt for choice. Look at the last World Cup; Anthony Martial didn't make the cut. He plays for Manchester United, which is not a small club. Alexandre Lacazette didn't make it. Basically they had too much choice! It's just a matter of finding the right balance because we have no problem with the quality of the individual players. If they find the right balance, and if the team is efficient, they can carry on winning major tournaments.

CHAPTER 1

MBAPPÉ, LE SAUVEUR

30 JUNE 2018

The air in the Kazan Arena feels heavy. Even the 23,000 bois-
terous Argentina supporters, beautifully decked out in their
Albiceleste colours, have somehow been calmed by the slow and
tentative start to this round of sixteen tie. The first glamour
match-up of the World Cup has been suitably hyped, but amid
the heat and humidity of this stifling afternoon, the reality of
France's hopes looks to be hitting home.

The French fans I had met in Kazan's vibrant city centre that
morning seemed largely resigned. Most complained about
Didier Deschamps's negative tactics and team selections, and
some had already booked flights home for the next day. Despite
boasting several of the most exciting attacking individuals on
the planet, *Les Bleus* had limped unconvincingly through the
group stage. Paul Pogba's deflected effort accounted for Australia, the team clung on grimly to a 1–0 lead against Peru and then
featured in one of the dullest games in the history of the World
Cup against Denmark.

As 7,000 France fans roundly booed their players off after
that stultifying goalless stalemate at Moscow's Luzhniki Stadium, it felt certain that the end was nigh for Deschamps. Indeed,
many in France were already looking forward to a brighter

future under the nation's favourite son Zinédine Zidane. The previous month, Zizou had surprised everybody by standing down as Real Madrid manager after overseeing a third consecutive Champions League win, and he was now odds-on for the France job.

Yet Argentina were not the force they used to be either. Yes, Lionel Messi had provided a timely reminder of his brilliance against Nigeria to edge the two-time world champions through their group, but this was an ageing team that looked incapable of executing the high-energy pressing game that their coach Jorge Sampaoli demanded. The South Americans had been held to a draw by Iceland and were trounced 3–0 by Croatia. Few expected them to repeat the feat of four years previously when they reached the final in Rio de Janeiro.

The opening exchanges in the match were in keeping with a tournament that is struggling to break free of an omnipresent political cloud. Vladimir Putin's Russia was a highly controversial choice to host the world's biggest, most watched and cherished sporting event, and the endless debates over security, engineered elections, racism, homophobia and human rights overshadowed the actual football for much of the group stage.

But then a nineteen-year-old changed the entire dynamic of the game, and ultimately the World Cup as a whole. With one devastating, insouciant, lung-bursting run, Kylian Mbappé captured the imagination of millions around the world and reminded everybody why football is such a wonderful sport.

Mbappé had only shown flashes of his brilliance in the group stage – although by scoring a tap-in against Peru he had become the youngest Frenchman ever to find the net at a World Cup. This was the knockout stage, though. This was Argentina and Messi. This was the kind of stage that Mbappé had been dreaming of shining on throughout his childhood.

In the ninth minute, the teenager showed that he was in the mood by surging past two defenders and winning a free-kick on the edge of the box that Antoine Griezmann duly curled against the crossbar. But nobody was ready for Mbappé's next trick just moments later.

When Éver Banega mis-controlled the ball deep inside the French half Mbappé pounced. He had one thing on his sharp mind. An initial burst took France's number ten clear of Nicolás Tagliafico and streaming over the halfway line. Javier Mascherano, a born fighter and veteran of four World Cups, barely even bothered trying to get back. He knew his tiring 34-year-old legs were not up to the task. As Mbappé eased through the gears, hitting a top speed of 37km/h – only fractionally slower than Usain Bolt in full flow – Argentina's last man Marcos Rojo looked vulnerable. Mbappé dropped a shoulder, exploded past Rojo on the outside, and in a moment of sheer panic, the defender thrust out his arm. Mbappé fell. Penalty to France.

Those few seconds were exhilarating. During my years reporting on *Les Bleus*, I have been fortunate to witness many extraordinary moments: Zidane's late heroics against England in 2004 provided extraordinary drama, Thierry Henry eliminating Brazil in 2006 felt like a monumental moment, and the scenes in Marseille when Antoine Griezmann stunned Germany in 2016 were unforgettable. Yet this was different. As the French journalists around me in the press stand jumped excitedly from their seats, it felt like we had just witnessed a seminal moment. Perhaps this was the start of a new era.

Mbappé's brilliance did not only thrill the French. Football lovers around the world were astounded by the sight of this bold, athletic, cool teenager from the Paris suburbs tearing through the heart of the Argentina team. 'When you see something like that, it doesn't matter if you're watching in the stadium, in your living room or in a bar on the other side of the world, you just want to scream out loud,' says UK football writer Amy Lawrence. 'You knew you'd just witnessed something important. It felt a bit like seeing the Sex Pistols or Rolling Stones in concert for the first time. You sensed you were watching something special, something new.'

'Mbappé's run felt like something from another time, another dimension,' explains a wide-eyed Vikash Dhorasoo. 'We'd never seen anything like it before. For a nineteen-year-old boy to do that, against Argentina, with Messi looking on, and to do it with this incredible coldness.' The former France midfielder, who played for Lyon, AC Milan and Paris Saint-Germain, pauses and puffs out his cheeks as he tries to find the words to do the moment justice. 'Personally, I found it almost troubling,' he says. 'I remember thinking: "This guy is not like the rest of us." It was scary.'

France winger Florian Thauvin was a substitute that day and had one of the best views. 'On the bench, we were in shock,' he stated after the match. 'We couldn't believe what he'd done. He ran so fast I wondered if he'd hopped onto a scooter or something.'

Thauvin had good reason to be incredulous. The smoothness of Mbappé's movement, the way in which he seemed to glide across the pitch, made the seventy-metre raid appear almost super-human. 'The scariest part,' says France legend Marcel Desailly, 'is that he destroyed Argentina by playing at about 60 per cent of his capacity.' Les Bleus' 1998 World Cup-winning defender was rarely troubled by an opponent during his playing days, but when I ask him if he would have fancied defending against Mbappé, the man known as 'the Rock' hesitates for a second. 'I'm not sure, you know, he's pretty quick.'

Within minutes of Mbappé taking the World Cup stage by storm, the biggest names in football had taken to social media to applaud the youngster. 'Fenomeno,' read the simple tweet from Italy legend Franco Baresi, employing a word reserved usually for ex-Brazil striker Ronaldo. Gary Lineker reacted similarly, tweeting: 'Phenomenal run from Mbappé. Reminds me so much of Brazilian Ronaldo'. Another ex-England striker,

Ian Wright, added perspective: 'A performance like that on world's stage ... At nineteen, I was being rejected by Brighton.'

The penalty Mbappé had earned was converted by Griez-mann, and it ignited the start of one of the most thrilling games the World Cup has ever seen. Mbappé's Paris Saint-Germain teammate Ángel di María levelled with a magnificent long-range strike before Gabriel Mercado diverted Messi's shot into the net to put Sampaoli's side ahead. Fans of *Les Bleus* had experienced their share of heartbreak over the previous fifteen, trophy-less years, and another disappointing exit looked like it was on the cards. However, out of the blue, right-back Benjamin Pavard scored the goal of the tournament, swerving a stunning shot into the top corner with the outside of his right boot to equalise at 2–2. Then Mbappé took matters into his own hands.

On sixty-four minutes, he latched on to a loose ball inside the box, took one touch to control, another to flick it beyond an onrushing defender and a third to rifle home. Three deadly touches in the blink of an eye. Argentina were still catching their breath when, four minutes later, Mbappé roared up the right flank, sprinted onto Olivier Giroud's through-ball, and calmly slotted a first-time shot beyond goalkeeper Franco Armani.

It was breathtaking. Mbappé had become the first teenager to score two goals in a World Cup match since Pelé, and in so doing had put his country on the path to glory. Although Sergio Agüero's late goal set up a grandstand finish, Deschamps's men held on to their 4–3 lead and celebrated as if they had won the World Cup. Indeed, the calmest France player was Mbappé, who seemed to have barely even broken a sweat during the match. As he swapped shirts with Messi near the touchline beneath us, it was hard not to feel the strong sense of symbolism in this act. Messi may well be the greatest player of all time, but he now looks destined to finish his career without winning the biggest prize of all. The Barcelona legend will be thirty-five when the World Cup takes place in Qatar. Mbappé will be twenty-three and by then could well have overtaken Messi at the very top of the pile of the world's best players.

What is clear is that his climb to the summit began in Kazan. 'There was a sense among the players that with Mbappé playing at this level, we could be contenders,' says Vincent Duluc, the chief football writer for *L'Équipe* newspaper. 'He had left everybody open-mouthed. Personally, this was the ninth World Cup I'd covered as a reporter, and I don't recall seeing another teenager make an impact like Mbappé did that day.'

Duluc, it should be said, did not witness Pelé in 1958. However, Arsène Wenger did, and the former Arsenal manager believes there are definite similarities between France's wonderkid and the Brazilian. In the restaurant of the Park Hyatt hotel in central Paris more than a year after that day in Kazan, Wenger's eyes still light up when he thinks back to Mbappé's performance. 'He was untouchable that day and, yes, there was something of Pelé about him,' Wenger states. 'You saw that mix of speed, power and the capacity to analyse the situation very quickly. These are qualities that only great players can combine.

'The difference between football now and then is that the pace of the game today is relentless. But physically Mbappé is a monster. We saw that in the World Cup: the longer the games went on, the more dangerous he became.'

It felt fitting that Pelé himself reacted to Mbappé's heroics by tweeting directly to his heir apparent: 'Congratulations @KMbappe! Two goals in a World Cup so young puts you in great company. Good luck for the rest of the tournament – except against Brazil!' Mbappé was quickly made aware of the tweet, but in keeping with his calm, assured manner, the Frenchman made light of any comparisons. 'It's flattering,' he told journalists before leaving the Kazan Arena. 'But let's put things in context here: Pelé is in a different category entirely!'

Mbappé's brilliance on the pitch is matched by his maturity off it. Indeed, his communication skills are almost as impressive as his capacity to devastate defences. 'That year, we kept having to remind ourselves that he was only nineteen,' Duluc says. 'The way he was playing, the way he was talking, it wasn't easy to believe it. It's like he is ageless.'

Philippe Tournon worked as the France team's head of media for much of the past two decades. Back in 1998, he managed the press conferences for such eminent figures as Deschamps, Desailly and Laurent Blanc. But Tournon insists none of those past greats had the ability to relate to an audience like Mbappé. 'I've never come across a player able to express himself with so much ease at that age,' Tournon told the television channel RMC Sport. 'The way Kylian engages with the press, the way he speaks so naturally, always from the heart, and you never hear a misplaced word or a hint of pretentiousness. It's remarkable and refreshing. I gained real pleasure from listening to him speak.'

•   •   •

For French football, the emergence of this well-spoken, likeable and brilliant black teenager from Bondy – a tough, underprivileged commune north-east of Paris – represented a hugely powerful symbol. This was an individual capable of singlehandedly transforming the image and fortunes of Les Bleus, while at the same time casting a wholly positive light on the country's many stigmatised suburbs.

In France, the national team represents so much more than just football. It is the pride of the nation, the pinnacle of French sport and one of the few remaining spheres where the expression of nationalism is accepted. As Didier Deschamps often states, 'there is nothing else above it'. Crucially, no other public entity in France reflects the country's rich diversity so clearly. The national team, with its mix of cultures, is often alluded to by politicians and media personalities as a mirror for society

– which is fine when things are going well but can create more troubling issues during the darker times.

Since winning the World Cup on home soil with a magnificent, multicultural team in 1998, and clinching the European Championship two years later, *Les Bleus* have stumbled from one crisis to the next and the image of the country's footballers has been dragged through the dirt. Just as Aimé Jacquet's much cherished *black-blanc-beur* (black-white-Arab) team was held up as a beacon for France's multi-ethnic society in the late 1990s, the scandal-filled era that followed was used as a stick with which to beat the nation's immigrant youth. 'A France team that wins is *black-blanc-beur*, and a France team that loses is scum from *les banlieues* [the suburbs],' mused Éric Cantona in the documentary *Les Bleus, une Autre Histoire de France (The Blues, an Alternative History of France)*.

These days, the majority of France's players hail from immigrant backgrounds and many have grown up in the relatively poor, humble world of French suburbia. When violent protests erupted on the outskirts of major cities for three long weeks in November 2005, the temptation to link the unrest with Raymond Domenech's struggling football team became too great for some. The outspoken philosopher Alain Finkielkraut chose this sensitive moment to question the make-up of *Les Bleus*. 'People say that our national team is admired because it is *black-blanc-beur*,' Finkielkraut began. 'In reality, the team is black-black-black and it's the laughing-stock of Europe.'

France's Minister of the Interior at the time, Nicolas Sarkozy, shocked millions – including *Les Bleus* defender Lilian Thuram – by remarking that it was time to 'flush the scum out of our suburbs with a power hose'. Thuram could not contain his fury. 'What does Sarkozy want to clean? Who does he want to flush out?' he raged during a France national team press conference. 'People used to call me scum when I was on the estate, but I wasn't scum. I just wanted to work. The situation makes me sick. Nobody's asking the right questions. Nobody's looking at the real problems.'

Indeed, ever since far-right leader Jean-Marie Le Pen began commenting on *Les Bleus* in the mid-1990s, describing France's increasingly multi-ethnic team as 'artificial' or even 'too black', the footballers have featured regularly on political agendas.

Former President Jacques Chirac gained popularity by associating himself closely with Jacquet's World Cup winners, but then both he and Prime Minister Lionel Jospin suffered in the polls when France's friendly against Algeria in 2001 was abandoned due to a mass pitch invasion by disaffected youths of North African origins.

For *Les Bleus*, the nadir arrived in 2010 when Domenech's players went on strike in the middle of the World Cup in South Africa, refusing to train in a disastrously misguided show of faith for the banished Nicolas Anelka. The Minister for Health and Sports, Roselyne Bachelot, appeared to insinuate that the players' antics reflected life in the suburbs, accusing Patrice Évra and friends of acting like 'immature thugs bullying frightened kids'. Finkielkraut went further, declaring: 'France has been invited to look into a mirror, a terrible mirror. We've gone from the Zidane generation to the scum generation.'

The country had fallen out of love with its football team, and with certain politicians pointing the finger at *les banlieues*, there was a clear racist undertone.

Over the past decade, the controversies surrounding Karim Benzema have only served to fuel the fire of negativity around the French football team. The Real Madrid striker, whose father was born in Algeria, has maintained links to his childhood mates from the Lyon suburbs, some of whom could be described, at best, as shady characters. Those associations have often landed him in hot water. In 2010, Benzema – along with another France player Franck Ribéry – was accused of sleeping with an underage prostitute. He later found himself linked to a scandal that would lead to several years of negative publicity, this time regarding the blackmailing of France teammate Mathieu Valbuena over a sex-tape.

The debate surrounding Benzema's selection became quite literally *une affaire d'état* (a state affair). In the build-up to Euro 2016, the country's Prime Minister Manuel Valls felt compelled to speak out, making it clear he did not want the striker involved. 'A great sportsman must be exemplary and if he isn't then he should have no place in the France team,' Valls declared. At the time the country was reeling from the November 2015 terrorist attacks on Paris and Saint-Denis, Islamophobia was mounting and the climate had become tense. Deschamps was accused of racism when he left Benzema out, yet nobody quite knows if that was truly the France manager's decision or if he was acting on orders from above.

In this context, the impact of Mbappé's rise cannot be reduced merely to his skills with a football. The day after the Argentina game in Kazan, *Le Monde* newspaper was already reflecting on the strong symbolism at play. 'The bad performances, the player strike and the scandals of 2010 now seem a long way away,' wrote the columnist Abdourahman Waberi. 'The critics have been forgotten. The boy from Bondy has well and truly kicked Alain Finkielkraut ... and [National Front leader] Marine Le Pen into the back of the net.'

That Mbappé comes across as such a kind, balanced individual is thanks largely to his parents. Wilfrid, Kylian's father, is a former amateur-level footballer of Cameroonian descent. He was his son's first coach at local club AS Bondy. Kylian's mother Fayza is of Algerian origin and is also from a sporting background having played top-level handball. Both were ever-present during Kylian's upbringing and remain fiercely protective of their boy.

Above all, though, Mbappé is a figure that everybody in France can relate to. 'We won our first World Cup with a *black-blanc-beur* team, but Mbappé seems to represent this diversity all on his own,' claims Duluc. 'He comes from the ninety-third *département* like so many black footballers, so he is recognised in those communities. He speaks well and is the son of middle-class parents so for many he is a little bit white as well. And, of course, his mother is from Algeria, so he ticks all of the boxes. The fact is Kylian Mbappé pleases everybody in France. You could say he is *black-blanc-beur* rolled into one.'

20 OCTOBER 2018

The train ride from Saint-Lazare in central Paris to the suburb of Bondy takes just eighteen minutes. Yet, when you arrive and step out of the station and into the market opposite you feel as if you have been transported a million miles away from the opulent boulevards of France's capital. Stalls selling exotic fruits, spices, mobile phones, roasted chestnuts and second-hand clothes do a roaring trade as emigrants of Maghrebi, West African, Indian, Pakistani and West Indian origins bustle about, joking and negotiating deals.

Surrounded by high-rise concrete towers, the setting feels poor and would not be out of place in the developing world. But this is the reality of modern-day France. This is the France that the tourists don't see and that the wealthy part of the country only sees on the news, usually after an outbreak of violence between local residents and the police. This is the France that Kylian Mbappé, and indeed most of the country's professional footballers, grew up in.

The sprawling suburbs of Paris represent the biggest reservoir of football talent in Europe. Eight of France's 2018 World Cup winners – Mbappé (Bondy), Paul Pogba (Lagny-sur-Marne), Benjamin Mendy (Longjumeau) and N'Golo Kanté (Suresnes) included – grew up in the hardened environs of *les banlieues*

Parisiennes. Bring the national teams for Tunisia, Morocco and Senegal into the equation and the Paris suburbs alone contributed fifteen players to the tournament in Russia.

From a population of just over 12 million, there are approximately 30,000 qualified football coaches and 235,000 licensed players from Paris and its suburbs, more than a third of whom are under eighteen. Football in these parts is quite literally a way of life.

Bondy is nestled in the heart of France's notoriously troubled ninety-third *département*. It has around 54,000 residents, most of whom are of foreign descent, and is one of the many 'rough areas' seen by some politicians and sections of the public to be a cancer on French society. Drug-trafficking, terrorism, crime, unemployment, you name it, if France has a problem the suburbs tend to get the blame. They have also become the scapegoat when the national football team is getting bad results.

On this particular October day, Bondy's streets don't feel the least bit unruly. Indeed, the atmosphere is far friendlier here than on many a Parisian pavement where commuters push and shove their way through life. Maybe the locals are in a particularly good mood because this is a special day. It is the day that Bondy's favourite son returns home.

When France beat Croatia to win the 2018 World Cup, the country exploded with joy. However, nowhere were the scenes more frenzied or heart-warming than in Bondy. Most of the town gathered to watch the final on a giant screen that had been erected at the Stade Léo Lagrange, where Kylian honed his craft. The local club, AS Bondy, is the beating heart of this football-obsessed town, so screening the match here seemed an obvious choice. Before Mbappé broke into the France fold, AS Bondy had already provided one international in Sébastien Corchia. Since the World Cup in 2018, it has provided another in Jonathan Ikoné. In 2019, the club's latest gem William Saliba signed for Arsenal from Saint-Étienne in a €29 million deal.

This is a proud community and veritable footballing hotbed. So, when Mbappé scored to seal France's 4–2 victory over Zlatko Dalić's side, the Stade Léo Lagrange absolutely erupted in ecstasy. Young and old partied long into the night as an unprecedented sense of happiness took over.

Three months later, that pride is palpable again as around 9,000 *Bondynois* return to the stadium, this time to witness the homecoming of their very own world champion. As an excited, expectant crowd sways to the sound of *'Ramenez la Coupe à la Maison'* ('Bring the Cup Home'), France's unofficial World Cup anthem by Vegedream, a hip-hop artist of Ivorian origins, it is impossible not to feel moved.

The PSG star's arrival on stage is greeted by a chorus of deafening screams and then chants of 'Mbappé! Mbappé!' The crowd represents a melting pot of cultures. Most of those present are children but even the adults heartily join in. Parents hoist their little ones aloft to offer them a glimpse of this superstar and role model.

For all his fame and riches, Mbappé has strived to maintain close links to Bondy. Twenty-five lucky children from Jean Renoir School in Bondy travelled to Russia and watched France play Australia in their first game, courtesy of Mbappé's generosity. As well as financing a large part of the trip, Mbappé treated the students to a prolonged autograph session after training. Just days after returning from Russia, he was back in Bondy to visit the children's hospital. His World Cup bonuses of around €350,000 were donated to the charity for which he is an ambassador, Premiers de Cordée, which helps disabled children through sport. 'I earn enough money – a lot of money,' Mbappé told *Time* magazine. 'I think it's important to help those who are in need. Lots of people suffer and have illnesses. For us, giving a helping hand is no big deal. It doesn't change my life, but it could change theirs.'

Today, as Mbappé steps up onto the stage with a broad smile, it is obvious that he feels a strong sense of duty to his hometown. 'You cannot imagine how happy it makes me feel to see so many of you here,' he tells his adoring fans. 'This is even better than winning the World Cup! Next time there's an event like this, I'll be down there in the crowd acclaiming one of you ... because you're all brilliant people and you will also go on to achieve great things.'

Standing next to him is the Mayor of Bondy, Sylvine Thomassin. No politician worth his or her salt would miss the opportunity to make a public appearance alongside Mbappé, but Thomassin's speech is genuine, even rousing, and is greeted by loud cheers. 'Kylian has shown the world that the ninety-third *département* develops brilliant individuals,' she declares. 'He is proof that – regardless of what the politicians say – it is possible to grow up in Bondy and become a successful, polite, kind, grounded and likeable person.' The message is clear. Mbappé is not just a footballer. This supremely gifted, impeccably behaved kid from an Algerian and Cameroonian family is the success story that French football – and indeed France as a whole – has been crying out for.

CHAPTER 2

BLACK-BLANC-BEUR

For footballers, and especially strikers, timing is everything, and Kylian Mbappé could hardly have timed his entrance to the world any better. When Mbappé was born on 20 December 1998, he arrived in a country that was freshly gripped by the wonders of the beautiful game. Just five months previously, a pair of Zinédine Zidane headers and Emmanuel Petit's clinical strike had clinched *Les Bleus*' inaugural World Cup win against Brazil inside a delirious Stade de France.

France '98 was a magnificent month-long football party. From David Beckham's stunning free-kick against Colombia to Davor Šuker's deadly finishing, Ronaldo's mystery illness or Dennis Bergkamp's flash of genius against Argentina, the games served up endless moments of drama and brilliance. When the hosts were in action the mix of tension and excitement was intoxicating.

As the tournament progressed towards its dizzy climax, France not only felt like a happy place, it appeared to be a united nation. People had been charmed and inspired by Aimé Jacquet's strong, skilful, multicultural team.

Winning the World Cup on home soil changed the way football was perceived in France. 'In 1998, it became fashionable and more acceptable to like football,' explains Joachim

Barbier, author of the book *Ce Pays Qui N'Aime Pas le Foot* (*This Country That Doesn't Like Football*), as he sips an espresso in a bustling Paris café. 'Previously the middle and upper classes looked down on it. But France's elite discovered the joys of football that summer, and suddenly politicians and media personalities all wanted to associate themselves with the World Cup victory.'

Businessmen on the Paris metro used to hide their copies of *L'Équipe*, the country's only daily sports newspaper, in order to maintain an image of respectability. Knowing about football did not bring you kudos. It was widely seen as an uncouth pastime for commoners. In the cult film *Le Dîner des Cons* (*The Dinner Game*), which enjoyed enormous success following its release in 1998, the idiocy and boorish behaviour of two characters, François Pignon (Jacques Villeret) and Lucien Cheval (Daniel Prévost), is depicted by their passion for football. In one scene, Pignon, an AJ Auxerre fan, trades insults with his Olympique de Marseille-supporting friend on the phone. When he hangs up and starts chanting 'Marseille, down the toilet!' at the telephone, his snobbish friends Pierre Brochant (Thierry Lhermitte) and Juste Leblanc (Francis Huster) stare at him with utter disdain.

But the stigma that was associated with football magically disappeared during that heady summer in 1998 as *Les Bleus* played their way into the nation's hearts. All of a sudden, even the more sophisticated newspapers began reporting on matches and interviewing the biggest names. France's World Cup stars became celebrities overnight.

Robert Pirès was a shy, young player enjoying the relative anonymity of life at FC Metz when his presence in the World Cup squad swiftly thrust him into the public eye. More than two decades later, when we meet in a Belsize Park café, in his adopted hometown of London, the former winger smiles at the memory of the tournament that changed his life. 'It was a crazy time,' Pirès recalls. 'We were suddenly like rock stars. Young people in France used to worship singers and actors, but now the footballers were the ones being idolised. Even the lifestyle magazines wanted to talk to us. They wanted to know everything about us from our musical tastes to our cultural backgrounds,' adds the Arsenal legend, whose mother is Spanish and father Portuguese. Pirès's parents both arrived in France in the 1960s in the middle of a prolonged period of economic prosperity during which the country welcomed immigrants from all corners of Europe and Africa. They met in Reims where Robert's father worked in a car factory and his mother was employed as a cleaning lady.

The origins of the players in the World Cup squad created particular intrigue and prompted open discussions and debates about race and the impact of immigration for the first time. Jacquet's class of '98 was a beautiful mix of cultures that reflected the diversity of modern-day France. The team included players with antecedents from Argentina (David Trezeguet), Armenia (Alain Boghossian and Youri Djorkaeff), Ghana (Marcel Desailly), Senegal (Patrick Vieira), Portugal and Spain (Robert Pirès). France's overseas territories were handsomely represented by Guadeloupe (Lilian Thuram, Bernard Diomède and Thierry Henry), French Guiana (Bernard Lama), New Caledonia (Christian Karembeu) and Martinique (through Thierry Henry's mother). And of course it was a virtuoso of Algerian origin (Zinédine Zidane) who knitted everything together. The team was an ideal example of what France could achieve through its rich diversity when everybody pulled in the same direction.

For many this was not merely a victory for French football, it was a victory for French society. President Jacques Chirac hailed France's 'tricolour and multi-colour' triumph, adding: 'A country needs, at certain moments, to come together, around an idea that makes it proud of itself. This victory has shown the solidarity, the cohesion ... that France had a soul, or more precisely that it was looking for a soul.' The term *black-blanc-beur* was adopted to describe this new positive identity. 'The *black-blanc-beur* slogan was first heard in France in 1983,' explains Yvan Gastaut, a historian who specialises in football and immigration. 'Back then, it was used to describe the participants of a fifty-day march from Marseille to Paris known as "The March for Equality and Against Racism". The English word "black" was used to describe a black person, as many felt it sounded less crude than "*noir*". Likewise, "*beur*" was seen as a friendly way to describe a French person of North African origin.'

As a feeling of unity and happiness swept across the country, it was clear that something of greater significance was happening. Four days after the final, the headline on the front page of weekly magazine *L'Express* read: 'The World Cup that changed France'. The lead article explained that:

> French people, all French people, were able to identify with this France team because it was a multi-racial team, because every one of its matches was thrilling, and because it was composed of great players, but above all good people. With idols like these, our kids can dream happily of a bright future.

Emmanuel Petit did not necessarily feel ready to become an idol for France's youth. The battling midfielder was enjoying a steady if unspectacular career when everything suddenly accelerated in the late 1990s. Petit captained Monaco to a Ligue 1 title in 1997, claimed a Premier League and FA Cup Double with Arsenal the following year, then, with a swing of his cultured left foot, sent an entire nation into raptures in the World Cup final against Brazil.

Petit and his blond ponytail immediately became part of French football folklore. He would never be looked at the same way by his countrymen again. 'The World Cup propelled us into a different dimension,' Petit, now working as a pundit on French television, tells me. 'We became national treasures and symbolic figures for so many people. Even now, I get stopped in the street on a daily basis by people who want to talk to me about the World Cup. I won many trophies in my club career too, but people rarely talk to me about Monaco, Arsenal, Chelsea or Barcelona. They want to talk about *Les Bleus*.'

The ex-Gunners favourite is immensely proud of his 1998 exploits, but being held up as a beacon for society does not sit so easily with him. 'The *black-blanc-beur* slogan always made me uncomfortable,' Petit states. 'It felt like people were telling me something I'd known already for twenty years. For me, the guys I played football with weren't black, white or Arab. They were just mates. We didn't take into consideration or even notice what colour a player was. This is France and this is the France I've always known.'

Marcel Desailly was also surprised by the racial categorisation, but there is a clear sense of pride in his voice when he discusses the impact that he and his teammates had on French society. 'For us, on the inside, this was nothing new. We'd grown up together and our origins or skin colour had never been a subject,' explains the former defender, who moved to France from Ghana aged three. 'But if we sent out a positive message, if this team helped people of different origins feel more comfortable about themselves, about their identity, then I am pleased. To see a nation of multiple origins decked out in the *Tricolore* flag is beautiful. Maybe it was just a fleeting moment, but at least for that time we gave the country a certain energy by showing that it was possible to succeed as sons of immigrants.'

Thanks to Zidane, the fresh sense of equality was keenly felt among the Maghrebi population too. Popular French comedian

Jamel Debbouze – who has a Moroccan background, and is one of the strongest voices on matters affecting France's North African communities – claims the World Cup triumph transformed the way people looked at him. In the France 2 documentary *12 Juillet 1998: Le Jour Parfait* (*12 July 1998: The Perfect Day*), Debbouze remembered: 'July 13, the day after the final, was even more pleasurable. All of us Arabs were now handsome. They'd abolished racism. It was the best summer of my life. We were in demand. The chicks all wanted to be with little Arabs or little black guys. It was our time.'

The 1998 vintage had a huge impact despite the fact they were not France's first multicultural team. Indeed, historically *Les Bleus* have always been a cultural melting pot. 'The composition of the France football team strongly reflects the country's immigration patterns,' notes the historian Yvan Gastaut. 'In 1904, the first-ever French national team was made up of English people living in France. You could say the French team was created by the English.'

Immigration allowed France to become a footballing heavyweight after the Second World War. *Les Trente Glorieuses*, a thirty-year period of economic boom, saw several million migrants flood into the country, boosting a depleted workforce and strengthening the football culture. 'France opened its doors to labourers from football countries like Poland, Italy, Portugal, Algeria, Tunisia and Morocco, and our national teams reaped the benefits,' explains Gastaut. 'It was a paradoxical period. On the one hand France was very open to immigration, but on the other hand society was not very open to diversity from a cultural point of view. Only native-born people were considered truly French. Even today, an immigrant in France can suffer from discrimination. Football has often served as a counterbalance because it gives everybody an equal chance. Immigrants have always thrived in French football.'

Les Bleus' first black player, Raoul Diagne, the son of a Senegalese minister, was selected way back in 1931, some forty-seven years before Viv Anderson became the first black player to represent England. Raymond Kopa, the son of Polish immigrants, was France's earliest international superstar. Kopa won the Ballon d'Or in 1958 after inspiring a France side that included the Moroccan-born forward Just Fontaine and Roger Piantoni, another forward who had Italian roots, to reach the World Cup semi-finals.

In 1984, *Les Bleus* claimed their first major prize on home soil. A son of Italian immigrants, Michel Platini, captained the hosts to glory in the UEFA European Championship, ably assisted by the Spanish-born Luis Fernández, Mali's Jean Tigana and the Frenchman Alain Giresse. 'That was a fantastic team,' Petit enthuses. 'The *carré magique* [magic square] of Fernandez, Tigana, Giresse and Platini was a wonderful midfield that I loved watching as a boy. Unfortunately for them they were born too early. The public don't remember Platini's team like they remember ours because they didn't get the same media coverage. We were lucky. In 1998, France was ready to embrace football like never before.'

•   •   •

When Aimé Jacquet took charge of *Les Bleus* in December 1993, the idea that his team might become an example for the rest of society must have felt laughable. France had just failed to qualify for the 1994 World Cup in the most disastrous and embarrassing fashion. Gérard Houllier's outfit needed only one point from their last two qualifiers at home to Israel and Bulgaria. For a side blessed with the talents of Laurent Blanc, Didier Deschamps, Jean-Pierre Papin and Éric Cantona, it should not have been a tall order.

Yet, a month after suffering a shock 3–2 defeat by Israel, the unthinkable happened. France were drawing 1–1 with Bulgaria in the dying moments when David Ginola, instead of keeping the ball in the corner of the Bulgarian half, attempted a cross. He overhit it, the visitors raided up the pitch, and within seconds Emil Kostadinov had drilled a shot high into the net. The Parc des Princes fell silent and Houllier hung Ginola out to dry. 'He's committed a crime against the France team,' the future Liverpool boss raged. 'Ginola has fired a missile through the heart of French football.'

Houllier's number two Jacquet got promoted to the top job, and he was no more forgiving towards Ginola. Despite the flamboyant winger's brilliant Premier League form with New-castle, he was left out of Jacquet's squad for Euro '96. There was no place for the 1991 Ballon d'Or winner Papin either, while, in-credibly, Cantona – the inspiration behind Manchester United's 1995/96 Double triumph – also missed out.

Cantona's performances since returning from a nine-month ban for kung-fu kicking a Crystal Palace supporter had been sensational. His omission from the French national side left English observers perplexed. 'It felt extraordinary to us,' says Amy Lawrence, who reported on *Les Bleus*' Euro '96 campaign for *The Observer*. 'That a player of Cantona's ability and person-ality could be deemed not good enough? Inexplicable. Utterly incomprehensible. As English people we were thinking "we'll have him if you don't want him!" From the outside, you thought "Jacquet must be a terribly conservative manager."'

Marcel Desailly is quick to defend Jacquet. A Champions League winner with Marseille in 1993, the powerful defender had joined AC Milan by the time *Les Bleus* suffered the Bulgar-ia humiliation. Like Cantona and Ginola, Desailly was on the pitch when Kostadinov plunged a dagger into French hearts. Yet he assures me Jacquet had little choice but to ring the changes after such a monumental disappointment. 'The 1994 campaign was the failure of a generation,' Desailly claims. 'Aimé came in and slowly began to identify players he wanted from the next generation. He wanted to make a clean break and build a new team.'

Jacquet used Euro '96 as an opportunity to mould that new side and, above all, prepare for the upcoming home World Cup. But he very nearly lost his job in doing so. France's performances at the tournament in England were distinctly lacking in panache. The high point proved a revenge-laden 3–1 win over Bulgaria in the group section, but *Les Bleus* failed to score a single goal in the knockout stages, edging past the Netherlands on penalties before limping out to the Czech Republic in the semi-finals.

Without the flair of Cantona or Ginola, the team lacked sparkle. Both players would have walked into any other national team, yet Jacquet's cautious mind told him he could not trust this pair of mavericks. For midfield creativity, he preferred to put his faith in two more conformist talents: Zinédine Zidane and Youri Djorkaeff. However, Zidane, then twenty-four, had little impact on the tournament, while Djorkaeff showed only glimpses of his exquisite skills.

French fans were fuming and the clamour for Cantona and Ginola to return intensified. But rather than looking back, Jacquet focused on the future, calling up a modest, unassuming 22-year-old playmaker from Metz. 'When I came into the side, the atmosphere was tense,' Robert Pirès recalls. 'Jacquet was already getting criticism before Euro '96, but when he refused to bring Cantona and Ginola back, he got hammered. It wasn't easy for me either. I knew people were comparing me with Ginola. We played in the same position, on the left flank, and he was flying at the time with Newcastle.'

Pirès coped just fine thanks to his own talent and the support he got from within the squad. 'The first time I arrived at Claire-fontaine, Didier Deschamps took me to one side and said, "Robert, I want you to know you're welcome here, and I hope you'll be coming to the château for as many years as possible." I don't know why he said that. He didn't need to. But he was the captain, he had an aura, and those words really stuck with me.'

Evidently, Deschamps was much more than the water carrier Cantona had once branded him. He was Jacquet's skipper and the team's general out on the pitch.

Few know France's World Cup-winning captain better than Desailly. The pair first met when competing against one another in the local junior leagues of western France, and they became inseparable after joining the FC Nantes academy, aged fourteen, in 1983. 'We were very different,' Desailly recalls, offering a nostalgic smile. 'Didier was so intense, so serious. I was always having a laugh and I think that Didier liked that. He fed off my insouciance.

'But at first Didier struggled at Nantes. He had stopped growing while the other kids were getting bigger and bigger. Didier was quite small and he wasn't athletic or agile. So he decided he'd have to compensate through hard work. He was obsessed with football and he did everything to succeed. Even as a boy his diet was perfect, he was always doing stretching exercises. He was the model professional.'

Deschamps's leadership skills were also evident back then, as he demonstrated on one tragic evening in November 1984. That night Desailly's half-brother and mentor when growing up in Ghana, Seth Adonkor, was killed in a car accident. Adonkor was twenty-three and a Nantes first-team player, but for Desailly he was so much more than that.

Breaking the news to the vulnerable sixteen-year-old would be no easy task. 'It was quickly obvious that Didier would take responsibility for talking to Marcel,' Nantes sporting director at the time Robert Budzynski told *So Foot* magazine. 'He was a leader then and he's never stopped being one. He was already exceptionally mature and with the other youngsters he behaved like the head of the family.' Desailly will never forget the moment that his teammate broke the terrible news to him in their shared bedroom. 'Some people don't like Didier,' the former Chelsea defender says. 'They think he's a cold, obsessive person. But I know him well and I know there is another warm, human side.'

Deschamps, it should be said, was not the only strong personality in France's characterful squad. 'All over the pitch we had big players who were playing for the biggest clubs in Europe,' Desailly stresses. 'There was [Bixente] Lizarazu at Bayern Munich, me at Milan, Zizou and Didier at Juventus, Djorkaeff at Inter, Petit who was phenomenal at Arsenal. That's why the criticism Jacquet was getting didn't really affect us. When you're a footballer, you have to be a bit selfish. You have to think about yourself and tell yourself just to focus on the job that you need to do.'

As the World Cup got nearer, the attacks on Jacquet grew nastier. Indeed, being depicted as a turnip on the front page of *The Sun* – as England boss Graham Taylor was in 1993 – would probably have been preferable to the treatment dished out to the former Bordeaux and Lyon manager. He could have lived with the accusations of being too defensive, but the personal barbs hurt. The proud son of a butcher, Jacquet grew up in the tiny village of Sail-sous-Couzan in south-east France, and his rural accent and mannerisms were continually mocked on the popular Canal Plus television show *Les Guignols de L'Info* (France's equivalent of *Spitting Image*). *L'Équipe* newspaper labelled him 'the country bumpkin' and called for his head in the spring of 1998.

Fortunately Jacquet's reputation within the squad was very different. 'We trusted Aimé 100 per cent, both on a technical and human level,' Petit argues forcefully. 'He had that skill of finding the right balance between discipline and kindness. On a human level, he's an exceptional man. We were aware of the criticism he was getting, and we wanted to help him rise above it.'

Jacquet had one other very powerful supporter in the form of Jacques Chirac, the French President, who was known to be a keen follower of sumo wrestling but had never before expressed any interest in football. As France's leader between 1995 and 2007, Chirac had been a controversial figure when it came to the subject of immigration. In 1991, during his time as Mayor of Paris, he questioned whether French workers living in Goutte d'Or – a poor neighbourhood in the north of the capital – should have to put up with the 'noise and smell' supposedly created by their immigrant neighbours.

By 1997, Chirac was languishing in the polls following a failed attempt to dissolve Parliament. His decision to throw his political weight behind Les Bleus was the first clear indication that this World Cup carried far more than just sporting significance. In March of that year, he told his sports adviser and future Minister of Sport Jean-François Lamour that he wanted to hold regular meetings with the team, and monthly briefings with Jacquet, in the run-up to the tournament.

After a 1–0 victory over Spain in January 1998, Chirac spent thirty minutes in the Stade de France home dressing room, discussing plans with Jacquet and motivating the players. 'Chirac was behind us from the start,' Pirès says. 'He told us we had a big responsibility because we were defending the colours of the nation. That had a real impact. When the head of state takes the time to come and see you and talk to you, it means that what you're doing is very important.' Petit agrees but adds a caveat: 'It felt strongly symbolic and it sent a powerful message. But we weren't naïve. We knew there was a political element there and that it was also about gaining popularity.'

Lamour feared that Chirac's association with Jacquet's beleaguered team could further damage his popularity. He warned the President against backing a horse that looked likely to lose. Yet Chirac seemed to genuinely believe in the squad. 'There's a spirit in this group, a coach who knows his players and a captain with a strong collective sense,' Chirac told Lamour after the Spain friendly, according to *Le Parisien* newspaper. 'Something special is brewing and I sense they can go all the way.' Lamour noted: 'Chirac was one of the first people, maybe the only person at that point, to truly believe in them.'

The doubters emphasised the fact that France lacked an established striker. AS Monaco pair Thierry Henry and David Trezeguet were just twenty, and while the former still operated as a winger, the latter was not yet ready to perform on the biggest stage. Searching for a solution, Jacquet even held an olive branch out to Cantona on the condition that he play as centre-forward. The United man allegedly refused.

'It's a pity,' muses ex-France boss Gérard Houllier, who, even today, cannot help thinking about what might have been. 'If Cantona had played just ahead of Zidane, he'd have scored plenty of goals. Éric wanted to be the number ten, but this role was reserved for Zidane. And with hindsight you can't say Aimé got that wrong.'

Auxerre striker Stéphane Guivarc'h, who had been Ligue 1's leading marksman for the past two seasons, started as Jacquet's first choice, but he went off injured in the twenty-sixth minute of France's opener against South Africa. When his replacement Christophe Dugarry took to the Stade Vélodrome pitch in Marseille he was greeted by vociferous boos. Dugarry, who had flopped at Barcelona, had been slammed in the French press. Many journalists felt he had only been included because of his close friendship with Zidane. The pressure looked to be getting to him as he fluffed his first chance, a one-on-one with the goalkeeper, then committed a careless foul on the edge of the France box.

Luckily for Dugarry and for France, the South African free-kick came to nothing and the substitute's fortunes quickly changed. Just moments later Zidane curled in a corner, Dugar-ry swivelled and nodded home. The maligned forward wheeled away gleefully, sticking his tongue out at the journalists who had been gunning for him. 'I felt both joy and hate,' Dugarry explained in the documentary covering the lives of the French team during the competition, *Les Yeux dans les Bleus*. 'You can see all the fucking journalists sitting in the stand. I thought: "I've screwed you all!" I felt hate.' The goal helped Dugarry to expel the negativity that had been building up and transformed the atmosphere both on the pitch and in the stands. *Les Bleus* won 3–0 and their campaign was up and running.

Henry slotted the third goal home in scintillating fashion that day. France's young number twelve exhausted the South African defenders with his relentless raids up the right, and in the ninetieth minute, Willem Jackson was powerless to stop the youngster from surging past him and coolly dinking a shot over the stranded goalkeeper Hans Vonk.

Monaco fans had already witnessed Henry's speed and slick movement when he helped them win the league as a teenager in 1996/97, but the World Cup represented the first opportu-nity for the world to feast its eyes on this modern footballing phenomenon. In the second game, Henry netted two more in the 4–0 demolition of Saudi Arabia, first steering home Liz-arazu's low cross left-footed, then sprinting in behind the Saudi defence with the elegance of a gazelle, before side-footing the ball beyond the goalkeeper.

The Stade de France crowd gave the electric winger a stand-ing ovation when he was replaced by an admiring Pirès late on in the game. 'People were raving about Kylian Mbappé in 2018, and understandably so, but I wasn't quite so amazed be-cause I'd seen exactly the same thing twenty years earlier,' Pirès tells me.

With Henry burning the full-backs for pace, and the elusive

Djorkaeff dribbling past opponents and accelerating forward with a trademark elegance that earned him the nickname 'the Snake', France's fans were starting to forget about Cantona and Ginola.

There were, however, stormclouds gathering. Once again, Zidane's performances were not matching the hype. The Juventus star's frustration got the better of him when he raked his studs down the thigh of Saudi skipper Fuad Amin and was sent off. Jacquet refused to meet Zidane's gaze as he trudged off, but Deschamps's damning post-match comments conveyed how angry he was. 'It's unforgivable,' the skipper fumed. 'Zidane's an impulsive player but that was a stupid reaction. Now the whole team will be penalised because he's a key man for us and we'll lose him for two or three games.'

Deschamps regretted making this public condemnation and apologised to Zidane the next day. Yet the incident, and the internal discussions that followed, proved to be a turning point in the playmaker's international career. 'Until then Zizou was very stressed,' Desailly remembers. 'He was putting himself under so much pressure, trying to do everything. So, as the leaders in the team, a few of us took him to one side. We told him he should stop tackling, stop chasing the ball. That's our job. He should focus on doing what he does best: expressing himself when he has the ball.'

Today when French people think about 1998, they think about Zidane. They think about his goals against Brazil and his face being beamed on to the Arc de Triomphe later that evening, accompanied by the words 'Zizou Président!' He is the figurehead of the *black-blanc-beur* generation. Yet, in reality his overall contribution was sporadic. 'Zizou? He only turned up on 12 July for the final,' laughs Pirès. 'You could say that's a sign of greatness. He was there when we needed him most. But he wasn't yet the great Zidane that we all grew to love and admire.

The true creative leader of that team was Djorkaeff, without question.'

The fact is *Les Bleus* weren't very creative at all. They scored nine goals against South Africa, Saudi Arabia and Denmark, but the knockout games were a different story. France rarely looked fluent going forward, but every time their future in the competition looked in jeopardy, something extraordinary and unexpected happened. Desailly believes his team's triumph was 'simply written in the stars', and at times it did feel as though they were being protected by some kind of spiritual force.

In the round of sixteen, it took Laurent Blanc's sudden decision to abandon defensive duties and play as a makeshift striker to break the deadlock against Paraguay deep in extra time. His defensive partners were imploring him to come back, but Blanc obstinately ignored them. In the 114th minute, after Trezeguet had nodded down a Pirès cross, the commanding, graceful centre-back with a keen eye for goal was perfectly placed to volley home.

In the quarter-finals, two normally reliable penalty-takers, Luigi Di Biagio and Demetrio Albertini, missed for Italy in the shootout that followed a goalless stalemate. And most incredibly of all, France came from behind to beat Croatia in the semi-finals thanks to two Lilian Thuram strikes in the space of twenty-three minutes. They were the only goals that Thuram scored in the 142 international appearances he made, and even today the right-back has no rational explanation. 'It wasn't really me,' he laughs. 'I've tried to find that person who scored two goals in a World Cup semi-final, but he's never surfaced again.' France had to protect their lead with only ten men for the final sixteen minutes after Blanc had been unfairly sent off for pushing out a hand and brushing Slaven Bilić on the chin. The Croatian defender fell theatrically, holding his forehead, and Blanc was suspended for the final.

What made France contenders was their defensive solidity

– and Blanc played a big part in that. He and Desailly were exceptional centre-halves who dovetailed beautifully. Desailly was all strength, aggression, speed and power. Blanc's game was about positioning, technique and finesse when passing or carrying the ball out of defence. Not that Desailly couldn't pass – after all, he played in central midfield for Fabio Capello's great AC Milan team. Likewise, Blanc could put his foot in when necessary. With Thuram on the right and Lizarazu on the left, *Les Bleus* boasted one of the most complete defensive units in history. Indeed, this back-four was never beaten, remaining invincible over twenty-eight games between 1996 and 2000. 'Is that the real stat?' Desailly asks with a mixture of surprise and pride. 'We formed an incredible block. The foundations of that team could not have been more solid.

'Above all, we complemented each other so well,' he continues. 'Thuram was immense, so strong, so athletic. Nobody got past Liza, and Laurent was a pleasure to play alongside. We were defenders but we always looked to impose ourselves on our opponents by playing with aggression, physicality and intensity. We'd push up and try to unsettle them, without ever over-committing or leaving space in behind.'

They were also afforded enviable protection. Jacquet always lined up his team with at least two defensive midfielders, usually Deschamps and Petit, sometimes even adding a third in Christian Karembeu or a young, hungry Patrick Vieira. No wonder goalkeeper Fabien Barthez conceded only twice in seven games. This defensive, risk-averse ethos would become the blueprint for French football for years to come, and it could even be argued that France's domestic league – which on average produces fewer goals than other major European leagues – is still suffering the consequences (as is explored in Chapter 11).

However, nobody in France was complaining on 12 July 1998 as Jacquet's confident, impenetrable team went into battle with Brazil for football's most coveted prize. Despite the presence of

80,000 roaring, partisan supporters inside the Stade de France, *Les Bleus* went into the game as slight underdogs. Not only had Brazil been there and done it before – they already had three world crowns and were the defending champions – Mário Zagallo's side was packed full with exceptional talent. Roberto Carlos and Cafu were among the best full-backs of that era, Rivaldo could create chances out of nothing, and the side possessed two of the most lethal finishers around in Ronaldo and Bebeto.

The evening began in somewhat comical fashion when one of *Les Bleus*' newest but most enthusiastic fans, Jacques Chirac, was captured by television cameras uncertainly mouthing the surnames of the France players as they were announced in the stadium. He did not dare shout for fear of getting one wrong.

Chirac could have been forgiven for failing to recognise an out-of-sorts Ronaldo. The Brazilian striker – who was later voted player of the tournament – was in no state to play a World Cup final and looked a shadow of his usual self amid reports he had suffered a fit shortly before kick-off. Ronaldo actually started fairly brightly, but after being dispossessed by a crunching tackle from Frank Lebœuf, who was standing in for the suspended Blanc, then getting knocked flat on his back by Barthez as the goalkeeper punched a ball clear, *El Fenomeno* faded away.

Another phenomenal talent became the star of the show instead. Zidane may have flattered to deceive at Euro '96, and got himself stupidly sent off against Saudi Arabia, but throughout his illustrious career this majestic footballer demonstrated a capacity to deliver the goods on the biggest stages of all. Twenty-seven minutes had been played when he leaped higher than Leonardo to nod Petit's right-sided corner into the back of the net. When Zidane repeated the feat on the stroke of half-time, this time from a Djorkaeff corner on the opposite flank, Zagallo's charges were in disarray.

The second half was incredibly tense for the French fans, particularly after Desailly was sent off for a second yellow card on sixty-eight minutes. Yet Brazil – for all their big names and occasional flashes of brilliance – created precious little. Then, deep in added time, the nation held its breath as Petit raced on to Vieira's through-pass. When he side-footed a finessed shot into the far corner, the party could begin. France had not only won the World Cup, they had done so in style by out-classing the biggest and most successful football nation on the planet. *'Et un, et deux, et trois-zéro!'* came the chant that would be heard long into the night and indeed still gets the odd airing in French stadiums today. The outpouring of joy was immense. Chirac handed the trophy to Deschamps and was down in the home dressing room celebrating with the players moments later.

The World Cup had an astonishing impact on the country. An unprecedented 26 million people were watching on television when Petit slotted past Claudio Taffarel, which smashed the previous television viewing record of 17.5 million. Tellingly 49.5 per cent of viewers were female. The next morning *L'Équipe* sold their print run of 1.6 million copies before lunch. The Champs-Élysées and its surrounding streets had been filling up throughout the second half. It is estimated that more than 1 million people descended on to the famous avenue, which was the biggest public gathering since 2.2 million came to acclaim Charles de Gaulle following the liberation of Paris on 26 August 1944.

The next day around 500,000 returned to cheer on the team as they paraded the trophy on an open-top bus. French author Joachim Barbier was among the crowd. 'I saw people of all backgrounds celebrating together, and it did feel special,' he recalls. 'Thousands had come from the suburbs to join in; people who are usually "invisible" in French society, people who would normally only come into Paris to clean the offices of *La Défense* [the business district in Paris] at 5 a.m. To witness such communal joy on the Champs-Élysées of all places, this avenue reserved usually for the elite and for tourists, felt very symbolic.'

The fact that Zidane, the son of Algerian immigrants, had been so crucial in this long-awaited victory filled France's North African communities with pride. There were nearly as many Algerian flags as French *Tricolore* flags on view that night. 'The North Africans came in numbers, both men and women,' Barbier describes. 'They joined in with the singing and dancing. The women were unleashing their famous "yoo-yoo" screams – the celebration you usually hear at Maghrebi weddings – and everybody laughed with them. They clearly felt that they were part of this event. Of course, that's thanks to Zidane. For the first time the country had a hero who was also a positive symbol for immigration.'

When you have witnessed the extraordinary, unifying effect that a football team can have on a country, it is difficult not to love the sport. Emmanuel Petit speaks with passion and emotion when I ask him if, having participated in such a landmark event for France in 1998, he is saddened by the spate of racist and homophobic incidents that have been reported in stadiums in recent years. 'There is a lot of hate in the world today – you only need to look at social media to see that,' he responds. 'But football does so much in the fight against discrimination, it is wrong to blame it for society's troubles.

'If all structures in society could carry the same values as football, the country would be much better off,' Petit continues. 'Football gives people from all walks of life a chance. Let's talk honestly about this: footballers in France are mainly black and Arab kids who come from suburbs. That's not a racist comment, it's an observation. They are mainly of African origin. They are French, OK, but of African origin. Football gives these people the chance that the other more traditional structures in French society don't give them. Football is more than just a sport. It has a social conscience.'

The day after the World Cup final the editor-in-chief of *Le Monde*, Jean-Marie Colombani, penned a thought-provoking lead for the newspaper's front page. He started in a cautious, even pessimistic fashion, stressing: 'Of course, everything remains the same. One football match cannot eradicate the sum of all our ills.' But he could not deny there was magic in the air: 'There is this overriding sense, amid the euphoria sweeping the country, that something has changed, or that something can change. Something in our collective conscience, relating to our own identity: multi-racial, or in other words black, white and Arab; something that could also symbolise the changing of an era.'

CHAPTER 3

BIENVENUE À CLAIREFONTAINE

In 1998, France was the envy of the football world. Not only had *Les Bleus* been crowned world champions, but the French game was in rude health. France had stolen a march on the competition by establishing ground-breaking youth structures that churned out an apparently endless supply of smart, strong, technical footballers.

As the Spanish, English and German football associations cast admiring, covetous glances at their Gallic neighbours, Europe's leading clubs began raiding French academies for elite young players. Meanwhile, Aimé Jacquet, the World Cup-winning coach, was reluctant to take the praise for *Les Bleus'* victory. The seeds of the success, he insisted, were sown at a lower level. 'This is, above all, a victory for French youth development,' Jacquet declared.

When Gérard Houllier welcomes me into his office at Red Bull's headquarters in Paris, the former Paris Saint-Germain, Lyon, Liverpool and France manager – who is now Head of Global Football for the Red Bull Group – is in a friendly mood. Yet, he is curious as to why a British journalist wants to speak to him about the visionary work that was carried out behind the scenes, in a sleepy village called Clairefontaine, more than thirty years ago. It is a subject close to Houllier's heart, and he is only too happy to revisit that fascinating time. 'The 1998 World

Cup win was the consequence of everything that we had put in place at Clairefontaine ten years previously,' he begins proudly.

Houllier is best-known internationally for his six seasons in charge of Liverpool between 1998 and 2004. However, arguably his most significant, impactful contribution to the game of football came before then. The former English teacher was appointed technical director by the *Fédération Française de Football* (FFF) in 1988; the same year that France's centre of excellence opened in Clairefontaine. He played a central role in establishing France as global leaders in the art of player development.

When you arrive at the complex in Clairefontaine, a rural town of 900 inhabitants situated 50km south-west of Paris, you are hit by a sense of quiet and tranquillity. Travelling down the windy roads that cut through the Rambouillet Forest there is a distinct feeling of nature taking over and it gladly replaces the noise and pollution of the capital. The entrance to the centre is grandiose with its elegantly pruned hedges. But once in the car park there is, frankly, not much to see. Essentially trees. In the distance a grand nineteenth-century castle, *le Château de Montjoye*, looks out regally at a series of modern buildings. And there are football pitches. Lots and lots of football pitches. But the overriding atmosphere is one of peace. The air is fresh and the silence absolute.

In the 1980s, FFF president Fernand Sastre decided French football needed a far more sophisticated, comprehensive headquarters than the basic structure they had in Vichy. By creating the Clairefontaine site, with its six full-size grass pitches, two artificial pitches, one floodlit stadium, sixteen changing rooms, numerous state-of-the-art gyms, a rehabilitation centre, balneotherapy centre, seven residences and 200 bedrooms, Sastre offered French football everything it could possibly need to develop and flourish.

The plan was not merely to create a luxurious getaway for France's senior team, but rather to design a single focal point for French football development – a haven where the sharpest minds and brightest talents could gather to plot a glorious future. 'We had a vision,' Houllier states. 'We wanted everyone to be in this same, unique place. A central hub. Clairefontaine became the headquarters, or you could say the nerve-centre for French football.' France's footballing strategy would be defined there, all national teams from the under-15s up to the senior side would train and reside there, French coaches would study for their coaching badges there, and, crucially, as of 1990 the most promising children from the Paris region would live and train there.

Houllier was the man responsible for coordinating the revolution. 'In France, the technical director is a very important position,' he says. 'You need to analyse trends, anticipate football's evolution, and ensure players are prepared for the demands they'll face in the future. I always say the job of the national team coach is to prepare for the match in ten days. The job of the technical director is to prepare for the match in ten years. As if by coincidence, ten years after we arrived and started working, France won the World Cup.'

Les Bleus followed up their World Cup triumph with another sensational victory at Euro 2000, and the rest of Europe turned to Clairefontaine for inspiration. Howard Wilkinson, the technical director of the English Football Association, spent several days there observing the facilities and techniques before submitting his proposal for England's very own national training centre, St George's Park, which finally opened after lengthy delays in 2012. England fans will no doubt be hoping that Houllier's ten-year theory works for the Three Lions at Qatar 2022.

But England were not the only ones taking note. Francisco Filho, a former Brazilian forward who coached for the FFF for twenty-nine years, recalls meeting a veteran Spanish midfielder named Pep Guardiola around the turn of the century. 'We were at a tournament in the Canary Islands,' Filho recalls. 'Guardiola was a great admirer of our methods, and he told me, "If ever I coach a team, I want them to play in exactly the same way as your kids."' Filho himself was recruited by Sir Alex Ferguson and joined the Manchester United coaching staff in 2002.

'People copied us, of course they did,' Houllier says. 'But that's OK. Football has always worked in cycles. Everybody looks at what their rivals are doing, and they try to take the best parts and adapt it to their own model. That's just part of the game.'

Back in 1966, France were the ones looking across the Channel for inspiration. *Les Bleus* had qualified for the World Cup in England, but they finished bottom of a group that included the hosts, Uruguay and Mexico. Despite this early elimination, France's technical staff stayed behind to watch the remainder of the competition. When England defeated West Germany 4–2 in an intensely gripping final at Wembley, the penny dropped. 'It was the day the people who ran French football realised that France had been left behind,' Filho states. 'The English and the West Germans were big, strong and quick, and they could run and run. Physically, they were light years ahead of France.'

French youth development was effectively born that day, and a certain Georges Boulogne became its instigator. Boulogne, dubbed 'the father of youth development' by Houllier, was part of the FFF's technical committee that began to address the problems at the grassroots level in 1966. Little improvement had been made, however, by the time Boulogne was appointed France manager three years later: his first game in charge ended in a 5–0 thrashing by the reigning world champions at Wembley.

Boulogne was able to wield more influence once he took on the all-encompassing, strategic role of technical director in 1970. He created the National Football Institute in Vichy in 1972. Located in the heart of the country, France's first centre of excellence looked to gather the most promising young players in the land, aged between seventeen and twenty, with the principal aim of raising their fitness levels. 'French teams were organised and defended well, but we needed to get in line physically,' explains Filho, who joined the staff in 1972. 'So we pushed the kids very hard. They trained in army gear. We provided them with bulletproof vests laced with metal. We were like a team of bulldozers. We never got tired.'

Even at that early stage, Boulogne recognised the importance of creating a centralised system. He wanted to instil a universal methodology, a French way, and he encouraged the professional clubs to set up their own academies based on the same principles.

AS Nancy Lorraine were the first to follow suit and one of their early graduates, Michel Platini, helped lift France out of the doldrums. *Les Bleus* were in a seriously dark place in the 1970s; they failed to qualify for the World Cups of 1970 and 1974 and also missed out on the Euros of 1972 and 1976. But the emergence of this exceptionally gifted midfielder, who won the Ballon d'Or in 1983, 1984 and 1985, sparked a revival. Michel Hidalgo's troops reached the World Cup semi-finals in 1982 and then claimed France's first major title by lifting the European trophy on home soil in 1984.

By this time, Boulogne had reduced the National Football Institute academy starting age to fifteen and made it compulsory for top-flight clubs to have their own centres. France were most definitely moving in the right direction, yet Vichy was still not producing top players. Indeed, when André Merelle joined the National Football Institute coaching staff in 1981, he was struck by the technical ineptitude of the interns. 'They were all fit, but I couldn't believe how low the standard was,' the former Bordeaux defender reveals. 'It was obvious they didn't have the skills required. That was partly our fault because we were working too much on endurance, but it was also because we were only getting second-choice players. Vichy didn't have the reputation or pulling power. So the clubs took all the top talent.'

The switch to Clairefontaine in 1988 proved to be an ideal time to move the goalposts. Upon his appointment as the French technical director, Houllier decided the national academy must get the best players first. He lobbied for the introduction of a *centre de préformation* (early training centre) for kids aged twelve to fifteen. 'When you want to become a doctor, you need to train for six or seven years,' Houllier reasons. 'An engineer or a teacher must study for five or six years. I believed that in order to be ready to play fifty or sixty games a season by the age of twenty, a footballer needs a similarly long period of grounding.'

The methodology also changed significantly. Houllier shifted the emphasis away from fitness and towards technique. He recalls taking inspiration from a conversation he had with Platini, who served as France manager from 1988 to 1992. Platini had observed that French players were physically and tactically strong, but lacked the creative spark that he himself had so often provided in the past. 'It got me thinking,' Houllier says. 'I went to speak to some neurologists, and they told me that when it comes to vision and creativity, a child's brain will develop most between the ages of twelve and fifteen.'

By recruiting players at the age of twelve, the FFF could get to the most gifted children early and work with them on a daily basis before any bad habits kicked in. For the sake of logistics, twelve more early training centres – all identical to the Clairefontaine model – were opened all around the country. 'We didn't want to uproot the children,' Houllier stresses. 'The kids would board from Monday to Friday, attend the local school and have just one training session a day. At weekends they went back to their parents, and if they wanted to play for their hometown teams they could.'

This centrally coordinated network of academies was the first of its kind and ultimately provided the foundations for France's success. The centre in Clairefontaine, which drew from the tens of thousands of football-crazy children in the Paris suburbs, proved to be the most fertile breeding ground.

The Clairefontaine academy could rely on three stalwarts of youth development: Claude Dusseau, the National Football Institute's technical director from 1984 to 2004, and Merelle and Filho, who were responsible for putting the youngsters through their paces on the training ground. All three dedicated the majority of their working lives to the National Football Institute. Today they are happy to share the secrets of France's success with me. 'When we moved to Clairefontaine, we changed the philosophy,' explains Merelle. 'We felt football was about technique above all, and we reasoned that if a child couldn't control or pass a ball then he would never become great. We repeated our technical drills over and over until they became second nature.'

This repetition of exercises became the Clairefontaine hallmark. Kids were never sent on runs and never practised fitness drills. 'Every minute a thirteen-year-old spends running without a football is a minute lost,' Filho states firmly. 'Our youngsters always had a ball at their feet. They learned how to control a ball that arrived from the side or from behind. They learned how to pass without altering their body shape. When they had growth spurts, the training drills we practised ensured that their bodies developed in a way that would help them as footballers.'

The first concrete evidence that the system was working arrived in 1996 when the France under-18 side coached by Houllier became European champions. Three Clairefontaine graduates – Thierry Henry, Nicolas Anelka and William Gallas – starred in that tournament and word began to spread that France was developing some special talents. 'We could see that our players had become more technically proficient,' Houllier argues. 'We beat Spain in that final because we passed the ball better than them. The methods were paying off. What we had done was simple: each year we found the best twelve-year-olds in the country. We selected twenty for each of the thirteen centres, so 260 in all. Every day they trained together, worked together and lived together. When you put the best with the best, the level rises. That's what happened.'

The France under-18s retained their European crown the following year, this time beating Portugal courtesy of a goal from another Clairefontaine alumnus Louis Saha. Meanwhile, Houllier began urging the French clubs to set up their own early training centres. 'Our role at the federation was to do the research and to give the clubs the tools they needed to train their own players,' he explains. 'Two factors convinced them to listen. Firstly, they could see the way our under-18s were playing. And secondly, we were able to provide evidence that the players who trained with us from the age of twelve were less susceptible to injuries.

'When a player has poor technique, and every time he controls the ball it bounces three metres away from him, he's more likely to be subjected to a tackle. Before, we were welcoming kids from amateur football who'd already suffered knee ligament damage. But when we started taking them at twelve, these problems disappeared.'

Early training centres began sprouting up at clubs throughout the land. The FFF maintained some control, though. Every youth academy chief was briefed on the methods at Clairefontaine, and clubs were obliged to employ at least one FFF-qualified youth coach. This meant even children who did not attend a National Football Institute academy benefited from the expertise that had been developed at Clairefontaine.

'There was clearly a French way,' Robert Pirès states. 'I spent three years at the Stade de Reims academy before moving to Metz, and I can say that the training methods at both clubs were the same. We always trained with a ball, repeating technical exercises over and over. We were taught that football is easy:

control, pass, move. That's what I was taught every day. If you wanted to dribble or try other things, you could. But first you had to master the basics: control, pass, move.'

The youth development techniques that had been introduced by Houllier's team in the late 1980s were now practised by clubs across the land as well as in the national academies. In 1998, the results were there for all to see. Watching Jacquet's team at the World Cup, it was obvious that every player had received an exceptional football grounding. Whether they had learned their trade at the famous FC Nantes academy (like Didier Deschamps and Marcel Desailly), at AS Cannes (Zinédine Zidane) or AS Monaco (Emmanuel Petit, Lilian Thuram and Thierry Henry), it did not seem to matter. Each and every player was technically, tactically and physically assured.

The Clairefontaine complex came into its own during the 1998 tournament. Jacquet's triumphant team resided in *le Château de Montjoye* throughout the competition, and unquestionably benefited from the cutting-edge facilities and peaceful surroundings. As the country worked itself into a neurotic frenzy between games, Deschamps and the squad could relax in one of the spas situated in the castle's basement, or simply enjoy a stroll in the forest. They were oblivious to the madness that was unfolding around them.

These days a sense of mystique hangs over the handsome château that has become an integral part of *Les Bleus'* story. The bedrooms are named after players from Jacquet's 1998 squad and Roger Lemerre's Euro 2000 winners. Players can have a game of pool or table football in the *salon Aimé Jacquet*, read a newspaper in the adjacent *salon Just Fontaine*, or attend a video session in the *salon Raymond Kopa*. In the *salon Roger Lemerre*, they assemble around a giant oval table to eat their meals before later heading out to train on the nearby *terrain Michel Platini*.

During this period the name Clairefontaine took on a mythical status, and by the turn of the century all of the most ambitious young footballers in the Paris region dreamed of joining the illustrious academy.

Ricardo Faty began his Clairefontaine odyssey in 1999. The tall midfielder from the Paris suburb of Villeneuve-Saint-Georges remembers how privileged he felt after getting through trials that started with around 800 children. 'I was so happy,' the former AS Roma man remembers. 'Clairefontaine was sacred. We'd all watched the World Cup, and now we were dreaming about following in the footsteps of our heroes. When you arrive you sense the magic straight away. You're immersed in football, surrounded by pitches, and you can see all the other France teams training there. For a young boy it's incredible!'

That the kids could see their heroes training on an adjacent pitch, and occasionally even get to meet them, provided extra motivation. 'We'd bump into the under-21s, guys like Frédéric Kanouté and William Gallas, and they'd give us words of advice,' Faty recalls, his voice still filled with wonder. 'Personally, I remember Thierry Henry coming over and talking to me. He was my hero and it was just an amazing moment.'

As France's record goal scorer with fifty-one strikes, Henry remains Clairefontaine's flagbearer and an idol for thousands of children from the *banlieues*. He grew up among the concrete tower blocks of Les Ulis, a tough neighbourhood situated a short drive along the A10 motorway from Clairefontaine. Yet, according to Claude Dusseau, Henry wasn't even the most talented boy of his generation. 'The most naturally gifted player we had was Anelka,' the former National Football Institute director says. 'That doesn't mean he was the best. There are other qualities you need besides talent. Henry was bright and attentive. He dreamed of becoming a star and he worked so hard to realise that dream.'

For Clairefontaine's coaching staff, helping the boys become responsible, rounded individuals was every bit as important as producing top footballers. The majority of those who were enlisted came from immigrant backgrounds and were often part of close-knit communities and strong family units. Being whisked away so young could be incredibly destabilising. The staff ensured that the boundaries were clear and discipline was respected. 'We had a big responsibility,' Filho muses. 'The boys were young and impressionable. We couldn't replace their parents, and we didn't try to, but we did spend a lot of time with them. We needed to make sure they remained grounded and stayed serious at school.'

Whenever they strayed, Faty and friends were quickly brought back into line. 'Claude Dusseau had a big influence,' Faty recalls. 'He had a father-son relationship with us. One day, Abou [Diaby], Olivier [N'Siabamfumu] and me got called into his office because we'd been naughty at school. I remember him telling us, very calmly: "You three will all have professional careers. No problem at all. But if you want to be top players, really top players, if you want to play for France, then you need to be even more demanding with yourselves. And you need to start now." Those words really stayed with me.'

When Thierry Henry was asked about his biggest managerial influences during an interview with Sky Sports in 2018, he began, rather predictably, by name checking the former Arsenal boss Arsène Wenger and Pep Guardiola, under whom the striker played at Barcelona. Viewers may then have been a little surprised when he added the names Francisco Filho and Claude Dusseau to his list of mentors. 'I'll never forget what those coaches at Clairefontaine did for me,' Henry said.

If Clairefontaine had given Henry the grounding, the Premier League provided him with the stage on which his career could flourish. Although he was a World Cup winner at the age of just twenty, Henry lost his way at Juventus when he moved there from Monaco. He even got dropped to the under-21 side by France coach Roger Lemerre. It was only when Wenger, the man who had handed Henry his professional debut with

Monaco, brought him to Arsenal that the forward's career truly ignited.

Wenger's arrival at Arsenal in 1996 proved to be hugely significant for the English game as a whole. For the first time, the Premier League was able to tap into France's know-how when it came to player development and coaching. The former Nancy and Monaco manager was closely followed by Gérard Houllier, who joined Liverpool in 1998. As well as opening English minds to fresh ideas and preparation techniques on the training ground, Wenger and Houllier lured a wealth of French talent across the Channel too.

Rémi Garde, the former Lyon captain, and a young midfielder from AC Milan, Patrick Vieira, were the first French players to join Arsenal. Their introduction to English football could hardly have been more brutal. In their very first training session, Arsenal's legendary captain Tony Adams called the squad together and announced that he was an alcoholic. The French duo were perplexed and unsure if they had heard correctly. They hoped, as much as anything, that they had misunderstood.

'It's a moment that epitomises this fascinating period in English football,' describes UK football writer and author Amy Lawrence. 'It was the old culture clashing with the new. There could be no greater symbol than Patrick Vieira – the future captain of Arsenal's invincible team – arriving in England and on his very first day being confronted by this. Tony Adams was Arsenal's talisman but he was also a symbol of English football, lifestyle and culture. I can't imagine what Patrick must have thought. It was incredible. The kind of thing you would normally only see in the theatre.'

Wenger would transform the way the Arsenal players looked after themselves and prepared for matches, notably urging them to cut out, or at least reduce, their alcohol consumption. 'There was a drinking culture, not just at Arsenal but throughout English football,' former Arsenal vice-chairman David Dein, the man behind Wenger's visionary appointment, tells me. 'In terms of diet, preparation and training methods, England had fallen behind. Arsène opened everybody's eyes to that.'

With the likes of Anelka, Henry, Emmanuel Petit, Gilles Grimandi, Robert Pirès, Sylvain Wiltord and Pascal Cygan joining Arsenal's French revolution, the Gunners won three league titles and four FA Cups over eight glorious seasons between 1997 and 2005. 'The French boys brought us something extra,' Dein reflects. 'We just didn't have players like Robert Pirès in England back then. Arsène possessed this wealth of knowledge and contacts in the French game. So when he told me he was interested in a French player I didn't hesitate. I knew that technically he'd be good and physically he'd be well prepared.'

French-trained players were ready to adapt to new surroundings, both from a football and cultural perspective. 'They had a touch of class about them,' Dein explains. 'I can still remember the first time Patrick Vieira came into the canteen. He walked around the room shaking everyone by the hand before sitting down to have his lunch. Everybody looked surprised but I remember thinking: "That's exactly the way it should be."'

By appointing Houllier, initially as joint-manager with Roy Evans in 1998, Liverpool opened their doors to Clairefontaine's expertise. Houllier took a more gradual approach to breaking with traditions, and the club's methods still felt very English by the time Bernard Diomède arrived from Auxerre in 2000. 'There were a lot of differences,' notes the 1998 World Cup winner. 'In the changing room there were sandwiches full of mayonnaise! And there was food everywhere. I'd never seen that before. In France, there'd just be some paracetamol, vitamin C and energy drinks. Gérard changed things slowly, but he also respected the existing culture. Michael Owen used to have a hot bath before the game. At Auxerre, we weren't allowed hot baths within forty-eight hours of a game. Jamie Carragher would even have a sauna the day before! My old

Auxerre coach Guy Roux would have flipped if he'd seen that,' Diomède laughs.

Scotland midfielder John Collins made the opposite journey, leaving Celtic for Monaco in 1996, and the two years he spent in the French league proved enlightening. 'When I started training at Monaco I couldn't tell which players were defenders, which were midfielders and which were forwards,' he recalls. 'They were all comfortable in possession, they all had good technique and could pass the ball. But overall what really struck me was the preparation. Everything was so professional. We had a fitness coach, we carried out different tests and our results were analysed. We did blood tests and we had vitamin supplements that were suited to individual needs.

'The day before a game we'd all stay in a hotel,' continues Collins, who was part of a Monaco side that won the title with Petit, Henry, Fabien Barthez and David Trezeguet. 'The food was carefully prepared – there was no butter, no fizzy water, no desserts. We had salads, rice, pasta, fresh meat or fish. The warm-ups were meticulous. The day after a game, we were in at training the next morning, warming down and defining the programme for the week. We had double sessions, triple sessions sometimes. There were no days off.'

Collins returned to the UK feeling like a new player, but re-adjusting to life at Everton proved difficult. 'It was like going back in time, back to the dark ages. There were days off again, overweight players in the dressing room ... the English were way behind.'

The sudden influx of French talent around the turn of the century helped to bring the Premier League up to speed. During this period Manchester United, who had already exploited the talents of Éric Cantona, signed goalkeeper Fabien Barthez and then later Laurent Blanc. Chelsea relied on France's centre-back pairing from the 1998 World Cup final of Marcel Desailly and Frank Lebœuf, plus the skipper Didier Deschamps, and they added the steel of midfielder Claude Makélélé in 2003. French internationals began to pop up all over the country: Olivier Dacourt moved to Leeds, Laurent Robert to Newcastle, Youri Djorkaeff and Bernard Mendy to Bolton, Christophe Dugarry to Birmingham.

Invariably, the French imports proved to be big hits, and the flow of French players to England, Spain, Italy and Germany has only increased through the years. So much so that France has now overtaken Brazil as the world's premier exporter of elite footballing talent. At the start of the 2019/20 season, there were more than 100 French players plying their trade in Europe's big four leagues, which is the first time any foreign nation has reached that landmark. The French footballer has become an established, adaptable and reliable brand. And all of that is largely down to the work that started in a sleepy little town in the middle of the Rambouillet Forest more than three decades ago.

CHAPTER 4

LIBERTÉ, ÉGALITÉ, FRATERNITÉ?

One man in France's 1998 World Cup-winning squad felt particularly affected by the sense of racial harmony that had descended on the country after that historic triumph. Ever since moving to France's mainland from Guadeloupe as a nine-year-old, Lilian Thuram was confronted by discrimination. The attitudes that he witnessed as a boy shocked him to such an extent that once his playing career ended, he decided to focus his energies on the fight against racism.

For those few happy weeks after the World Cup win, Thuram was delighted to see people in France treated equally regardless of race. 'The *black-blanc-beur* symbol we created was positive and I liked it,' he says. 'It wasn't only a reference to the football team, it was about all of society. I'm not naïve. I know very well that outside football people aren't treated the same. They are not allowed to dream about the same things. Depending on your skin colour, depending on your origins, you do not have access to the same opportunities. So this is why I'm very happy that for a period at least there was this recognition.'

I am talking to Thuram at the headquarters of his association in the Odéon district of central Paris. He launched the Fondation Lilian Thuram after quitting his final club, FC Barcelona, in 2008 with the aim of educating young people on the roots of racism and why it is wrong. France's most capped player now fights racism with the same kind of ferocious determination that made him one of the leading defenders of his generation, and travels the world to deliver talks at schools, universities and conferences.

Securing a meeting with Thuram has proved difficult – and not just because he is extremely busy. Thuram has found himself at the centre of a media storm following an interview he gave to the Italian newspaper *Corriere dello Sport*. Contacted to discuss the ongoing racism in Serie A, he was reflecting on the history of the problem when he said: 'It is necessary to have the courage to say that white people believe they are superior.' This sentence upset some of his compatriots and notably prompted the influential football journalist Pierre Ménès to claim: 'The real problem in France, in football in any case, is anti-white racism.'

The controversy made Thuram reluctant to accept another interview, but a month later he has agreed to meet and seems to be more relaxed. 'Listen, the fact that the subject of racism is being debated more and more is good,' Thuram states. 'And if I'm being attacked then it means that in some way my actions are making certain people uncomfortable. They feel in danger, which, again, is a good sign. Don't forget that back in the day, Nelson Mandela was accused of being an anti-white racist. Martin Luther King, too.'

The bespectacled Frenchman does not consider himself to be the next Nelson Mandela or Martin Luther King, but the number of books on the shelves of his office dedicated to those two historical figures suggest that he is deeply inspired by them. Born in Guadeloupe in the French West Indies, Thuram has been intrigued by the subject of racism ever since his mother moved the family to the greater Paris region in 1981. 'What struck me when I arrived was that some of my classmates judged me because of my skin colour. They made me believe my skin colour was inferior to theirs and that being white was better,' Thuram recalls.

'These were nine-year-old kids. They weren't born racist, but they'd already developed a superiority complex. From that moment, I started to ask myself questions: "Why are they teasing me? Where does this come from?" My mother couldn't provide me with answers. For her, this was just the way it was. There are racists and it won't change.'

Unsatisfied with that response, Thuram buried himself in history books to try to find a better explanation, studying events that had created this damaging mindset. 'Historically we ranked people, we created hierarchies according to skin colour,' he says. 'We educated the white person to think he is dominant over others. Just as we educated men to feel dominant over women. These are intellectual and ideological mechanisms that were constructed in order to exploit other people.'

Thuram speaks in a calm, intelligent manner. His gentle demeanour contrasts with the aggressive way in which he defended on the football field. It is also very different to the stereotypical image that some individuals in France have of black people who come from the suburbs. 'People like to fantasise,' Thuram muses, allowing himself a throaty chuckle. 'They like to think the suburbs are full of violent thugs. But they're not. The majority of people are just like me. They try to live well in a calm, peaceful way.'

Raised by his mother, who was a cleaning lady, in the modest council estate of Les Fougères in Avon, south of Paris, Thuram knows what it is like to struggle on the periphery of French society. Football helped him gain respect in a tough local community made up of immigrants from all corners of the globe. 'I played with kids from Pakistan, Lebanon, Vietnam, Congo, Algeria ... the whole world was there! Football has this great strength of bringing people together and making you feel part of something.'

His first club, Portugais de Fontainebleau, was founded by Portuguese expats but its players hailed from many different cultures. 'At the weekends, I became Portuguese,' Thuram jokes. 'Opponents used to insult me by calling me a "dirty Portuguese", which, as a West Indian, I found pretty funny.' Like many of his peers, Thuram spent every spare moment during his childhood with a ball at his feet. 'The best way to be good at something is to do it a lot. When you're in the suburbs, you play a lot of football. You don't have access to piano or violin lessons. During the school holidays, you don't go away, you stay at home and you play football all day long. That's the reason why so many players emerge from these areas.'

Thuram's world changed when Arsène Wenger brought him to AS Monaco aged seventeen. This proved to be the start of a long, trophy-laden career. Yet, for all his success, the spectre of racism never went away. At Monaco, despite being a regular in Wenger's title-chasing team, Thuram would often get refused entry to nightclubs and exclusive restaurants. During the ten seasons he spent in Italy with Parma and Juventus after leaving Monaco, he heard monkey chants on a regular basis.

It must have been difficult to bear, but Thuram insists he had the tools necessary to rise above it. 'I was lucky that from a young age I understood the mechanism behind racism,' describes the two-time Serie A winner. 'So, when I heard the monkey chants, there was no doubt in my mind that the people with the problem were the ones making monkey noises, not me. I didn't get angry, I tried to understand why they did it.'

Thuram has a burning desire to share his knowledge, and much like the marauding raids that he launched on the right flank with *Les Bleus*, he is difficult to stop when he gets into his stride:

'Racism stems from a feeling that you are superior to the other person. You think you're "normal" and they aren't. It's the same with homophobia. Heterosexuals were educated to think they are normal and gay people aren't. Well, we need to explain very nicely to these people that they are not "the norm". There is no norm. I understood that very early, and when you understand racism, you know you are not the one with a problem.'

Sadly, the abuse of black players has continued well into the twenty-first century.

When I suggest to Thuram that racism in football looks to be escalating because more incidents are being reported, he describes the suggestion as naïve. But surely the terrible scenes in Bulgaria the week before our interview, when England's players were racially abused throughout their Euro 2020 qualifier, are evidence that the situation has deteriorated? 'People often try to analyse racism through their own country or through their own personal feelings, but you have to consider racism on a global scale and take on board the historical depth,' Thuram insists. 'European societies were built on racism. It has been integrated into the collective subconscious for centuries.'

To illustrate the progress humanity has made, Thuram takes the example of his own family: 'My grandfather was born in 1908, sixty years after the abolition of slavery in Guadeloupe. When my mother was born, in 1947, there was segregation in the United States. When I was born, in 1972, there was Apartheid in South Africa. In France, state racism ended in the 1960s. If you're not aware of this deep history, you may think there's more racism today. But I can tell you there isn't. There's far less.'

• • •

Unfortunately, the unity that emerged in France during the summer of 1998 proved to be short-lived. As the sceptics had predicted, normal life resumed, society remained divided, and the suburbs continued to suffer from political and economic neglect.

National Front leader Jean-Marie Le Pen had lost popularity when *Les Bleus* triumphed. But the far-right politician, who had complained about the number of black players in the France side, duly recovered and his anti-immigration campaigns even saw him emerge as a serious candidate in the 2002 presidential elections.

By the turn of the millennium, Thuram had also become a household name, and his willingness to speak out about major societal issues positioned him as a voice for France's ethnic minorities. His problem, he claims modestly, is that he always feels obliged to give honest answers when asked questions. Increasingly, journalists began quizzing the France defender on matters beyond the realms of football. 'I remember being asked in a press conference about Jean-Marie Le Pen saying there are too many blacks,' he recalls. 'In reply, I said I was surprised that somebody who wanted to become President of France wasn't aware of the fact that there are black French people. In France, politicians often try to instrumentalise football. I merely try to balance things out.'

On 8 October 2001, an eagerly anticipated friendly match staged at the Stade de France would severely damage the reputation of the immigrant communities, and provide Le Pen with significant traction. For the first time since Algeria gained independence from France in 1962, the two nations agreed to play one another in a contest that politicians hoped would symbolise their reconciliation.

It was less than a month after the 9/11 attacks in New York and the climate around the world was tense, with France's Muslim communities being viewed with suspicion. Young people of North African descent poured into the ground in their thousands, vastly outnumbering the fans of *Les Bleus*. Indeed, it is estimated that around 60,000 people (around three-quarters of the stadium) were there to support the 'away' side. The night got off to an inauspicious start when, for the first time in a home international, the French national anthem was roundly jeered.

The world champions roared to a 4–1 lead, but the victory was never completed. In the seventy-sixth minute, hundreds of fans invaded the pitch and the game had to be abandoned. To this day it is the only France international match that could not be concluded. Even the friendly against Germany in November 2015 was played out despite the terrorist attacks that were simultaneously unfolding just outside the stadium and in the capital.

One of the lasting images from the game was of Thuram remonstrating with young fans on the pitch, as he tried his best to explain the harm that their actions were doing. 'I was very angry,' he tells me. 'I knew how these scenes would be interpreted. I knew that the young French guys who had come onto the pitch would soon be described as young Algerians – people would quickly forget that actually they are French. Then the Algerians would become Muslims. That's the way it works in our society: when an Arabic person does something negative, it reflects badly on all Arabic people.'

The timing of these disturbances was significant. 'This was such an important night,' Thuram stresses. 'Firstly, because we'd just had the 9/11 attacks. And secondly, because France has a unique, deep-rooted history with Algeria. A lot of people don't even realise that France began to colonise Algeria way back in 1830 and acted in a brutal manner for so long. Some think there was just a six- or seven-year war. This game was a chance for people to mourn and a chance to calm the tensions.'

As the players headed down the tunnel, Thuram remained out on the pitch. The crowds did not present any danger. There was no violence. In fact, they were just laughing and joking, apparently pleased to have stopped a match that had become embarrassing for Algeria. Visibly upset, Thuram attempted to repair the damage singlehandedly, he even grabbed one youngster by the scruff of the neck and tried to talk sense into him. 'I think that boy was a bit surprised,' Thuram laughs. 'He was thinking: "Why is Lilian Thuram shouting at me?" They didn't understand that their actions would have political consequences. I was saying to them: "You guys cry all the time about being discriminated against, but you need to be careful how you act here."

'Sometimes, as adults, we need to play our role,' Thuram continues. 'I'm from Guadeloupe, and in my village every person had a role in educating children. It's up to us to instil values in young people. That's why I felt we should stay out on the pitch to talk to them. But we live in a society where adults no longer have responsibility.'

Thuram's hands-on approach contrasted with the reaction, or lack of one, from the government members in the VIP seats in the Stade de France that night. Prime Minister Lionel Jospin, the Minister of Youth Affairs and Sports Marie-George Buffet and the Interior Minister Daniel Vaillant were among those looking displeased when *La Marseillaise* was booed. Later, during the pitch invasion, Jospin and his colleagues remained in their seats, totally inactive, clearly uncertain as to what action should be taken.

As Thuram feared, the pitch invasion had serious ramifications. The chaotic scenes witnessed by millions of television viewers strengthened a growing impression that France's immigrant youth represented a disruptive presence in society. Six months later, Le Pen received 4.8 million votes in the first round of the presidential elections, only slightly fewer than Jacques Chirac and, crucially, more than Jospin. For the first time, France's extreme right had a candidate in the second round.

'The France-Algeria game was one of the most important factors in Le Pen getting through to the second round,' says the journalist and author Daniel Riolo. 'The jeering of *La Marseillaise* and the pitch invasion were a rejection of the French identity, but the image of the government just sitting there, watching, saying nothing, not condemning anything, was even more damaging. They looked totally incapable of reacting.'

Four years after *Les Bleus* had lifted the spirits of a nation, France appeared unhappy and disunited again. There was no more talk of the magnificent *black-blanc-beur* team. Working out how best to expel illegal immigrants was now a far more popular news topic. 'The *black-blanc-beur* rhetoric was overly simplistic, and politicians used it for their own convenience,' reflects the author Joachim Barbier. 'France v. Algeria at least made us understand this once and for all. The World Cup win was never going to repair society's problems, and that night we saw the limits of football.'

Not that Barbier blames the perpetrators. 'France's motto is *Liberté, Égalité, Fraternité*, but you know what? If I was an Algerian immigrant living in poor, cramped conditions in the suburbs and being excluded from society, I might feel a bit less free, a bit less fraternal and a bit less equal.'

This feeling of exclusion snowballed until it reached a head in November 2005. Young people in France's many underprivileged suburbs were tired of battling against a system that set them up as second-class citizens. Unless you were an extremely talented footballer or a rapper, it was near impossible for young people from Seine-Saint-Denis – a congested agglomeration of suburbs, just north of Paris, which houses more than 1.6 million people – to ascend the social ladder.

Job applications would be dismissed purely on the basis of the applicant's postcode. As unemployment spiralled to over 20 per cent in the toughest areas – and more than 40 per cent for those aged between eighteen and twenty-four – relationships with the police became increasingly tense. Accusations of structural racism were now a daily occurrence. When one considers that people of black and Maghrebi origin are twenty times more likely to be stopped for a routine police check than the rest of the French population, it is easy to understand where this growing sense of victimisation was coming from.

The tipping point arrived on 27 October 2005 when two boys, Zyed Benna (who was seventeen years old) and Bouna Traoré (who was fifteen), lost their lives on one terrible evening in Clichy-sous-Bois, a suburb in Seine-Saint-Denis. They were making their way home from football training when the police approached them for a routine check. Despite having committed no crime, the boys fled. They were electrocuted while hiding in a power substation.

The locals decided enough was enough, and what followed was three weeks of serious violence: thousands of youths protested against the police harassment they felt they were being subjected to and the lack of job opportunities. The unrest spread through the troubled neighbourhoods of greater Paris to the suburbs of other major cities. Overall, 8,973 cars were burned, 144 buses ransacked, 217 police officers wounded and 2,888 arrests made during the relentless disturbances. France was placed into a state of emergency.

From the moments the riots began, the government vowed to respond unequivocally, but the Minister of the Interior Nicolas Sarkozy merely inflamed tensions. Sarkozy had already spoken of his desire to 'flush out the scum' and 'to wash out the estates with a pressure hose' by the time he visited the suburb of Argenteuil, just four days after the deaths in Clichy-sous-Bois. Again, the future President of France shocked many with his crude, threatening language. 'You've had enough, haven't you?' he shouted up at the inhabitants of a tower block. 'You've had enough of that scummy mob. We'll get rid of them for you.'

At the same time that France's suburbs were going up in flames, *Les Bleus* flew out to the West Indies for an historic friendly against Costa Rica in Martinique. The *Fédération Française de Football* had agreed to play an international in one of the French overseas territories to pay homage to the 151

Martiniquais who had perished in a plane crash two months previously. Many felt the trip was long overdue, especially considering the high number of players that the overseas territories had contributed to the French national team through the years. 'West Indians had been waiting for that moment for centuries,' Thuram claims.

In Fort-de-France, *Les Bleus* lined up with six players of West Indian origin: Thuram, Éric Abidal, Florent Malouda, Thierry Henry, Nicolas Anelka and Sylvain Wiltord. For Henry and Abidal, whose families are from Martinique, the moment was especially poignant.

But if the warmth of the Caribbean climate transported the players both physically and mentally away from France, Thuram found it hard to forget what was happening back home. Indeed, he was still fuming when he stepped off the plane in Martinique. 'During the flight,' he states, 'I remember thinking: "I really hope nobody asks me a question about Sarkozy." But of course, in the press conference, somebody asked, and I couldn't help myself. I got very emotional.'

In front of a room of surprised football journalists, Thuram mounted a fierce attack on Sarkozy, and an equally stirring defence of the so-called 'scum' that stood accused of bringing French society down. 'I was fed up with the politicians always stigmatising people,' he explains. 'It's too easy. When they don't have a solution to society's problems, they look to stigmatise the people who do not have a voice in that society.

'These people are a minority, they are the people who vote least, so they are easy to attack. At some stage, you have to say "stop". The politicians don't even know the people they are talking about. What on earth does Sarkozy know about life in the suburbs?'

Like many of the most impoverished areas, Mbappé's hometown of Bondy – which borders on Clichy-sous-Bois – was being transformed into a battleground night upon night in November

2005. There is a good chance that Thierry Henry's late winner against Costa Rica lifted spirits in the Mbappé household that evening. But there is little doubt that the country that little Kylian was seeing through his six-year-old eyes did not look nearly as happy or as friendly as the one he was born into.

CHAPTER 5

L'ENFANT DE BONDY

'Here in Seine-Saint-Denis, we don't call them "riots". We prefer to describe the 2005 movement as a "social revolt".' Sylvine Thomassin is quick to correct my faux pas. The Mayor of Bondy is a fiercely determined socialist who, since she was elected in 2011, has led a relentless fight to improve living conditions in *les banlieues* and to subvert the stereotypes. She is proud of her town and even prouder of its favourite son. 'Kylian is our symbol, our ambassador,' she enthuses. 'He put Bondy on the map, he represents us in a wonderful way, and we're so happy to be able to call him one of our own.'

Thomassin is speaking from her office in Bondy Town Hall, one of the commune's most striking and elegant buildings situated in the large, pleasant central square. In the lobby, young mothers gather for a post-natal group. A middle-aged man is cursing under his breath after being told he does not have the right documents for his driving licence application. On one side of the room there is a stand with information on the Christmas market that is due to open in Bondy the following week. As settings go, this could not feel more normal.

For some reason, I had expected something different. When you make the trip to the other side of the *périphérique* – the Paris ring road that represents a distinct social divide – you apparently do so at your own risk. Especially when venturing into the notorious ninety-third *département*. Well, that is what many people would have you believe. The reality is of course far more mundane. 'This town is full of normal, friendly people who are just trying to live and earn their keep like anybody else,' Thomassin states. 'But because the politicians don't come this side of the *périphérique* they imagine things very differently.'

Thomassin has lived in Seine-Saint-Denis all her life. She is well aware that the *département* of around 1.6 million people, who are mainly from immigrant backgrounds, has a bad reputation. But thanks to Mbappé, Bondy is at last attracting positive publicity. Indeed, since his heroics in Russia, Thomassin has been inundated with interview requests. She does her best to accept every invitation. But the irony of Bondy suddenly gaining nationwide recognition – and even being described as part of Paris by certain media outlets – is not lost on this veteran politician. 'The *périphérique* just melted away after the World Cup,' Thomassin laughs. 'I keep hearing people say that Mbappé is a Parisian. Well, he may play for PSG, but we've only loaned him out. The Parisians can have him for now, but he'll always be a *Bondynois* at heart.'

Mbappé is proud of his roots and he remains in close contact with his friends from Bondy. By teaming up with Nike to launch his own clothing range Bondy Dreams in December 2019, he was reiterating the fact that for all his fame and success he has not forgotten his roots. They certainly haven't forgotten him. When drivers turn off the A3 motorway and enter a busy slip-road that leads into Bondy town centre, they cannot fail to see the enormous mural of Kylian Mbappé that is plastered onto the side of La Résidence des Potagers, a high-rise building.

This particular advertising space first featured Mbappé in 2017, when a giant mural was erected by local authorities depicting the striker in a PSG shirt. '*Bondy, ville des possibles*' (Bondy, town of opportunities), announced the accompanying slogan. When that was replaced by an advert for the hardware store Castorama in the middle of the 2018 World Cup, there was uproar. Popular demand ensured that Mbappé's face quickly returned, this time with Nike – who sponsor the player, PSG and France – erecting a stunning poster of Kylian in a France shirt, posing in front of a blue, white and red background. The message alongside read: '*98 a été une grande année pour le football français. Kylian est né*' (98 was a great year for French football. Kylian was born). In December 2019, Nike unveiled their second offering, featuring a young Kylian, lying asleep on his bed dressed in an AS Bondy shirt, dreaming of the grown-up Kylian who stands proudly over him in the France number ten shirt.

This latest mural is an advertisement for the Bondy Dreams clothing range, which includes a green pair of football boots, Mercurial Superfly, which are available for €290. It is safe to assume that Nike will not be selling masses of these shoes in this town. Bondy is a poor commune. During the unrest in 2005, it was one of the most turbulent zones in Seine-Saint-Denis. But Thomassin claims the media coverage merely reinforced national stereotypes. Yes, there was violence, yes, some demonstrators went too far, but the cry for help that was being made by so many disillusioned youths got lost among the reports of vandalism and thuggery.

'It was a time when the young people spoke up and said: "What about us?"' Thomassin explains. 'They don't want to live separately in their own communities, cut off from society, they want to be part of the republic. Young people here don't have the same opportunities. They were fed up with that and they were tired of not having a voice.'

Thomassin was deputy mayor at the time and spent her days out on the streets listening to young people. 'We wanted things to evolve,' she says with an undertone of frustration in her voice. 'We didn't want to just put the lid back on the cooking pot as we knew the issues would bubble back to the surface.'

She received plenty of local support. One couple that helped her to alleviate the tensions on the streets were Fayza Lamari and Wilfrid Mbappé-Lottin.

Kylian Mbappé's parents were already respected members of the Bondy community. Fayza, who worked on youth projects with the local council, became a close friend of Thomassin. 'They were both very active during those few weeks,' the mayor tells me. 'They always paid a lot of attention to what was happening in the town. Their belief was that the young people should be allowed to express their anger. The Mbappés lived in the centre of Bondy. Kylian was at the heart of it all. He was young at the time, but he witnessed this collective expression of anger.'

It was not an easy time for the inhabitants of France's troubled suburbs, or for the police, but for the rest of France life continued as normal. Indeed, as a foreigner living in central Paris, I had a feeling that the violent scenes taking place just a few kilometres from my flat existed in a different world to mine. The images on the news of buses on fire in Bondy and Montfermeil were shocking, but no more so than the latest car bombing in Baghdad. The only time I crossed the *périphérique* would be to go to see a football match at the Stade de France or to visit PSG's training ground in the lush western suburb of Saint-Germain-en-Laye. To put it bluntly, the riots did not affect my life.

It is telling that the only newspaper to provide in-depth coverage of the social revolt taking place around Paris was a Swiss publication. Serge Michel, a Swiss journalist who worked for the magazine *L'Hebdo*, was so struck by the lack of information being provided by the French press, he decided to go and see what was happening for himself. Michel rented a small flat in the heart of one of the town's poorest districts, and along with a handful of colleagues, spent three months immersing himself in Bondy life.

During that period, he learned about the plight of France's

underprivileged youth. 'We recounted the story of everyday life in the suburbs: the kebab shops, the transport, the football,' Michel told *Le Nouvel Observateur* magazine. 'We tried to understand the people who worked and the people who didn't. We tried to find the root of the malaise.'

Michel came across all sorts of people in Bondy, but interestingly he did not meet a single French journalist. Travelling to the suburbs, it seems, was not high up on the agendas of the French correspondents. 'For reporters, the suburbs are just the place you go through when you catch a plane from Roissy [Charles de Gaulle] airport,' Michel stated. 'The French reporters came to Bondy to report on specific events. But they stayed on the other side of the police barriers. They were reporting from the outside, looking in.'

Before leaving, Michel wanted to make a positive contribution. He decided to launch the Bondy Blog, a website that went on to become a valuable source of local information and an opportunity for an otherwise invisible section of the population to express itself. He set up a training scheme to allow aspiring local journalists to work for the website.

Today Bondy Blog is thriving and is recognised in media circles as 'the voice of the suburbs'. The website's editor-in-chief Ilyes Ramdani encourages contributors to write about subjects that are close to their heart and affect their daily lives. This is another, more peaceful and productive platform to voice and discuss the injustices that many Bondy residents feel they are still subjected to. But don't go onto the site expecting to find a feature on the next Mbappé, or sensationalist nonsense about gang warfare in the cities. 'We try to tell the real story of everyday life,' Ramdani tells me. 'We talk about what happens in *les quartiers* when cars aren't being burned and when Kylian Mbappé isn't winning the World Cup.'

•   •   •

For every Mbappé, there are hundreds of tales of disappointment. One report on Bondy Blog tells the story of a young *Bondynois* named Mokhtar Bakli. He shared similar passions to the PSG star; he trained every day and dreamed of becoming the next Thierry Henry. Mokhtar, however, lost his way. In 2003, aged just thirteen, he was shot dead by police after reportedly attempting to steal a car. The 2006 article explains that an annual football match is organised in Bondy to commemorate Mokhtar's tragically short life.

Those who knew Kylian as a child believe that he too could have veered off the straight and narrow. He was a bright boy with a cheeky, infectious smile, but he needed constant stimulation, regarded schoolwork as a chore and had to be brought into line frequently. 'School was always a problem,' Alain Mboma, a football coach and close family friend, told *L'Équipe* magazine. 'It wasn't that he struggled with the work, he was intelligent, it's just that his ambitions didn't lie in the classroom.'

Indeed, Kylian seemed to know from an early age that he was destined for a career in football. He was confident, joyful and had no problem making friends at school. But sitting in a classroom was not his idea of fun, and his frustration would often manifest itself through a kind of cheekiness that bordered on insolence. 'Sometimes when he arrived in the morning, I'd see this little spark in his eye, and think: "It's not going to be your day, is it,"' Nicole Lefèvre, Mbappé's secondary school French teacher, described in *L'Équipe* magazine. 'Kylian was good at misbehaving. But he mainly teased his teachers. He didn't tease the other boys so much.'

The former headteacher of Mbappé's first school Yannick Saint-Aubert remembers telling a six-year-old Kylian to pick up ten pieces of rubbish in the playground as punishment for misbehaving. Through the window, he saw the boy tearing the scraps of paper he found in half. 'When he came in with ten pieces, I said: "Well done, you've acquired basic aptitude in multiplication and division. Now get back out there and find me ten more,'" Saint-Aubert said in Arnaud Hermant's book, *Mbappé: Le Phénomène*.

Kylian's great advantage, and probably his saving grace, was the exceptional support network that he had around him. His parents paid extremely close attention to his schoolwork and ensured their boy always had plenty to keep him occupied. 'Fayza realised very early that Kylian was an exceptional boy but not particularly scholarly,' Thomassin explains to me. 'He didn't have a long attention span and always needed to be on the move. The state education system isn't always good for children who are a bit different, be it kids who struggle to keep up or kids who need constant stimulation. So Fayza was careful to choose the schools that could offer Kylian the support he needed, and she kept a very close eye on things.'

Indeed, Fayza went above and beyond her role as a mother. The former professional handball player arranged for Kylian to meet a psychologist aged five, and was reassured to learn that he was 'advanced' and had no apparent behavioural problems. The following year, he sat an IQ test at school. Kylian's results in the first part were outstanding. Then, upon hearing the school bell and being told that he could not go out to play, he messed up the second part on purpose.

No other pupil benefited from the kind of attention that Kylian received. 'We would see Fayza every evening,' Saint-Aubert said. 'She came to see me, spoke to Marc, the teacher, and asked how the day had gone. We spent a lot of time talking about Kylian.'

When Kylian was ten and set for secondary school, Fayza feared he was getting in with a bad crowd. His football skills were earning him considerable kudos, and he was in danger of becoming big-headed. Saint-Aubert admitted Kylian's behaviour was borderline: 'He could lose the plot if he didn't get what he wanted. He was exactly the type of kid who could have gone off the rails in a council estate, no doubt.'

Instead of moving to the state *collège*, he was enrolled in a nearby private Catholic school. At his new school, L'Assomption, Kylian was the only pupil equipped with a report card that had to be signed off by the teacher after every class. 'Fayza wanted us to write a comment about how he had behaved,' explained Lefèvre in *L'Équipe*. 'Then in the evening, his mother would say to me: "He's had eight hours of lessons today, and he's got eight [negative] comments!" Several teachers wanted Kylian expelled. 'His attitude, that smirk in the corner of his mouth, and the scathing comments he made to teachers got him in more and more trouble,' Lefèvre stated. 'He felt like people were against him.'

Yet, the French teacher liked Kylian and fought his corner. He could be naughty but Lefèvre knew that his mother was trying hard. She had also taken a shine to his dry sense of humour. 'One day a kid was having a go at him, and Kylian reacted by making fun of his pullover,' she described. 'To make him understand his error, his mother sent him to school wearing flared trousers and velcro-strap trainers for a whole week. He looked at me and said: "Am I handsome, Miss?" When I told him he looked fine, he replied: "It's thanks to you, Miss." He knew I liked him, and I think he liked me too. Even when he was being punished, there was a fun kind of complicity between us.'

When he was not at school, or at football training, Kylian would be taken to swimming and tennis lessons. He also attended the *École de Musique de Bondy* (Bondy Music School) between the ages of eight and thirteen. He was not especially gifted at music, but happily sang in a choir and learned to play the drums before undertaking flute lessons for two years.

This was not your typical working-class education. Kylian was a black boy in a tough neighbourhood, but he did not have the kind of upbringing that many assume.

When Kylian featured on the front cover of *Time* magazine's European edition in October 2018, under the headline 'Next

Generation Leaders', the strap above the interview claimed this was a remarkable rags-to-riches tale. Yet, however you spin it, and however much the media wants to turn Mbappé's life into a dreamy fairytale, this is simply not the case. He had a happy, comfortable, middle-class childhood and was provided with everything that any young person could hope for.

'What's interesting about Kylian is he's clearly not a typical *Bondynois*,' notes Bondy Blog editor-in-chief Ilyes Ramdani. 'If you look at his parents' social standing and the education he received, he's privileged. He lived in a fancy apartment and went to a private school. He was among the 5 to 10 per cent in Bondy who are quite well off.'

As a town, Bondy is effectively separated in two halves by the N3 road, a busy thoroughfare that cuts from east to west through Seine-Saint-Denis and into Paris's nineteenth *arrondissement*. The north of the city is mainly a dense collection of council estates. It is a poor area and crime is rife. The south is leafier and the housing consists of semi-detached houses as well as high-rises.

In keeping with their own social rise, Fayza and Wilfrid started out in north Bondy, then moved to the centre – to a flat that overlooked the AS Bondy stadium – when Kylian was born. They moved again, to south Bondy, when Kylian's younger brother Ethan arrived. Kylian's parents have been part of the Bondy community for several decades and they have earned widespread respect for the immense contribution they have made to their hometown. The couple first met in the late 1980s at *La Maison de Quartier Daniel-Balavoine*, a drop-in centre where youngsters from north Bondy would hang out.

Wilfrid, who was then twenty, worked at the centre as a helper, but quickly grew frustrated by the lack of facilities and began to campaign for the creation of a real youth club. He and his friends found another site, and after convincing the local authorities to invest some funds, they launched *Le Petit Bar*.

It was painted by volunteers, equipped with table football and table tennis tables and quickly began to attract dozens of kids. By the time they built an extension – converting the disused cinema next door into a concert hall – *Le Petit Bar* had 130 members.

Football began to play a central part in the association. Wilfrid organised Saturday kickabouts on a nearby concrete pitch, and within weeks they had enough teams to set up their own league. Mbappé Sr was in his element. On top of the Saturday games, he staged tournaments in the local gymnasium and – sensing the kids had an appetite for more – began running his own private training sessions. This was in the late 1980s, and the local football club *L'Association Sportive de Bondy* (AS Bondy) was suffering in comparison. One of the AS Bondy coaches, Jean-François Suner, decided something needed to be done. He recruited Wilfrid and several of his colleagues to coach the AS Bondy youth teams.

This decision effectively launched the modern-day AS Bondy. Youngsters swarmed to the club and the number of registrations swelled. Today, AS Bondy have more than 900 members, including three girls' sections, and each year they are forced to turn several hundred applications down. Wilfrid, who coached there for the best part of three decades, became reputed as one of the leading youth trainers in the Paris region.

In addition to Kylian, two more current French internationals – Jonathan Ikoné (who currently plays for Lille) and Sébastien Corchia (who is currently at Espanyol) – benefited from Wilfrid's sessions at the Stade Léo Lagrange. The list of professional players who developed under him at AS Bondy is mightily impressive. If Fabrice N'Sakala (Alanyaspor), Jamel Zahiri (ex-Angers), Mourad Satli (ex-Red Star), Steven Joseph-Monrose (ex-Brest) and Ben Amadou Sangaré (ex-Sedan) all enjoyed solid professional careers, emerging talents like Metehan Güçlü (ex-PSG and now Rennes), Joé Kobo (Lille) and

William Saliba, who signed for Arsenal for €29 million in 2019 before being loaned back to Saint-Étienne, look set for big things.

Wilfrid's former pupils remain grateful to him. When I spoke to Sébastien Corchia, the France right-back was effusive in his praise for Kylian's father. 'Wilfrid has this formidable presence,' describes the former Lille, Benfica and Sevilla defender, who spent one season at Bondy. 'He was very demanding, and he has a strong, deep voice. If we didn't give our all, he'd give us a severe dressing down. For a twelve-year-old he could be quite frightening. But he was close to the players and he was always fair.' Wilfrid's long-time friend Dominique Mendy, who helped create *Le Petit Bar* before also moving to AS Bondy, is puzzled as to why Wilfrid was never picked up by a professional club. 'There aren't many coaches in amateur football who have developed as many pro players as him,' Mendy said in Hermant's book, *Mbappé: Le Phénomène.* 'Wilfrid was ahead of his time. He was one of the first coaches to promote kids to higher age groups to accelerate their development.'

Wilfrid's success with young talents was extraordinary, yet arguably his biggest achievement of all lay elsewhere. The football club, which is situated in the heart of Bondy, just south of the N3, became the social epicentre of the town. Thanks to Wilfrid's human values, warmth, generosity and extraordinary commitment to the club, young people always felt welcome. Birthdays would be celebrated after training sessions, and families were urged to spend time there. Every summer, Wilfrid hosted a barbecue and staged a football match between parents and the coaching staff.

On one of my visits to AS Bondy, one freezing Sunday in November, the community spirit is warm and welcoming. As the under-14 boys battle it out against their local rivals FCM Aubervilliers on the main pitch, parents, brothers, sisters and club staff crack jokes on the sidelines. The arrival of under-12 coach Rayane Abdelli sparks a wave of banter. 'Hey, Giroud, what did you think of Benzema's goals last night?' a man in an AS Bondy tracksuit shouts at Abdelli. It soon becomes apparent that everybody here refers to Abdelli as Giroud. 'It's because I'm the only person in Bondy who likes Olivier Giroud,' the young coach tells me.

The former Arsenal forward is not especially popular among France's immigrant communities. Not since he took Karim Benzema's place in the national team. A heated discussion then breaks out regarding the merits of the two strikers, and most come to the conclusion that Didier Deschamps must indeed be blind. Eventually I manage to drag Abdelli away for a chat. 'This club is like a second home to me, and it's the same for a lot of people,' explains the tall 22-year-old. 'I used to play here – I even played with Kylian – and now I'm a coach. It's a family club. Everybody knows everybody and we look after our own. That's the philosophy Wilfrid wanted to instil.'

Wilfrid highlighted this family ethos in remarkable fashion at the turn of the century when he invited a lost soul into his own home. Jirès Kembo Ekoko was born in the Democratic Republic of Congo but at the age of six his parents sent him to France to live with an uncle and aunt. Kembo Ekoko says he was 'moved about a lot' during his early months in France, but he ended up playing for AS Bondy. Then one day, after a training session, nobody came to pick him up. Wilfrid took him home that evening and investigated the situation. Upon discovering that Kembo Ekoko's supposed uncle and aunt were not actually related to the boy's parents, Wilfrid and Fayza agreed to take Jirès in on a formal basis.

They raised him as one of their own. 'Wilfrid was my first coach, and he became my legal guardian and father,' Kembo Ekoko told *So Foot* magazine. 'It feels as if I was always destined to be with this person. He was the father figure that I never had.'

A skilful dribbler with pace and a low centre of gravity,

Kembo Ekoko blossomed as a footballer, initially under Wilfrid's watch. The winger was accepted to Clairefontaine at the age of twelve, represented France's junior teams up to the under-21 level, and made 110 Ligue 1 appearances for Rennes. At twenty-four, after being offered an opportunity to secure his financial future, he chose to move to Saudi Arabia.

For Kylian, who is eleven years younger, Jirès became a big brother and a role model. The future World Cup winner set his heart on going to Clairefontaine, just like Jirès, but he was not happy about his mentor's decision to move to the Middle East so young. 'I didn't agree with his choice and I found that hard to accept,' Mbappé told *L'Équipe* newspaper. 'He'd just had a great season at Rennes and wasn't far off the France team. I cried about it. It was brotherly love. But I supported him and I still do.'

Kylian could not have grown up in a more football-centric environment. The family home, a two-bedroom flat on the second floor of a large block, was adjacent to the Stade Léo Lagrange. His father was a coach, as was his uncle Pierre, his brother Jirès was one of AS Bondy's best players, and his mother Fayza had not only played top-flight handball, she was also a keen football fan. As a toddler, Kylian wore his France replica shirt to the local crèche. When he was at home, he would spend hours gazing out of his window at the training sessions and matches taking place below.

Even the Mbappés' friends were from the football world. Alain Mboma, the brother of former PSG and Cameroon striker Patrick Mboma, coached another local team called Blanc-Mesnil. He was often round at the Mbappés' flat, and his wife used to provide Kylian with extra tuition at weekends. 'Like all parents, Fayza and Wilfrid wanted to be sure he had a back-up plan in case football didn't work out,' Mboma explained in the documentary *Kylian, Hors Normes* (*Kylian, Out of the Ordinary*) on *La Chaîne L'Équipe*.

'But he was so sure he'd succeed. He was in his own world, his own little bubble. We could see he had quality, but only he believed he'd go as far as he has.' Mboma was particularly taken by Kylian's habit of interviewing himself. 'At five, he was capable of answering questions. It was like he had trained himself up. He used to watch players being interviewed on TV and then he had fun mimicking them. I think in his head, he used to think: "How would Cristiano Ronaldo answer this question?"'

At six, Kylian obtained his first football licence. His mother allowed him to walk to training on his own – although she insisted that a coach texted her when he arrived – and he started spending all of his spare time at the club.

Sébastien Corchia is eight years older than Kylian, but he distinctly remembers him as a tiny boy with a football shadowing the team. 'Kylian was always there,' he recalls. 'He used to listen to all the team-talks, he'd watch all of the games and he'd be in the dressing room with us all afterwards. He always had a ball at his feet and didn't hesitate in challenging us to dribbling contests.' Ex-France under-21 left-back Fabrice N'Sakala, who played in the same side as Corchia at Bondy, described Kylian as the club mascot. 'He would come on away trips with us when his dad was coach,' N'Sakala explained in *Mbappé: Le Phénomène*. 'I can still see him now, sitting in the corner of the dressing room with his oversized baseball cap. He listened to everything. His eyes didn't miss a thing. On the team bus he'd sit at the back with us, and our coach would tell stories about different players and teams. Kylian lapped it up. He loved it.'

Even then, Mbappé was at ease when he was among older kids. Wilfrid quickly recognised this and insisted that he played with more senior age groups. 'We noticed how comfortable he was with the ball. He did everything quicker than everyone else,' Jean-François Suner, who is now AS Bondy sporting director, tells me. 'We put him in the year above, and he was still the best player. So we put him two years up and he coped just fine.

But it wasn't just the way he played that stood out. The way he acted was different too. He seemed to be desperate to succeed as a footballer and he had this confidence, this conviction that he would.'

By the age of eleven, Mbappé was the talk of the football club. 'He was so good, I couldn't keep up with him,' laughs Abdelli. 'I was two years older than him, but he played at a much higher level than me. It was quite hard to take actually because everything he did seemed to be so easy. He'd run past you for fun and he was always laughing and joking.'

As Kylian won games singlehandedly on a weekly basis, scouts flocked to see the boy wonder in action. During the 2009/10 season, PSG, Monaco, Bordeaux, Caen, Rennes, Lens, Sochaux, Chelsea and Real Madrid all sent representatives to Bondy to watch Kylian, and they all established contact with Wilfrid.

The youngster knew he was homing in on his goal. AS Bondy's coaching staff tried to keep his feet on the ground, but it was not always easy. On one occasion, with Bondy's under-15s struggling against Bobigny, and the contest deadlocked at 0–0, the coach changed tactics at half-time. 'He told everybody to just pass the ball to Kylian,' Abdelli explains. 'That's all he wanted us to do; forget the original plan, just give it to the kid on the wing. We won 4–0 and Kylian scored all four.'

Kylian has a self-confidence that sometimes gets interpreted as arrogance. Some people believe that he has developed a big head since joining PSG and rubbing shoulders with Neymar. But those who know him best insist that this is utter nonsense. 'He's always been like that,' Abdelli states. 'He's always been sure of himself. He knows his qualities and he knows what he wants to achieve. But he hasn't changed. The Kylian you see scoring every week for PSG is the same Kylian who used to score every week for Bondy.'

Ramdani, who has followed Mbappé's progress since the

striker was eleven, agrees wholeheartedly. 'He has the mentality of a kid from *les quartiers*,' says the Bondy Blog editor. 'Nobody has opened doors for him. Kylian has always had to force doors open to get anywhere. What sets him apart is his ambition and his fierce determination. He wants to succeed at all cost. So far, he's done exactly what he promised he would: he's succeeded in Ligue 1 and he's won the World Cup. Next, he says he wants to win the Euros or the Olympics with France. Then move to Real Madrid and win the Champions League. Then win the Ballon d'Or. And you know what? I'm almost certain he'll succeed.'

CHAPTER 6

ZIZOU, LA LÉGENDE

By choosing to wear the number ten shirt in Russia, Kylian Mbappé was inviting pressure on himself. 'I won't pretend I don't know what it signifies,' Mbappé said before the World Cup. 'It's a number that carries the weight of history.'

For more than a decade, that blue number ten shirt was synonymous with grace, skill, class and success. Zinédine Zidane was voted France's greatest ever player by *L'Équipe* newspaper in 2018, seeing off competition from Michel Platini and Raymond Kopa. Many, including ex-Real Madrid teammates David Beckham and Roberto Carlos, consider him to be the best of all time. Few would contest he was the greatest player of his generation.

From the moment Zidane made his France debut – as a substitute against the Czech Republic on 17 August 1994 – it was clear that he was special. *Les Bleus* were in the midst of a fallow period. They had failed to reach the 1990 World Cup, crashed out at the group stage of Euro '92, and missed out on 1994 World Cup qualification in ignominious fashion. Indeed, Zidane's entrance in the sixty-third minute of this friendly game, staged at the playmaker's home stadium in Bordeaux, was the turning point in France's modern history.

The hosts were trailing 2–0 when Aimé Jacquet beckoned the

debutant from the bench. There was a roar from the crowd when the 22-year-old replaced Corentin Martins, and jogged on to the pitch in that now iconic, languid manner. Within minutes, the game was transformed. By knocking simple, early, accurate passes forward to Christophe Dugarry or Éric Cantona, Zidane got France playing in the opposition's half. He instantly looked like he belonged.

Zidane may have been sporting virtually a full head of hair, but he is otherwise easily recognisable on the blurred highlights footage from that night in Bordeaux. The effortless ball control, his elegance in possession and the way his body moved rhythmically as he danced away from opponents and into space gave him a unique, majestic air.

With five minutes left, Zidane offered the French public a mouth-watering glimpse of the future. Accelerating onto Laurent Blanc's pass, he used one of his famous stepovers to eliminate his first opponent before a drop of the shoulder took him beyond the second. The left-footed strike that flew past Petr Kouba into the net from twenty-five metres was a thing of pure beauty. Three minutes later, the comeback was complete when Zidane headed Jocelyn Angloma's corner powerfully home. 'It's Zidane again!' screamed Thierry Roland, the commentator on French television. 'Zidane at the double!'

If Roland and viewers around the country were amazed, Zidane's closest friends knew what was coming. Lilian Thuram, who also made his debut that day, already knew that Zidane was a star in the making. 'I'd seen him do that kind of thing in every training session and every game that we'd played together with the France under-21s,' Thuram states.

Thuram's first sight of Zizou came when he was called up to train with France's under-18s. 'I got changed and as I walked out I saw this guy in the distance juggling a ball,' the former AS Monaco defender explains. 'He'd kick it high up in the air, control it, then start juggling again. He did this for minutes on end. The ball never touched the ground. I remember thinking "who the hell is this guy?" I'd never seen anyone as technical as him. That evening I called my mates and told them I'd seen a phenomenon.'

In this pre-internet age, reputations were built through word of mouth rather than YouTube compilations. Bernard Diomède remembers hearing whispers about 'this incredible number ten' when he was at AJ Auxerre's academy. During a training camp at Clairefontaine with the France under-17s, the winger managed to sneak a look at his future teammate. 'We used to hide and watch the older teams train,' Diomède laughs. 'I still remember the first time I saw Zizou. He dribbled around everyone, and with the goal almost empty, he decided to pass to a team-mate to let him score. I thought it was amazing. Nobody else did that!'

By the time Euro '96 came around, everybody in France knew who Zidane was. That season, he had been the inspiration behind Bordeaux's run to the UEFA Cup final, and after scooping the Ligue 1 Player of the Year award, he was on his way to Juventus and the big time. Outside of France, however, his talents remained largely unknown. 'There was a lot of noise surrounding Zidane,' remembers Amy Lawrence, who reported on Euro '96 for *The Observer*. 'But it wasn't easy to watch the foreign leagues back then and I hadn't yet seen him play. So when I was asked to report on France against Spain, the thing I was most interested in was seeing what Zidane was really like in the flesh.'

That match was played at Elland Road and finished 1–1, and in keeping with the overall campaign, neither Zidane nor France performed at their best. The playmaker had been involved in a car accident just before the tournament and, according to *L'Équipe* journalist Vincent Duluc, was only '60 or 70 per cent' fit. Yet, there were still glimpses of the magic that was waiting to be unleashed. 'He already had that laconic style,' Lawrence points out. 'He had that flourish, beauty and eloquence. But he was unable to express his full talent. He wasn't yet ready to be the team's fulcrum.'

Zidane had not reached his peak by 1998 either. But his two goals in the showpiece against Brazil, coupled with an excellent season at Juventus where he claimed the *scudetto* and reached the Champions League final, proved enough to win him the Ballon d'Or. 'Those two goals propelled him to another level,' Emmanuel Petit tells me. 'They gave him star status and from there he simply took off. In France, he became the symbol. Everybody wanted him to be the figurehead of the team and he carried that mantle.'

• • •

To fully comprehend the power of that symbolism it is important to consider where Zidane comes from. His father, Smaïl, emigrated from Algeria in 1953, leaving behind his rural village of Aguemoune, nestled in the northern hills of the Kabylie region. Initially working as a labourer in the Paris suburb of Saint-Denis, Smaïl wanted to return to his homeland after Algeria's independence in 1962, but he only made it as far as Marseille. There he met his future wife Malika, who was also of Kabyle origins but had moved to Marseille. The couple settled in the Mediterranean town and raised their five children there.

Smaïl and Malika lived in La Castellane, one of the toughest, poorest corners of Marseille's drug-filled northern suburbs. Rumour has it that the siblings had to take turns to sit at the table to eat their dinner, so small and cramped was their apartment in Tour G, one of the tower blocks that surrounded Place de la Tartane. It was on this long, narrow, concrete courtyard that the youngest boy, known to his parents as Yazid, developed his extraordinary skills, cutting his teeth with tough kids from a variety of backgrounds. North Africans, West Africans, Turks, Albanians, Iraqis and Kurds, this bleak public housing estate was a veritable melting pot of cultures.

There is nothing special or glamorous about Zidane's story. Indeed, many immigrant families in France shared similar experiences. Smaïl worked tirelessly to provide for his children in Marseille, first in a warehouse, then at the local supermarket. Modest, hard-working and respectful, he was a role model to his fourth son. 'I'm very inspired by him,' Zidane told *The Guardian* in 2004. 'It was my father who taught us that an immigrant must work twice as hard as anybody else, that he must never give up.'

Zidane's humility and the work ethic that his father had instilled in him played a key role in his success. He was given nothing on a plate, and his life in La Castellane taught him to fight. 'Zidane enjoyed such a great career firstly because he was a strong character, which is something people don't necessarily realise, but also because he was humble,' Thuram stresses. 'Having that humility is crucial because it creates doubt, it pushes you to work; and Zizou worked a huge amount.'

Although Zidane's skills stood out during those feisty kickabouts on Place de la Tartane, it was never certain that he would secure a professional contract. Like most of his peers, he worshipped Olympique de Marseille, the southern giants who absolutely dominated the French game between 1988 and 1993. The shy teenager dreamed of emulating his hero Enzo Francescoli, who, along with Jean-Pierre Papin and Chris Waddle, dazzled the Stade Vélodrome crowd in the 1989/90 season. Later, Zidane named his first son Enzo after the wonderfully skilful Uruguayan playmaker.

Zidane's chances of representing France's most popular club looked strong when, aged ten, he scored four second-half goals for his local junior team US Saint-Henri against Marseille to win the semi-final in a regional cup competition. He was invited to attend a trial with Marseille, but reportedly got turned away after being told he was not quick enough.

At fourteen, Zidane trialled with AS Cannes. During his first match he was surprisingly positioned as a sweeper and attempted a nutmeg inside his own penalty area, lost possession and allowed the opposition to score. Luckily, the scouts overlooked this glaring error and he was offered a place in the academy. There, Zidane worked harder than anyone else to make the step up. 'He listened to everything we told him,' former Cannes youth coach Guy Lacombe told *So Foot* magazine. 'He had this ability to soak up all our advice and transfer it onto the pitch. That's a rare quality, and it's what makes him the person he is.'

The ability to remain silent and absorb everything happening around him could be almost unnerving. Raymond Domenech recalls feeling this 'secretive, voiceless' presence among his ranks when he was the France under-21 coach. 'Zidane possessed an incredible aura, fascinating even,' Domenech wrote in his book *Tout Seul* (*All Alone*), a fascinating account of his time in charge of *Les Bleus*. 'He used to hide behind Christophe Dugarry, who was more famous than him back then. But it was clear who the leader was in that duo. Zidane was the leader of the team already, with a natural authority that you cannot explain.'

In Stéphane Meunier's wonderfully revealing film *Les Yeux dans les Bleus*, a fly-on-the-wall documentary that follows Jacquet's side throughout the 1998 World Cup, Zidane is always in the background, yet at the same time he seems to be omnipresent. On the few occasions he speaks up – almost whispering with his impossibly soft voice and unmistakable Marseille accent – his teammates hang on every word. 'When he talked, we listened,' Petit states. 'Firstly, because he didn't talk often, and when he did, he chose his words carefully. And secondly, because he was Zizou.'

Pirès has no recollection of Zidane speaking in the dressing room at all. 'I only recall him talking out on the pitch,' Pirès states, before laughing at the memory of the advice Zizou used to give him. 'He'd just say: "Hey, *le Portugais*! If you don't know what to do with the ball, give it to me."'

For Amy Lawrence, Zidane's leadership provided an ideal foil for Didier Deschamps's far more vocal, animated captaincy. 'You can see through the documentary the way that Zidane carried the team in an almost gentle way,' she suggests. 'It was quite beautiful actually. It demonstrated how somebody can be a leader in a quiet way. Deschamps was a phenomenal captain. Zidane was more spiritual.'

Zidane was as coy with the press as he was with his teammates. He very rarely gave interviews, and after the 1998 win, refused to make even a passing comment on the social or cultural implications of the *black-blanc-beur* triumph.

Historically, France's relationship with Algeria is extremely complex, and political lobbyists from both nations have tried to get Zidane on their side. He is fiercely proud of his father's Berber roots, but in 2001 Zidane refused to speak out in support of his ancestors during Algeria's 'black spring', a three-month period of violent conflict between the Algerian government and Kabylie's Berber people. His reluctance to offer words of comfort to the long-suffering Berbers became a source of frustration and even resentment in the region where his parents were born.

In France, the extreme-right party the National Front began using *Les Bleus* as a political tool in the 1990s. When Zidane's popularity soared, National Front leader Jean-Marie Le Pen made a point of describing him as 'a son of French Algeria'. The term 'French Algeria' is a clear reference to French colonialism, and by employing it Le Pen insinuated that Zidane's family had somehow been on France's side during the brutal seven-year war of independence. One of Le Pen's followers then claimed Zidane's father was a *harki*, the Arabic word used to describe the Algerians who fought for the French during the battle for independence and who were massacred or fled to France once the conflict was over.

Zidane finally broke his silence after seeing banners labelling him a traitor during France's ill-fated friendly with Algeria in 2001. 'I say this once for all time: my father is not a *harki*,' he told the press. 'My father is an Algerian, proud of who he is, and I am proud that my father is Algerian. My father never fought against his country.'

For this unassuming young footballer who had emerged from the humblest of beginnings, it was all a lot to carry. As well as having his face beamed onto the Arc de Triomphe in Paris, Zidane's green eyes gazed out over the Mediterranean Sea after adidas installed a giant mural on the coastal road running south of Marseille. 'Made in Marseille' read the message on the 170-square-metre poster that was only supposed to stay for a month, but ended up dominating the coastline for six years such was its popularity. 'He is a national icon and the pride of Marseille,' the sports brand argued.

Yet the only place Zidane truly wanted to express himself was on the football pitch, and he did that brilliantly at the turn of the century. France went into Euro 2000 as favourites along-side the Netherlands, who were co-hosts with Belgium, and they lived up to their billing. The immense back-four that had provided the cornerstone of their World Cup success remained resolute, Patrick Vieira was now one of Europe's most dominant midfielders, while in attack Nicolas Anelka and Sylvain Wiltord joined up with Thierry Henry and David Trezeguet, both of whom had matured into deadly strikers.

Weaving everything together was a playmaker at the very peak of his powers and widely considered the best footballer on the planet. 'In all my years of covering football, watching Zidane at Euro 2000 will always be one of the highlights,' enthuses Amy Lawrence. 'It was one of life's great pleasures. He produced a masterclass in that tournament.'

Les Bleus opened with a 3–0 win over Denmark, Blanc, Henry and Wiltord providing the goals. An electric Henry netted again against the Czech Republic, before Youri Djorkaeff's strike clinched a 2–1 victory. It felt very different to two years previously. The shackles had been removed and this France team – now coached by Jacquet's former assistant Roger Lemerre – attacked with extraordinary verve. 'It wasn't arrogance, but we did feel very sure of ourselves,' Pirès says. 'We were two years older, we had more experience, more quality and we were absolutely ready to conquer Europe.' Marcel Desailly remembers feeling invincible during that period. 'I would say that between 1999 and 2001, we walked over the world of football. We were playing like real world champions and had no doubt we could win the Euros,' Desailly insists.

Lemerre felt confident enough to rest players for the third group match against the Netherlands, but a 3–2 defeat cost *Les Bleus* top spot. Spain represented a stern test in the quarter-finals, although with Zidane back and at his imperious best there would be no stopping Lemerre's men. Experts had predicted that the battle between Zidane and his direct adversary Pep Guardiola, who pulled the strings from a deep-lying midfield role for Spain, would define the result – and so it proved. Zidane's sublime free-kick opened the scoring, but it was his control, his movement, his laser-like passing and his persistent, faultless dribbling that drove Spain to distraction.

'Zizou had this presence with the ball,' explains Desailly, 'a kind of elegance that he created through the movement of his hips. It was just magnificent, almost like art, and when he played like that, he gave us so much confidence. He was like a ballet dancer. But he was not a nice ballet dancer – he was a killer ballet dancer.'

For all Zidane's magic, *Les Bleus* suffered a nervy finish against Spain. Gaizka Mendieta's penalty drew José Antonio Camacho's charges level before Djorkaeff's vicious, swerving strike restored the lead before the interval. France failed to make their superiority count in the second half and were fortunate that Raúl González missed a last-minute penalty.

Zidane certainly deserved to be on the winning side. His performance was mesmerising, as close to perfection as you could get, and as a defeated Guardiola swapped shirts with his chief tormentor, you could see the respect in the eyes of the defeated Catalan. This was the day that Spain truly recognised the talents of Zidane, and the moment that he caught the eye of Florentino Pérez. The following month, when Pérez was elected Real Madrid president, he made it his priority to recruit the Frenchman.

Pérez had to wait until 2001 to get his man, but before then he captured the signature of another *galáctico*: Luís Figo. Like Zidane, the Portuguese was outstanding at Euro 2000, helping his country defeat England, Romania and Germany in the group stage, and Turkey in the quarter-finals. Figo's Portugal proved formidable opponents for France in a semi-final that was filled with tension and controversy. Thierry Henry cancelled out Nuno Gomes's early opener in Brussels, collecting Nicolas Anelka's cutback and shooting on the turn past Vítor Baía. But the true drama was reserved for extra-time.

With both sides labouring in the heat, the quality of France's bench gave them a crucial edge: Pirès, Wiltord and Trezeguet were all sent on, the latter two combining to earn a penalty with only minutes left. Abel Xavier was beside himself when the linesman informed referee Günter Benkö that he had handled Wiltord's shot. The Austrian official struggled to maintain control as a cluster of furious Portuguese players crowded around him in protest. The disgraceful scenes that took place both before and after the penalty were unprecedented – as were the sanctions dished out by UEFA. Xavier received an initial nine-month ban for manhandling officials and spitting at the linesman, Nuno Gomes was suspended for eight months and Paulo Bento six.

Amid the madness, one person remained totally calm. As he stood, hands on hips, waiting to take the penalty, Zidane appeared oblivious to the mayhem that was unfolding around him. 'It's one of my favourite goals of all time, even though it was a penalty,' Amy Lawrence says. 'I remember during the two or three minutes between the penalty being awarded and it being taken, I watched only Zidane. It was like I was watching him through a magnifying glass, with everything else around him blurred out. Amid this maelstrom of chaos, with players losing their minds, Zidane was just standing there like a zen master. It looked like he was meditating or something. The contrast between the tornado that was raging around him and his concentrated calm was just incredible. Then he smashed home the penalty and to me it felt like one of the great sporting moments.'

The final, against Italy, was always going to be a tight affair. The teams knew each other inside out. Nine of the starting eleven for France had played in Serie A, and the nations had been separated only by penalties two years previously. When Marco Delvecchio took advantage of a rare chance, turning home Gianluca Pessotto's cross on fifty-five minutes, *Les Bleus* were in trouble. Again, Lemerre turned to his substitutes. First

Wiltord ran on. Then Trezeguet. Then Pirès. The ninety minutes were up, the Italy substitutes and coaching staff lined up
arm-in-arm on the touchline, ready to explode with joy, and the
Italian supporters inside Rotterdam's De Kuip stadium began
singing the national anthem.

'We had to keep on believing until the end,' Pirès describes,
'but honestly, only one of us truly believed: Didier Deschamps.
He kept on shouting at us, barking instructions, urging us to
fight until the very end. Like the Italians always do.'

Deep in added time, Wiltord picked up a loose ball on the
left side of the box, surged forward and rifled home a vicious
low shot beyond Francesco Toldo from a tight angle. The atmosphere changed, and as extra-time commenced, the momentum was suddenly with the French. Pirès saw his drilled
effort saved by Toldo at the second attempt, then moments later
he embarked on a run that has been etched into the annals of
French football history. The winger feigned a pass inside to
Zidane, jinked past two Italian defenders, then pushed the ball
towards the byline. His cutback was just behind Trezeguet, but
the Juventus striker swivelled brilliantly to smash a left-footed
strike into the top corner. As Trezeguet ripped his shirt off to
celebrate his golden goal, the man who had set him up stood
motionless in front of the France supporters. 'I had a blackout,'
Pirès nonchalantly explains with a shrug. 'I don't know what
happened. I should've been happy, but my brain just switched
off for a few moments. Psychologically, the match had been so
intense, I felt drained.'

Following the incredible standards that he set during that
mesmerising month, Zidane had a relatively quiet final, but
he was inevitably voted player of the tournament. L'Équipe
journalist Erik Bielderman struck a chord with many when
he likened watching Zidane at Euro 2000 to falling in love. In
France, he was now rivalling Johnny Hallyday as the nation's

favourite son. Indeed, Zizou edged ahead of the beloved rocker for a period, winning the French personality of the year award, as designated by *Le Journal du Dimanche* newspaper, six times between 2000 and 2007.

CHAPTER 7

LA ZIZOU DÉPENDANCE

It is a measure of just how good Zinédine Zidane was that *Les Bleus* seemed incapable of performing when he was not in the team. For an entire decade, between 1996 and 2006, there was a clear correlation between the presence, or otherwise, of a fully fit Zidane and the national team's results. France struggled with an injured Zizou in their ranks at Euro '96, yet he was the hero of the 1998 World Cup win and then the star of Euro 2000. The playmaker's aura, leadership and his ability on the ball gave the team supreme confidence and allowed France's many other talented players to express themselves fully.

When he was absent, the side appeared rudderless. 'You cannot replace Zinédine Zidane,' France boss Aimé Jacquet had argued in 1998 after Zizou's red card against Saudi Arabia led to a two-match ban. 'He's an exceptional player who is on another level.' During the early 2000s, Jacquet's words would resonate strongly with his successors Roger Lemerre, Jacques Santini and Raymond Domenech.

On 26 May 2002, when the 29-year-old schemer limped out of France's final World Cup warm-up game with a thigh injury, just five days before the competition commenced, there was a sense of genuine panic inside the camp. 'Zizou's given us a real fright,' right-back Willy Sagnol told journalists immediately after the 3–2 friendly win over South Korea in Suwon. 'We're not sure what he's done.'

The injury, which put Zidane's World Cup participation in jeopardy, became a huge story, not just in France but around the world. The Frenchman was not only the best footballer on the planet, he had also become the world's most expensive player after Real Madrid President Florentino Pérez signed him from Juventus for €77.5 million in 2001.

A fortnight before the tournament in Japan and South Korea, Zidane showed that he was worth every cent by scoring the greatest ever Champions League final goal against Bayer Leverkusen at Hampden Park. The contest was poised at 1–1 when Roberto Carlos lobbed a cross from the left flank back to the edge of the Leverkusen penalty area. Zidane moved himself into a side-on position, then brought his left leg around to execute an exquisite, waist-high volley into the top corner. The acrobatic strike required an extraordinary level of technique, but Zidane appeared to be in total control. This moment of pure artistry, which earned the Spanish giants their ninth Champions League crown, prompted fresh discussion as to whether the fantasti- cally balanced footballer really was actually right-footed, as the experts claimed. 'I'm more accurate with my right foot, but I feel more comfortable with my left,' came Zidane's ambiguous answer, leaving the subject very much open for debate.

When *Les Bleus* arrived in Seoul, the day after their friend- ly against South Korea, they were greeted by a media frenzy as the international press looked to ascertain whether Zidane would miss the tournament. More than two hundred journal- ists attended a press conference with the France team doctor Jean-Marcel Ferret.

Back home, everyone in the country became well informed on matters of human anatomy, particularly in the upper-leg region, and when it was announced that Zizou had torn his quadriceps, most already understood he would require between ten and twenty days' rest. He would definitely miss the opening group games against Senegal and Uruguay, and only had an outside chance of featuring against Denmark in fifteen days' time. Any other player would have been sent home and replaced in the squad. But this is Zidane we are talking about, and it was decided he should stay on in South Korea.

The feeling was that Lemerre's team had more than enough quality to get through the group, even without Zidane. This was, after all, a star-studded unit. Fabien Barthez, Marcel Desailly, Lilian Thuram, Bixente Lizarazu, Patrick Vieira and Emmanuel Petit were still in the side, offering *Les Bleus* a solid platform. While in attack they were spoilt for choice: Lemerre could call upon the 2001/02 top goal scorer from the Premier League (Thierry Henry), from Serie A (David Trezeguet) and from Ligue 1 (Djibril Cissé).

Incredibly, though, this team of champions fell flat on its face. Without Zidane tying everything together, France were a rabble. They suffered a 1–0 loss to World Cup debutants Senegal – a defeat that was made all the more embarrassing for the fact that their opponents consisted mainly of players from mid-ranking teams in Ligue 1.

At twenty-four, Henry was close to his peak, yet any hope Lemerre had of his striker assuming a starring role evaporated in the second game against Uruguay when he was sent off for a dangerous challenge just twenty-five minutes in. The ten men could only muster a 0–0 draw and found themselves on the brink of an early exit from the competition. Knowing that only a victory by two clear goals against Denmark would do, Lemerre issued a clear message to his medical team: get Zidane fit, whatever it takes. An entire nation prayed for a medical miracle.

Three days before the showdown, Dr Ferret announced the good news: Zidane, he said, would be available to face the Danes. 'There's a risk of worsening the injury, of course,' the

France doctor admitted in an interview with *Le Monde*. 'But given the situation, it's a risk we must take.' The fact that nobody believed France could possibly see off Denmark without their creative leader was a measure of just how irreplaceable he had become.

Early on Tuesday morning, thousands of fans gathered on the immense square in front of the splendid Hôtel de Ville in Paris to watch on a giant screen as *Les Bleus* scrapped for their World Cup lives. It may have been 7 a.m. in France when the pre-match coverage started, but the roar from the crowd was loud and raucous when the pictures showed Zidane stepping off the team bus and walking happily into the bowl-shaped Incheon stadium in Seoul. However, there was an obvious sense of disquiet when the camera focused in on Zidane during the warm-up, and the extent of the strapping on his left leg became apparent: Zidane could barely run, let alone orchestrate the team's play.

Still, where there is Zidane there is hope. The fans continued to believe – even after Dennis Rommedahl had ghosted in at the far post to give Morten Olsen's side a lead in the twenty-second minute. Zidane's every touch provoked a buzz of excitement outside the Hôtel de Ville, and when he fizzed a powerful shot fractionally wide of the top corner of Thomas Sørensen's goal on thirty-nine minutes the masses responded with a resolute rendition of *La Marseillaise*.

Yet the footballing gods were not with the French. Desailly headed Zidane's 51st-minute corner powerfully against the crossbar – the fourth time Lemerre's misfiring side had hit the woodwork in the competition – and when moments later Zizou lost his balance inside the Danish box, and then spent several seconds motionless with his nose buried in the Seoul turf, it felt like the end of the road. Jon Dahl Tomasson duly finished the defending champions off by making it 2–0 to Denmark. There were still twenty-three minutes remaining, but the French fans watching on the big screen had seen enough and began to file away glumly to begin a long day at the office.

France's bubble had been burst in spectacular fashion, and as the monthly publication *So Foot* explained so poetically, this dramatic, unexpected failure left many fans shell-shocked and disillusioned: 'For an entire generation of supporters who only discovered football in 1998, France represented an invincible armada, a kind of blue dream personified by Zidane, this genius who could overcome anything with a touch of magic,' the magazine noted. 'He was like a Greek hero, a demi-god. But if Achilles succumbed because of his wounded heel, Zidane's thigh would gently crush the illusions of France's youth.'

It would be disingenuous to claim that France's disastrous, goalless 2002 World Cup campaign was all down to Zidane's injury. As Lilian Thuram points out: 'We were missing another extremely important creative player in Robert Pirès. He had been phenomenal for Arsenal that year, but he got injured just before the tournament.'

Thuram also believes *Les Bleus* and their supporters had become complacent. The muscular defender points to the euphoric send-off they were given at the Stade de France before leaving for Asia. After the 2–1 defeat by Belgium, a giant banner depicting a blue France shirt with two stars on – symbolising a second World Cup win – was unveiled in the stands. 'We had just lost a friendly, and yet people were celebrating the World Cup that, apparently, we were going to win,' Thuram says, shaking his head in disbelief. 'We lacked humility; each and every one of us. We turned up thinking we'd already won the World Cup. We were not mentally or physically prepared for the battles ahead.'

Lemerre was sacked and replaced by the former Lyon coach Jacques Santini, who took charge for France's Euro 2004 qualifying campaign and naturally built his side around Zidane. But the harmony of 1998 had long since evaporated and there were cliques developing within the camp. It was reported that Thierry Henry, in particular, felt Zidane was wielding too much power. The Arsenal striker was by now the best player in the Premier League and received a steady stream of adulation from English football fans. Yet in his homeland he was always seen as second-best.

The ex-AS Monaco forward was extremely unfortunate to be pipped by Pavel Nedvěd of Juventus to the 2003 Ballon d'Or, but he responded to this personal setback by raising his game a notch further. In 2003/04, Henry netted thirty Premier League goals and, along with his fellow countrymen Pirès, Vieira and Sylvain Wiltord, helped the Gunners go an entire league campaign unbeaten. Voted player of the season in England, he finished second, behind Zidane, in the 2003 FIFA World Player of the Year award.

Henry respected Zidane, but the two rarely clicked on the pitch. It was telling that this brilliant playmaker had not yet provided Henry with a single assist. 'At Euro 2004, we heard that Henry was complaining a lot about not getting passes from Zidane,' states L'Équipe's chief football writer Vincent Duluc. 'At the same time, Trezeguet was complaining that Henry was the team's centre-forward. There were a lot of issues.'

While Henry struck up a near telepathic partnership with Dennis Bergkamp at Arsenal, he never achieved that level of understanding with Zidane. 'They didn't hate each other but they weren't friends either, and you could sense that out on the pitch,' Duluc explains. 'There was a mutual respect, but also a kind of mutual jealousy.'

At the Euro 2004 finals in Portugal, Santini's side struggled for cohesion against England in their opening match. Frank Lampard put Sven-Göran Eriksson's charges ahead, and David Beckham could have finished France off, but had his penalty saved by Barthez in the seventy-third minute.

Then, in the dying moments of the game, Zidane decided to

take matters into his own hands. As added time began, Emile Heskey fouled Claude Makélélé around five metres outside the England box, to the right of centre. The free-kick favoured a left-footer, but Zidane stepped up and clipped a sumptuous right-footed shot over the wall, across David James and inside the far post. 'The great man produces a great moment,' declared a somewhat deflated Martin Tyler, the English commentator.

Incredibly, that was not the end of it. Seconds after the restart, Henry latched on to Steven Gerrard's loose back-pass, James fouled him, and Zidane was presented with a chance to win the game from the spot. From my seat behind the goal, I vividly recall a young English boy next to me who started crying uncontrollably and turned his back on the action. His father was not happy and insisted he put on a brave face. It was all very unpleasant, but as this stranger forced his son to watch Zidane take the penalty, I thought maybe, just maybe, this was good parenting. The dad wanted to teach his boy a lesson: sometimes in life you lose but losing to someone as great as Zidane is nothing to be ashamed of.

Despite the fact that Zidane vomited before taking the penalty, he looked calm and unfazed as he ran up and fully smashed the ball home. As England's players put their heads in their hands, and the devastated kid next to me wailed deliriously, France's fans started to believe that Zidane could guide Les Bleus to glory once again.

However, this time the optimism did not last long. The incredible late comeback against England proved the high point for Santini's side. France drew with Croatia 2–2 and beat a weak Swiss side 3–1, but the defending European champions went out with a whimper in the quarter-finals, losing 1–0 to Greece. Besides those three minutes of bliss against England, it had not been a happy experience. 'We lost pathetically,' Thuram remarks. 'I didn't enjoy that tournament, and I no longer felt I belonged in that squad. There was a new generation coming and I thought it was the right time to stop.'

12 AUGUST 2004

The news arrives like a bombshell. With a simple statement published on his personal website, Zinédine Zidane announces his retirement from international football. At the age of thirty-two, having earned ninety-three caps over a trophy-laden ten-year period, the greatest player in France's history has decided he does not wish to continue. 'Playing for France has been the most beautiful experience of my career. [But] something happened after the 2002 World Cup,' the statement read cryptically. 'Euro 2004 provided confirmation.' Speaking to Canal Plus, Zizou hinted that the departures of France's long-serving general manager Henri Emile and the physiotherapist Philippe Boixel had swayed his choice. 'Something is a little bit broken,' he added.

A week before the announcement, Zidane had met with France's new coach Raymond Domenech for talks in Madrid. Many experts blamed Domenech for the outcome, claiming that the manager was so intent on building his own team from scratch he did not try hard enough to convince the legendary midfielder to stay on in the team. With Desailly, Lizarazu and Thuram also calling it a day that summer, *Les Bleus* were patently lacking in experience and quality in Domenech's first season in charge.

Twelve months on from Zidane's retirement, France were languishing in fourth place in their 2006 World Cup qualifying group having failed to beat Switzerland, the Republic of Ireland and Israel (twice). The overriding sense that Domenech's ship was sinking grew when the vastly experienced Makélélé also leaped overboard, hanging up his boots after being left on the bench for an away game in the Faroe Islands.

Then suddenly, one sunny summer's morning, the unexpected happened: on 3 August 2005, out of the blue, Zidane announced his return. He added that Makélélé was also coming back, and it later emerged that Thuram would follow them. 'The coach has come to see me in Madrid two or three times,' Zidane explained. 'That was significant. And as I've always said, France is the most important thing that's happened to me.'

The U-turn sent a wave of happiness and excitement across the country and reignited France's passion for *Les Bleus*. '*Il revient*' (He's coming back) was the simple headline on the front page of *L'Équipe*, accompanied by a photo of Zidane raging in celebration after his free-kick goal against England. There was no need to cite his name. The 'He' in the headline felt very much like a biblical 'He'. The Messiah was returning. 'The papers talked about the return of the Beatles,' Domenech noted. 'That was an exaggeration, but I understood the idea.'

Yet, even John, Paul, George and Ringo would have struggled to generate an atmosphere to match the one that greeted Zidane, Makélélé and Thuram in Montpellier on 17 August 2005. At the Stade de la Mosson, where the revered trio made their comeback in a friendly against Côte d'Ivoire, a sell-out crowd roared its appreciation and cheered every single touch from France's prodigal captain in the first half.

With Zizou back on centre stage, the transformation was instant. Never before have I witnessed a player who has so much presence on a football pitch. The 33-year-old was like a magnet for the ball. The other players, previously bereft of confidence, knew that if they were in trouble they could look to their new leader, and that's exactly what they did: passes were fired in the general direction of the playmaker, who would stretch out a leg, kill the ball dead and retain possession.

The crowd was in such a noisy, festive mood, the game felt like a seminal moment. 'The fervour in the stands took me back to the communal scenes of joy in 1998,' Domenech wrote in his book *Tout Seul*. 'We won 3–0 and Zidane scored. Between the transformation of the team and the atmosphere around us, I had this vague impression that I'd switched teams and jobs. It felt like the start of something. I began to believe we could go a very long way.'

Buoyed by the thrilling emergence of Franck Ribéry – an insouciant, fearless winger who brought directness to the pitch and a sense of fun and mischief off it – *Les Bleus* travelled to Germany in the summer of 2006 filled with hope. However, many of the past issues remained. The tactics were prosaic and after draws with Switzerland and South Korea, the team were staring at another premature exit. Nevertheless, with Zidane suspended after picking up yellow cards in the first two games, Domenech's team secured the 2–0 win they needed against Togo to progress courtesy of goals from Vieira and Henry.

Throughout his career Zidane saved his best performances for the biggest games, and he stamped his class all over the knockout stages of the 2006 World Cup.

France's round of sixteen opponents Spain made the mistake of winding the maestro up. 'We're going to retire Zidane,' boasted *Marca*'s front page on the day of the game, which looked like it was a solid prediction as Luis Aragonés's squad dominated early on and took the lead through a David Villa penalty. But France reacted through their livewire Ribéry. The 23-year-old chose an ideal moment to score his first international goal, racing clear after a one-two with Vieira, dribbling around Iker Casillas and gleefully rolling the ball home.

Ribéry's breathtaking strike seemed to liberate his teammates, and in the second half, with Zidane rolling back the years, *Les Bleus* roared into the quarter-finals. Vieira pounced to head home a Zidane free-kick on eighty-three minutes, and then the skipper added the *coup de grâce* himself, surging onto Sylvain Wiltord's pass, twisting inside Carles Puyol and hammering a low shot beyond Casillas to make it 3–1. 'I just want to say to the Spanish, it's not yet time for my testimonial,' declared a joyous Zidane. 'The adventure continues.'

Zidane's career was still very much alive, although the quarter-final against Brazil would spell the end for one modern great: like Zizou, Ronaldo had vowed to quit international football after the tournament. The Real Madrid striker had just established a new World Cup record by taking his overall tally of goals to fifteen, and he had no intention of stopping there. 'Just before kick-off, Zidane and Ronaldo caught each other's eye and exchanged knowing smiles,' recalls the journalist and author Amy Lawrence. 'It was like a flashback to 1998. They must have been thinking, "Here we are again, after everything we've been through." There was this obvious respect between these two sporting warriors.'

There remained, however, a question mark over Zidane's fitness, as he had been feeling pain in his right thigh ever since the Spain game. Domenech recalls watching his captain during the warm-up and noticing that he was unwilling, or unable, to strike the ball with his right foot. Yet, those concerns evaporated in the second minute when Zidane had his first touch of the ball. Three Brazilians rapidly descended on him, boxing him in. The midfielder bamboozled them with a double drag-back to find space, then released a perfect pass to launch a France attack. 'At that moment,' Domenech reflected, 'I looked at my assistant Pierre Mankowski, and I told him: "We've won this."'

Zidane turned in a number of wonderful performances while wearing the blue shirt of France. But the masterclass he produced in Frankfurt that night in July 2006, against the reigning world champions, was the best of the lot. 'It was simply mind-blowing,' enthuses Amy Lawrence. 'He was pirouetting through tackles, spraying passes all over the pitch – he was a level apart. There was a perfection about him during this game.' Domenech was of the same view: 'I don't think I'd ever seen Zidane at that level,' he said.

Zidane was taking football to another dimension. That day,

watching him move so gracefully across the pitch, caressing the ball with the lightness of an impressionist applying the finishing brush strokes to a masterpiece, it was easy to understand why, in 2005, two film directors, Douglas Gordon and Philippe Parreno, had decided to make a documentary (*Zidane: A 21st-Century Portrait*) by tracking this veritable artist with seventeen cameras during a Spanish league game between Real Madrid and Villarreal.

It was somewhat fitting that on that memorable day Zidane provided his first assist for Henry, in his 106th appearance for France and the fifty-seventh time the pair had lined up together. Noticing that his clubmate Roberto Carlos was distracted as he was busy pulling up his socks, the elegant number ten whipped a free-kick towards the far post and Henry ghosted in unmarked to score with a clinical volley.

The holders had been dumped out, yet the post-match talk centred on France's ageless playmaker. 'Zizou played like a Brazilian today,' laughed winger Florent Malouda. Left-back Éric Abidal seemed to be in awe, stating: 'Before I turned professional, he used to make me dream. Today, he's still doing that.' Pelé insisted Brazil need not feel ashamed after succumbing to 'such a veritable magician', and Franz Beckenbauer called on Zidane to continue. 'Why is he retiring?' the Germany legend asked. 'He's just as good as he was four years ago. If he's playing well, he has to carry on.'

In his head, though, the plan was clear: Zidane would retire after winning the World Cup for a second time, in Berlin, on 9 July. When he fired *Les Bleus* through to the showpiece by scoring the only goal, from the penalty spot, in yet another tight, tense semi-final against Portugal, the stage was set.

It all looked like it was going to script too. Against Italy, Zidane broke the deadlock in the Olympiastadion with another spot kick on seven minutes, this time dinking an audacious Panenka (a cheeky chip from the penalty spot made famous by the Czech midfielder Antonín Panenka at the 1976 European

Championship), which hit the underside of the bar and just about crossed Gianluigi Buffon's goal line. But Marcello Lippi's tenacious players, and Marco Materazzi in particular, had no intention of letting this final turn into a farewell party for Zidane. The Internazionale defender equalised on nineteen minutes, nodding in a corner from Andrea Pirlo's delivery. Luca Toni then struck the bar, but it was France who came closest to winning in extra-time when a brilliant header from Zidane produced an even better save from Buffon. Indeed, had it not been for the Italian goalkeeper's tremendous agility, Zidane's career would have ended in glorious fashion.

Instead it ended in ignominy.

There were thirteen minutes left when Zidane's coolness suddenly deserted him. Upon hearing an insult from Materazzi, the red mist descended, and France's captain squared up to the Italian and thrust his head powerfully into the defender's chest. It was a moment of pure theatre, the violence as raw as it was unexpected. The referee, after consultation with his assistant, produced the inevitable red card, and Zidane embarked on a long, lonely, painful walk off the pitch, passing the World Cup trophy, which had been tantalisingly positioned in front of the tunnel, without so much as a glance. He was ruminating in the dressing room when Fabio Grosso won the World Cup for Italy, sending Barthez the wrong way in the shootout after Trezeguet had smashed his penalty against the bar.

It is impossible to know if France would have won had their talisman remained on the pitch, but Zidane's dismissal clearly did not help. Regardless, few back home blamed the now retired footballer. In fact, there was an overwhelming desire to understand, and even justify, his violent actions. In an address to the players, France President Jacques Chirac even praised Zidane, saying: 'You are a man of heart, commitment and conviction. That's why France admires and loves you so much.' Four days after the final, a survey conducted by Institut CSA revealed that 61 per cent of French people had already forgiven him. Six years on, the head-butt was immortalised by the Algerian-born French artist Adel Abdessemed, who sculpted a five-metre-high statue depicting the moment.

The public's response can be explained partially by Zidane's immense popularity, his enormous contribution to *Les Bleus* over twelve years, and the fact that his brilliant swansong had sparked such a thrilling, enjoyable and unexpected story. But there was more to it than that. There had always been an endearing, vulnerable side to Zidane, and this moment of weakness displayed on the biggest stage of all comforted people in their conviction that he is, after all, a human being who makes mistakes just like everybody else. 'The incident turned him into a human god,' Raymond Domenech observed. 'Head-butting somebody who has just insulted you – you can't get more human than that.'

As a boy, Zidane learned to fend for himself in one of the toughest environments imaginable. He had to be hard to survive, and he carried that aggressive, violent edge into his playing career. A terrible haul of fourteen career red cards testifies to this. For that split-second in Berlin, amid the intense scrutiny and pressure of a World Cup final, Zidane's mask fell. The global superstar and role model that the French media had been happily deifying throughout the tournament momentarily disappeared. In his place stood an angry kid from La Castellane.

Back in his youth, the insults would fly during games on Place de la Tartane and the language was colourful. Yet bad-mouthing someone's family remained taboo. When explaining his reaction, Zidane still seemed to be going by those rules from his childhood. '[Materazzi] said some very serious things, personal things that touched me deep down, about my mother, my sister,' Zidane said. 'I'd have preferred being punched in the mouth than have to hear that.'

In France, Zidane's legacy was not tarnished by this violent outburst. It might have even grown stronger. He is certainly not remembered as a hot-headed individual who cost his country the World Cup. Zinédine Zidane is seen as the nation's greatest ever footballer; a magician with a football and a kind, humble person who – when all is said and done – was just trying to protect the name of his mother and his sister, as any good person should.

CHAPTER 8

LIGUE I – LA LIGUE DES TALENTS

Kylian Mbappé first crossed paths with Zinédine Zidane on a frosty December morning in the Spanish capital in 2012. Mbappé was thirteen and had been invited for a trial with the mighty Real Madrid. Zidane, the club legend who was earning his coaching badges at the time, had been asked to show the wide-eyed teenager around the training ground.

This was not Mbappé's first trial at a big foreign club – he had gone to train at Chelsea two years earlier – but Real Madrid were pulling out all of the stops. During those few dreamy days, Real Madrid laid out the red carpet for a player they knew was special. As well as persuading France's greatest ever footballer to work as a tour guide, the European giants invited Mbappé and his entourage to attend that weekend's game, a 2–2 draw with Espanyol, in one of the Santiago Bernabéu's VIP boxes.

Zidane even introduced Mbappé to his hero, Cristiano Ronaldo, and the photo he got with the Portuguese star would take pride of place in his bedroom back in Bondy.

It was exciting, but Mbappé did not feel overawed. If anything, his uncle, the former CS Sedan sporting director Pierre

Mbappé, who travelled to Madrid with his nephew, was more star-struck. 'I never imagined my thirteen-year-old nephew would take me to Real Madrid or to Chelsea,' he told *L'Équipe* magazine. 'But Kylian did it and I want to thank him for that. Selfishly, I gained a lot of pleasure from talking to coaches like Carlo Ancelotti and Zinédine Zidane.'

Pierre Mbappé should not have been surprised. After all, Kylian had already promised that he would take his inner circle to Real Madrid one day. From a young age, he went around telling anybody who would listen that he was destined to play for *Los Merengues*. There was no doubt in his eager mind.

In a documentary produced for *L'Équipe*'s television channel *La Chaîne L'Équipe*, Alain Mboma, the brother of ex-Cameroon striker Patrick Mboma and a close friend of the Mbappé family, recounted the moment that he gave Kylian a model of the Bernabéu for his tenth birthday. 'Kylian kept saying he was going to play for Real Madrid, so we gave him this model and told him that we'd buy him tickets for a game,' Mboma explains. 'We were gently teasing him. But he turned it around, saying: "One day I'll take you all to Real Madrid and we'll sit in the VIP seats."' Everybody burst out laughing. But Kylian was not joking.

This astonishing self-assurance is something Mbappé was born with, but the fact that his parents were so present, so supportive and also shared his unwavering belief in his abilities, strengthened his convictions further. His mother, Fayza, demonstrated her steely faith in her son's talents when, at the end of Kylian's trial at Chelsea, the English club told her they would like to invite him back for a second look. Aged eleven at the time, he had trained at Cobham for a whole week and even played a game for Chelsea's under-12s against Charlton. With Mbappé lining up alongside future England striker Tammy Abraham in attack, the Charlton kids did not know what had hit them. Fayza thought Chelsea had been afforded plenty of time to recognise her son's ability. She was unimpressed by their reluctance to make an immediate offer, and curtly informed them there would be no second trial.

Yet, Kylian remains grateful to Chelsea for giving him that experience. 'Chelsea was the first great club, the first big club, that I went to visit,' he told the *Daily Telegraph* in 2017. 'So it was a real discovery for me. We played against Charlton, and we won maybe seven or eight nil. I also got to meet some of the first-team players – [Didier] Drogba, [Florent] Malouda – the French-speaking ones and took some pictures with them.'

That Mbappé was dreaming of following his idol Ronaldo to the Bernabéu, or of one day replacing Drogba at Stamford Bridge, is hardly surprising. In modern times, the ultimate dream for all aspiring footballers in France has been to leave their home country to play in one of Europe's four biggest leagues.

Serie A had already started exploiting France's elite talent in the 1990s. Come 1998, seven members of *Les Bleus*' World Cup-winning squad played their club football in Italy. By the time the 2002 competition came around, there were just five Ligue 1 players in Roger Lemerre's squad. Five others were based in Serie A, three in La Liga, two in the Bundesliga and eight played their club football on the other side of the English Channel.

The Premier League revolution was in full swing and England became the destination of choice. Football enthusiasts in France were charmed by the English game. The stadiums were full, the football chaotic, and the deep culture and history of English football was intriguing. Furthermore, Arsène Wenger's Arsenal were proving that French players could flourish in this colourful environment.

Mbappé's strike partner in the France team, Olivier Giroud,

grew up in the southern region of Isère. As a boy, he was enchanted by the aura of Olympique de Marseille. But for Giroud, who was thirteen at the turn of the century, the pull of the Premier League took over during his teenage years. 'I wanted to play in Ligue 1, but the Premier League represented an even bigger dream,' explains Giroud, who is talking with me in the plush surrounds of Chelsea's training ground. 'When I was a teenager, I was a big fan of Arsenal and also Liverpool. I used to love watching the French guys who were succeeding at Arsenal ... Robert [Pirès], Titi [Henry], Pat [Vieira], Manu [Petit] and everyone. I said to myself: "Wow! Football is different over there."'

With Henry conquering English football in glorious style, Arsenal became everybody's second favourite team in France. In 2002, the year of the Gunners' second Double under Wenger, the television network Canal Plus launched a new version of their Sunday night show *L'Équipe du Dimanche* (*The Sunday Team*). The programme featured highlights from Europe's top four leagues, but the presenter Hervé Mathoux introduced an original twist: each league would be represented by an expert from that particular country.

Suddenly, with five different nationalities around the table, the show had colour, local knowledge, amusing foreign accents and bags of charm. England's representative Darren Tulett was a particularly big hit. With his tweed jackets, Beatles haircut and carefully placed references to the Queen, cups of tea and Britpop, Tulett brought the delights of English culture into French living rooms in a deeply entertaining way.

L'Équipe du Dimanche gathered a cult following and its ratings rocketed, despite its late 11 p.m. screening time. 'It was an important moment of the week,' describes Giroud. '*L'Équipe du Dimanche* was part of the ritual before going back to school on a Monday morning. I had to negotiate with my dad but luckily he let me stay up to watch. It was such a pleasure to see all the best teams from around Europe.'

If Henry was the most famous Frenchman in England, Tulett became France's most cherished Englishman. French footballers, in particular, took a shine to the person who enlightened them with his weekly English football stories. 'When I started going to the stadiums, I couldn't believe it: everybody knew me,' Tulett, who is now a colleague of mine at beIN Sports, remembers with a smile. 'I was only on television once a week, and I was on late in the evening, but England was the place to be at that time, and the show became really popular.'

Usually journalists have to fight to get the attention of footballers. But for the man who represented the Premier League in France, the opposite was true. 'The players were coming up to *me*,' he laughs. 'They'd come and chat about the show. Then, they might casually say: "So Darren, can you get me a move to England?" They were laughing but they genuinely wanted to know if I had any ins. Some would ask me what I thought about a particular club. They wanted my advice before signing.'

Flush with cash thanks mainly to lucrative television deals, Premier League clubs could cherry-pick talent from France – and they did not hold back. The floodgates opened and by 2010 there were fifty-one French footballers playing in England's top tier.

Not all of these transfers ended well, however. Young French players, in particular, struggled. For every Nicolas Anelka, Gaël Clichy or Abou Diaby – all of whom succeeded after moving to England in their teens – there were many more players who sank without trace.

Gaël Kakuta was regarded as one of the world's most exciting young talents when he signed for Chelsea aged sixteen. He was later voted best player of the Under-19 European Championship that France won in 2010. But Kakuta made just sixteen appearances for Chelsea during the eight years that he was on the club's books. Likewise, Florent Sinama-Pongolle and Anthony Le Tallec never reached their potential at Liverpool after leaving France aged eighteen. Teenage forward David Bellion struggled at Sunderland, while the hugely promising Gabriel Obertan floundered after signing for Manchester United.

Mbappé's parents were aware of the dangers and were therefore reluctant for Kylian to leave France before he was ready. So, when Real Madrid offered him the chance to sign his first professional contract with them following the trial in 2012, the Spanish giants were told they would have to wait. 'Wilfrid manages Kylian in a very careful, intelligent way,' says AS Bondy's sporting director Jean-François Suner. 'From a young age, Kylian was in demand. There was always interest from French and foreign clubs. He could have gone anywhere he wanted. But his dad made sure he kept his head on his shoulders and took one step at a time.'

Kylian was a Real Madrid fan but he accepted his parents' opinions. 'People talk about "the Mbappé clan", but the boss, the one who decides, is Kylian,' Pierre Mbappé told L'Équipe magazine. 'Anybody who believes people impose decisions on him are wrong. If he didn't join Real Madrid, it's because he decided not to.' Indeed, even as a kid he knew how important it was to cut his teeth in France. Alain Mboma claims Kylian had already mapped his career out by the time he started primary school. 'From the age of four, he knew what he wanted,' Mboma explained. 'He used to tell us that he wanted to go to Clairefontaine first of all, then play for a French club, then end up at Real Madrid.'

On his decision to reject Real Madrid, Mbappé told Le Parisien newspaper: 'I wasn't ready to go abroad. Leaving my friends and my country behind, coping with the language barrier ...

Les Bleus line up ahead of the 1998 World Cup final against Brazil in Paris. The tournament changed the way football is perceived in France, and Aimé Jacquet's much cherished *black-blanc-beur* (black-white-Arab) team was held up as a beacon for the country's multi-ethnic society.
© CHRISTIAN LIEWIG/TEMPSPORT/CORBIS VIA GETTY IMAGES

Lilian Thuram leads the celebrations after France's thrilling 2–1 victory over Italy in the Euro 2000 final in Rotterdam. The first nation to follow up a World Cup triumph with a European title, *Les Bleus* set new standards in international football at the turn of the century.
© POPPERFOTO VIA GETTY IMAGES

The giant Zinédine Zidane billboard in Marseille was only supposed to stay for one month but ended up dominating this coastal road for six years, such was its popularity. Widely considered the nation's greatest ever footballer, the Marseille-born legend is also a much-loved personality in France and a symbolic figure for its immigrant communities.
© PASCAL PARROT/SYGMA/SYGMA VIA GETTY IMAGES

France's 2001 friendly against Algeria is forced to be abandoned after hundreds of youths, mainly of North African descent, invade the pitch. Politicians had hoped that the first meeting between the nations since Algeria's independence in 1962 would symbolise their reconciliation. Instead it stoked racial tensions and is believed to have helped far-right leader Jean-Marie Le Pen reach the second round of the presidential elections in 2002. © OLIVIER MORIN/AFP VIA GETTY IMAGES

Thierry Henry, Nicolas Anelka and David Trezeguet (*from left to right*) prepare for a training session at Clairefontaine in 1998. The renowned centre of excellence, which was established in 1988, provided the foundations for France's success, churning out a seemingly endless supply of talent. COURTESY OF SPORTS PRESSE

Karim Benzema, Hatem Ben Arfa and Samir Nasri (*from left to right*) celebrate winning the 2004 European Under-17 Championship on home soil. The so-called *Génération '87* was tipped for greatness but failed to live up to expectations at the senior level for France, and off the field controversies were rarely far away. COURTESY OF SPORTS PRESSE

Kylian Mbappé (*furthest right, bottom row*) lines up for AS Bondy, his local team, which was coached by his father Wilfrid (*furthest left, top row*). Bondy, one of the toughest *banlieues* in the Paris region, suffers from high rates of crime and unemployment, but its football club continues to produce exceptional players, from France internationals Sébastien Corchia, Jonathan Ikoné and Mbappé to Arsenal's William Saliba. COURTESY OF KYLIAN MBAPPÉ

A ten-year-old Mbappé kisses the Gif Cup after helping the Rennes under-12 side win the international youth tournament in May 2009. Although still an AS Bondy player, Kylian was invited to participate in the competition by Ligue 1 club Rennes. COURTESY OF GIF CUP

Mbappé is all smiles after joining the prestigious AS Monaco academy, aged fourteen, in 2013. An avid fan of Cristiano Ronaldo, he decorated his bedroom with posters of the Portuguese star, having already enjoyed the pleasure of meeting his hero during a trial with Real Madrid in 2012. COURTESY OF SPORTS PRESSE

Mbappé poses with his father Wilfrid after enrolling at the world-famous Clairefontaine academy in 2011. He was one of the smallest boys in his year and even got the nickname Mbébé (M-baby) because of his tendency to sulk. But Kylian had a growth spurt in his second year and, according to the academy director, 'just exploded' in his last six months there. COURTESY OF KYLIAN MBAPPÉ

Brazil's players try to stop Zinédine Zidane during the 2006 World Cup quarter-final. The playmaker, who had come out of retirement the previous year, carried *Les Bleus* all the way to the final in Germany. Against Brazil, the 34-year-old was untouchable, producing one of *the* great World Cup displays.
© CONTRAST/BEHRENDT/ULLSTEIN BILD VIA GETTY IMAGES

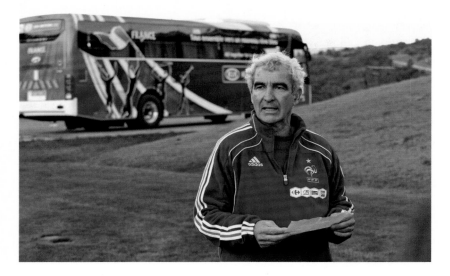

France's maligned manager Raymond Domenech reads out a letter written by his players after they decided to go on strike during the 2010 World Cup in South Africa. The behaviour of the mutinous players, who sat obstinately on the bus near the team base in Knysna, refusing to train, brought shame on the country and is considered to be the darkest episode in the history of *Les Bleus*. © DAVE WINTER/ICON SPORT VIA GETTY IMAGES

France coach Didier Deschamps is given the bumps after a dramatic 3–2 aggregate triumph over Ukraine in the play-off for the 2014 World Cup. The stirring performance – during which they overturned a 2–0 deficit from the first leg – signalled the end of years of failure and embarrassment, and marked the start of a new dawn for *Les Bleus*. It sparked an immense outpouring of joy both on the Stade de France pitch and in the stands. © LIONEL BONAVENTURE/AFP VIA GETTY IMAGES

Kylian Mbappé surges away from Argentina's Javier Mascherano at the 2018 World Cup. The nineteen-year-old hit speeds of 37 km/h in this breath-taking seventy-metre burst, which earned France a penalty and left a global audience open-mouthed. The insouciant forward upstaged Lionel Messi in the round of sixteen clash, becoming the first teenager to score twice in a World Cup match since Pelé and inspiring an unforgettable 4–3 victory. © ROBBIE JAY BARRATT/AMA VIA GETTY IMAGES

Les Bleus captain Hugo Lloris lifts the World Cup trophy and the celebrations can begin. Twenty years after France's first title, Didier Deschamps's fiercely determined and united team – the youngest victors since Brazil in 1970 – were worthy winners in Russia after seeing off Argentina, Uruguay, Belgium and Croatia. France fans hope 2018 will prove to be the start of a new legacy. © SHAUN BOTTERILL VIA GETTY IMAGES

Kylian Mbappé makes his first public appearance in Bondy since winning the World Cup. On 17 October 2018, thousands of proud *Bondynois* gathered at AS Bondy's Stade Léo Lagrange to see the new national hero and role model. The town mayor, Sylvine Thomassin (*left*), presented Kylian with a flute, the instrument he used to play as a boy at Bondy's music academy. © BAPTISTE FERNANDEZ/ICON SPORT VIA GETTY IMAGES

adapting would probably have been difficult. My objective was always to start in France and to succeed in my homeland.'

These days, Ligue 1 is an ideal breeding ground for young players. France's culture of youth development and its expertise in that particular field remains strong, and with an ever-increasing number of players moving abroad, there is invariably room for the academy kids to play. 'Our great strength is that we blood our young players,' says the former Lyon coach Hubert Fournier, who became the FFF technical director in 2017. 'Youngsters play for professional clubs at an early stage, and that's a key part of their development. It's essential that they play.'

As somebody who has been commentating on Ligue 1 matches for the English world feed since 2004, one of the great pleasures I get comes from discovering tomorrow's superstars. Seeing Eden Hazard make his first confident steps as a sixteen-year-old with Lille, observing Raphaël Varane's commanding debut with RC Lens at seventeen, or commentating on Karim Benzema's first Ligue 1 goals for Lyon aged eighteen, all remain vivid memories. In each case, I knew instantly that I was witnessing the start of something special.

France continues to unearth fresh gems on a weekly basis. In each of the last three seasons, teenage players have made more than 700 Ligue 1 appearances between them, approximately double the number in La Liga, the Bundesliga and Serie A, and more than three times the Premier League figure.

It came as no surprise to me or to other Ligue 1 observers that Arsenal signed Saint-Étienne's impressive centre-back William Saliba, aged eighteen, in 2019. In the handful of Ligue 1 games he played in the 2018/19 season, it was obvious that he had immense qualities both as a defender and as a leader. The arrival of midfielder Eduardo Camavinga, who broke into the Rennes side at sixteen, was equally impressive. Camavinga, much like Lyon's latest prodigy Rayan Cherki, will be the focus of attention from Europe's biggest and wealthiest clubs during the forthcoming transfer windows.

'We are a very good country for youth development, but we are even better at integrating the youngsters,' argues *L'Équipe* journalist Vincent Duluc. 'For players aged between eighteen and twenty-two, France is brilliant because if you are good enough, you play week in week out. Our youngsters get the grounding they need. By the time a player is twenty-one or twenty-two, he has already played 150 top-flight matches and he's ready to play anywhere.'

In the summer of 2019, Ligue 1 again lost a cohort of fine players. Lyon sold left-back Ferland Mendy to Real Madrid for €48 million, midfielder Tanguy Ndombélé to Tottenham for €62 million and forward Nabil Fekir to Real Betis for €21 million. Saliba signed for Arsenal along with Lille forward Nicolas Pépé for a combined fee of €110 million. Of Europe's top five leagues, Ligue 1 was the only one to recoup more money on transfers than it spent. 'Every year people get alarmed and say: "Look at all the players leaving! Surely Ligue 1 is going to get weaker." But then every season new kids arrive and we have different talents to get excited about,' enthuses Duluc.

The *Ligue de Football Professionnel* (the governing body that oversees the major professional football leagues in France) rightly branded Ligue 1 'The League of Talents' in 2018. Other European leagues – and especially the Premier League – should be grateful for the player development that is part of football in France.

In a list of the 100 greatest players in Premier League history, compiled by *The Independent* in 2019, ten Ligue 1 alumni featured in the top fifty: Thierry Henry, Patrick Vieira, Éric Cantona, Didier Drogba, Eden Hazard, Petr Čech, N'Golo Kanté, Robert Pirès, Claude Makélélé and Nicolas Anelka. Nine more players – Michael Essien, David Ginola, Jürgen Klinsmann,

William Gallas, Jay-Jay Okocha, Patrice Évra, Emmanuel Petit, Marcel Desailly and César Azpilicueta – also made the longlist. If the Premier League is the biggest and most watched league in the world, it owes a healthy dose of its appeal to the French-trained talent that thrives in it.

However, the fact is that Ligue 1 has become a development league, or to put it more crudely, a selling league. It is still considered to be one of the continent's top five divisions, but in recent years the poor performances of French clubs in Europe has meant that France has found itself scrapping with Portugal and Russia to hold on to fifth position in the UEFA rankings. This is the modern-day reality. It is the reason why Mbappé grew up supporting Real Madrid rather than PSG. It is the reason why French children are more likely to be spotted in a Barcelona, Chelsea or Liverpool shirt than in the colours of their local team.

This was not always the case. When the Bosman ruling came into effect in 1995, Ligue 1 was strong and sat second in the UEFA rankings, behind only Italy. French clubs had an abundance of gifted homegrown players but could also attract foreign stars.

Marseille were the prime example. They reached the Champions League final in 1991, then won the competition two years later by beating AC Milan 1–0 in Munich. Belgian coach Raymond Goethals relied on an outstanding French core that included Fabien Barthez, Didier Deschamps, Marcel Desailly and Basile Boli, while in attack Ghana's Abedi Pelé, Germany's Rudi Völler and Croatian star Alen Bokšić formed a deadly trio.

PSG, who were then owned by Canal Plus and received considerable financial backing from the pay-television network, emerged as Marseille's biggest rival. They too had a tremendous team. Between 1992 and 1996, the side reached four consecutive

European semi-finals. With Brazilian maestro Raí pulling the strings in midfield, David Ginola providing the trickery and George Weah plundering the goals, they got to the Champions League last four in 1995. The following year, having brought in the majestic Youri Djorkaeff, PSG lifted the UEFA Cup Winners' Cup.

Marseille and PSG were the glamour clubs, yet the Ligue 1 title race invariably involved a host of contenders and was fiercely competitive. AS Monaco were a force both domestically and on the continent. Title holders in 1988, Wenger's side got to the Cup Winners' Cup final in 1992, then, with Jürgen Klinsmann's goals to the fore, they reached the Champions League semi-finals two years later.

Under Jean Tigana, the principality club enjoyed putting English sides to the sword. Ali Benarbia, Sonny Anderson, Thierry Henry and Enzo Scifo were in the team that beat Newcastle home and away in the UEFA Cup in 1997, and the following year David Trezeguet's stunning strike silenced Old Trafford and fired Monaco through to the last four of the Champions League at the expense of the Red Devils.

FC Nantes enjoyed a wonderful tussle with Juventus in the Champions League semi-finals in 1996. Although their former captain Deschamps was by now playing for the *Bianconeri*, Nantes – who had Claude Makélélé in their midfield – came very close to upsetting the Italian giants. The Bordeaux team of Zinédine Zidane, Christophe Dugarry and Bixente Lizarazu were UEFA Cup finalists in 1996, and even AJ Auxerre claimed major continental scalps. Between 1994 and 1998, the tiny provincial club – guided by their inimitable trainer Guy Roux – battled their way to three European quarter-finals.

Then the Bosman ruling kicked in. By insisting that football clubs respect the freedom of movement for workers, the European Court of Justice changed the face of the French game.

There was a major shift in power away from the clubs and towards the players, and Ligue 1 – along with the Dutch and Belgian leagues – gradually became feeder divisions for Europe's economic superleagues.

Before 1995, clubs could have no more than three foreign players in their squad. This meant that the vast majority of French players remained in France. But when those restrictions were lifted, Ligue 1 clubs were powerless. A trickle turned into a steady flow and by 2018 a mind-boggling 821 French-trained footballers were plying their trade outside France.

French football does not have the economic structures necessary to compete. Historically, the sport in France was regarded as a social tool rather than an economic force. The French league only turned professional in 1932, and even then there was a fear that money could harm the game. 'In every period, footballers in France have been considered overpaid, even when their salaries were modest,' explained *L'Équipe* historian Didier Braun. 'Even before the professional game arrived, there were objections.' In 1921, *Le Miroir des Sports* expressed concern that businesses had started investing in football clubs. After the Casino supermarket group agreed to back AS Saint-Étienne, and Peugeot began funding FC Sochaux, the journal warned: 'Money will damage the purity of the sport and its noble role of educating the masses.'

Even today the economic activities of French clubs are monitored closely by the *Ligue de Football Professionnel*'s very own financial watchdog *La Direction Nationale du Contrôle de Gestion* (the National Board for Management Control). At the end of the season, every professional club must present its accounts and prove that they have remained within their annual budget.

PSG have no trouble with the board simply because the French governing body – unlike UEFA – allows its clubs to balance their books through private owners or investors. But the huge sums that the Qatar Sports Investments group has pumped into the capital outfit – already well in excess of €1 billion – have drawn more frowns than smiles. When Zlatan Ibrahimović signed for PSG in 2012, soon after the arrival of the Qatari investors, there was as much talk in the French newspapers about his obscene €14 million annual salary as there was his presence on the football pitch and his immense skills. Ligue 1 had secured the services of a global superstar, but the figures involved created a negative reaction.

France has always had trouble warming to ostentatious footballers. Nicolas Anelka recalls the jealous looks he attracted after returning for a second spell at PSG. 'I was twenty and drove a Ferrari,' the France striker said in 2014. 'A lot of people couldn't accept this. In Spain or England, people with expensive cars don't have to hide. In France, there's a weak mentality. You have to hide what you have. There is a problem with money.'

The state has maintained a certain influence in French football. Local councils traditionally own the stadiums and in general each town is represented by just one club. This is why there are no local derbies in France and why even the capital has just one major team. Although public–private partnerships have emerged, not having full control of their own stadiums has been a major handicap for clubs. This helps explain why Olympique Lyonnais president Jean-Michel Aulas fought tooth and nail in the courts for a decade to get permission for the club to build its own ground. The Parc Olympique Lyonnais finally opened in 2016 – making Lyon the only French club with exclusive stadium rights – and Aulas hopes the revenues generated will allow the team to compete in Europe in the long term.

The other major handicap is the extremely prohibitive fiscal regime. Tax rates in France are high for top earners. When the socialist President François Hollande introduced a 75 per cent 'millionaire tax' in 2012, French clubs knew that competing for players with their European counterparts would be nigh on impossible. The tax proved to be short-lived, but the real burden for Ligue 1 remains the enormous sums they must pay in employer contributions.

In 2018, a report released by 'Première League', an independent syndicate for Ligue 1 clubs, revealed that PSG had paid more in employer contributions (around €77.6 million) over the past season than all La Liga, Bundesliga and Serie A clubs put together. Even a modest French club like Angers SCO paid twelve times more than Real Madrid. In France, an annual salary for a footballer of €1.8 million costs the club €3.4 million. In England that figure is €3 million, in Italy €2.8 million, and in Spain and Germany it is €2.6 million.

These factors have left clubs with little choice. Besides PSG, who have enjoyed the backing of the Qatar Sports Investments group since 2011, every French club bases its economic model on television rights and player sales. As negotiating TV deals is out of their hands, they focus much of their efforts on ensuring their academies are productive.

But as well as spotting, recruiting and developing the talent, clubs need to ensure they secure the signatures of players once they turn sixteen and are allowed to sign a professional deal. In 2009, Le Havre accused Manchester United of 'stealing' a sixteen-year-old Paul Pogba when the future France dynamo penned his first professional contract with the Red Devils rather than with the club that had developed him. Losing top talent in exchange for minor compensation remains a major concern for French clubs.

In modern times, Lyon have been France's most successful club when it comes to youth development. Karim Benzema, Nabil Fekir, Hatem Ben Arfa, Maxime Gonalons, Samuel Umtiti, Alexandre Lacazette, Corentin Tolisso, Anthony Martial, Clément Grenier, François Clerc and Loïc Rémy have all played for France after coming through the ranks at Lyon. Along with

Ajax, they are regarded as European leaders in developing elite footballers. Yet, even Lyon came close to losing their latest gem: Rayan Cherki.

The sensationally skilful forward had Europe's biggest clubs on red alert when he produced a series of mesmerising performances for Lyon in the UEFA Youth League. Barcelona, Real Madrid, Manchester City and Manchester United were all circling, knowing full well that Cherki's three-year trainee contract was nearing expiry. Lyon had to dig deep, very deep, to convince the local lad to stay. 'Cherki's the future star of French football, maybe even the future Mbappé,' states *L'Équipe*'s chief football writer Vincent Duluc. 'At fifteen, Lyon had to put a million euros on the table just to get him to say "hello".'

On 6 July 2019, Manchester United were reportedly waiting for Cherki at Bron airport, near the Parc OL, with a private jet and a cheque for €10 million. But to Lyon's relief, he resisted the lure of the English giants and signed for his boyhood team the following day. 'It's good for Lyon and for Ligue 1 that Cherki stayed,' explains the FFF's technical director Hubert Fournier. 'We're in a system of free movement so we cannot stop young players from going. But we encourage them to at least start their careers in France. Leaving can have a destabilising effect. We try to alert the kids, the families and the clubs to the problems that can arise when you leave too young.'

But remaining in France presents dangers of its own. The fact that players are already on big money by the age of sixteen takes away one of the main sources of motivation for a trainee footballer: financial reward. Whereas previously clubs would start players on a basic salary at eighteen, then offer a more lucrative deal once they had established themselves two or three years later, now players command huge salaries before they have even made their first appearance in the first team. 'Today you get your reward before you have even started your training,' Duluc says.

Ligue 1 clubs have become so reliant on their youngsters that they are prepared to do almost anything to keep them happy. But when a rich teenager believes he can behave in whatever way he wants without suffering consequences, it creates problems. 'The clubs base their entire economy on selling players, so they can't afford to punish an eighteen-year-old who's full of talent,' the journalist Daniel Riolo describes. 'The club needs to keep him sweet so that they can sell him in two years when an English club offers €30 million.'

Often, a young player who has caused problems with his French club transforms into a respectful, perfectly behaved individual when he moves abroad. 'It's like a kid in secondary school who plays the fool,' Riolo continues. 'His parents send him off to boarding school, and all of a sudden he behaves well.'

Competition to secure the best young talent in the land is fierce. On a Saturday morning, the pitches of the Paris suburbs will be crawling with scouts, agents and individuals looking for a chance to make money out of football. Likewise, for the kids, playing football has become a business opportunity rather than a source of pleasure.

The editor-in-chief of Bondy Blog, Ilyes Ramdani, also works as a youth coach for FCM Aubervilliers, the club that developed the talents of Abou Diaby. Ramdani has noticed a shift in behaviour in *les banlieues* over the last decade. 'What is interesting is that the *city stades* [small caged football pitches] are no longer full,' he notes. 'Kids in the suburbs no longer play football 24/7. They're like all youngsters: they prefer to stay in and play FIFA or Fortnite on the console. Nowadays, when they go to play football, they're not doing it for the pleasure, they're doing it to try to get spotted.'

For many, football is one of the few credible ways of escaping poverty. 'Most kids in the suburbs are poor and they don't have many role models,' Ramdani explains. 'They don't know any doctors or lawyers. In their family circle, they'll know a cleaning lady, a builder, someone who's run into trouble with the police, maybe a rap artist ... and they'll know two or three footballers. They grow up thinking: "I don't want to struggle on the minimum wage like mum and dad, I don't want to study and then end up on the dole like my big brother. I want to make it in football." The relationship with football has changed. It's no longer: "I want to make it in football." It's become: "I *have* to make it in football."'

Statistically one out of roughly 5,000 boys who play junior football in France will get to play professionally. The chances are minuscule, yet many families place all of their hopes on their boy making the grade. Ramdani is shocked by the increasingly complex strategies that parents, brothers and agents develop to try to ensure their prodigy gets spotted: 'Boys get transferred from one club to the next if the dad or agent thinks they'll get more visibility. It's all about making sure their boy is playing where the scouts are. Also, if the parents can afford it, they'll pay for a private coach. The kids are made to feel they have to make it and they put themselves under huge pressure.'

Former Arsenal midfielder Rémi Garde headed up Lyon's academy before taking charge of the first team in 2011. He played a pivotal role in the emergence of Lacazette, Tolisso, Gonalons and Umtiti. But Garde often spares a thought for the many others who slipped through the net. 'I witnessed some unbelievable things,' he stated in Riolo's book *Racaille Football Club* (*Scum Football Club*). 'I'd go to visit a fourteen- or fifteen-year-old boy, speak to him and to his parents, and very quickly it'd become clear that everyone was counting on this boy to keep the family afloat. Everything was resting on his shoulders. He was the head of the family. How is a kid supposed to remain grounded in these circumstances? How can this shift in responsibility within a household not destabilise a teenager? How can the notion of authority survive such a radical change in roles, when a fifteen-year-old boy is earning more than his unemployed dad?'

Some of the boys succeed, make their family proud, and provide them with financial security. The vast majority fall short and have to deal with the crushing disappointment and guilt that comes with this. 'They feel like they've let everyone down,' Ramdani remarks. The worst cases are often the ones who actually get picked up by a youth academy, only to be among the two-thirds who fail to earn a professional contract. 'We see those guys all the time here in Bondy,' Ramdani continues. 'They're the most affected. They come back to *les quartiers* and they've lost their love of football. They don't know what to do. Mum and dad don't have a plan B. Everything, absolutely everything, was riding on them becoming a footballer.'

CHAPTER 9

LE DÉSASTRE DOMENECH

When Vikash Dhorasoo arrives at the bustling Nazir café in Abbesses, an energetic, bohemian corner of northern Paris, nobody bats an eyelid. He may be a former France midfielder who shone for two of the country's biggest clubs – Olympique Lyonnais and Paris Saint-Germain – and played for AC Milan, but Dhorasoo doesn't stand out from the crowd. In fact, this diminutive, dishevelled man in faded jeans and a brown hoodie blends in perfectly well in the eclectic surroundings of Paris's eighteenth *arrondissement*.

Dhorasoo is not like the rest of the football pack. There is nothing ostentatious about the way he dresses or acts. He is down to earth and enjoys living in the foothills of Sacré-Cœur, mingling with people from all corners of the globe amid the backdrop of sex shops, kebab restaurants, cabaret joints and trendy bars. 'What I love about this country is the mix of cultures,' explains Dhorasoo, whose great-grandparents are from India and whose parents grew up in Mauritius. 'My kids are mixed race. These days, one in four marriages is mixed. It's the history of this country and people should embrace that. Most have the same outlook as me, we live happily together. But when there are problems people try to blame immigration. The news at the moment is all about Muslims. The politicians are telling us there's an issue with [Muslim women wearing] hijabs.

They're trying to convince us that Islam is a problem here. But the last time I checked, Islam wasn't in power in France. [President Emmanuel] Macron isn't a Muslim. [François] Hollande wasn't either. Nor was [Nicolas] Sarkozy,' scoffs Dhorasoo, who would love to have the chance to make a difference himself. He is currently campaigning to become a mayor of Paris in 2020, having put himself forward as a candidate for the eighteenth *arrondissement*. But he has already been confronted by many obstacles, and the 46-year-old is not getting his hopes up. 'People like me aren't supposed to go into politics but I'm giving it a go,' he smiles.

Les Bleus' first international of Indian descent is not afraid to speak out against the establishment and he does so on a regular basis. His frank, unconventional manner frequently landed him in trouble during his playing career. Dhorasoo fell out with a number of his coaches, was allegedly punched in the face by Lyon teammate Grégory Coupet during half-time in a Champions League match with Arsenal, and famously became the first Ligue 1 player to get 'sacked', by PSG, in 2006. The club declared they were severing their ties with Dhorasoo because of 'his refusal to play for the reserves, his lack of loyalty, also his insubordination, disobedience and his permanent air of provocation.'

When Dhorasoo received his first international call-up in 1999, he remembers feeling different to the other France players. 'It was hard,' he admits. 'Most of the others were world champions, playing for Europe's biggest clubs in the Champions League. I was playing for Lyon in the UEFA Cup. I didn't know how to act in training. If I ran too hard the others would look at me and think "who's this little Indian guy and what's he trying to prove?" If I didn't run hard enough the coach [Roger Lemerre] shouted at me.'

Legend has it that the devilishly skilful playmaker resorted to doing what he did best: nutmegging opponents. Unfortunately, one such flash of talent in training did not sit well with France's World Cup-winning skipper Didier Deschamps. 'Honestly I don't know if that nutmeg on Deschamps really happened,' Dhorasoo smiles. 'But I hope I did it. For me, nutmegs are the essence of football. Maybe I did it and he took it badly. But if nutmegs weren't allowed, somebody should have told me. I wouldn't have bothered coming.'

By supposedly humiliating Deschamps in training, Dhorasoo might have been seeking revenge for the skipper mispronouncing his first name on the team bus, allegedly referring to the newcomer as 'Vishcach'. *Libération* newspaper affirmed that the infamous nutmeg *did* happen and claims it led to Dhorasoo being ostracised from the group. 'Vikash is an … interesting boy,' Desailly is quoted as saying. 'As for the nutmeg on Didier, given the quality of Vikash's performances in training and his implication, I would say it was not especially appropriate.' Dhorasoo got dropped from the squad and it took him five years to get back into the fold.

Raymond Domenech was the man who offered him a reprieve. The newly appointed France coach was charged with the task of bringing in fresh faces following the Euro 2004 disappointment and the departure of Jacques Santini, and Dhorasoo, with his exceptional technique, close skills and ability to link midfield with attack, found himself at the heart of a younger team. The first year was difficult, though, and home draws with Israel, Republic of Ireland and Switzerland left France in danger of missing out on the 2006 World Cup.

Then Zinédine Zidane came out of retirement and the whole country celebrated. Well, almost the whole country. Dhorasoo, never shy of adopting an alternative view, saw things differently. He felt Zidane's U-turn undermined the work that Domenech had been doing and interrupted the team's momentum. 'It was all quite surreal,' Dhorasoo recalls. 'Zidane decides to stop playing, then he decides he wants to come back – so basically he does what he wants – and everybody thinks it's great. It was hard for me. I knew I could lose my place, but I had to pretend I was happy. In France, Zidane is unattackable. You can't say anything against him. He was a fantastic player and, of course, it's better to have him. But we had been writing our own story, we hadn't actually lost a game, and who knows what we might have done without him.'

Dhorasoo's words offer a glimpse into the deeper malaise that was developing within the squad. Domenech had arrived at a difficult time. The backbone of France's all-conquering team had gone. Deschamps, Desailly, Bixente Lizarazu and Laurent Blanc had all left along with Zidane and Lilian Thuram. Claude Makélélé announced his international retirement just weeks into Domenech's reign.

By opting for Domenech – who was an FFF stalwart – the authorities were banking on the same in-house methodology that had worked so well a decade earlier with Aimé Jacquet. They felt that they were turning to a safe pair of hands. Domenech had coached France's under-21s for eleven years, which meant that he possessed expert knowledge of the younger players, and had worked with most of the older ones further down the line. If anybody was qualified to manage the transition from one generation to the next it was surely him. Furthermore, his close relationship with Jacquet, and the fact they shared similar footballing philosophies, strengthened his hand.

In reality, however, the appointment of this fiercely stubborn, confrontational and eccentric man turned out to be a trigger for the most spectacular car crash in the history of French football. 'Domenech was appointed because of his work with the under-21s,' explains the journalist Daniel Riolo. 'Yet the fact is he wasn't even good with the under-21s. He had some of the best generations that France has ever produced, and he won nothing with them. It's like having a schoolteacher who keeps on changing schools and every time he's hopeless. Then all of a sudden he gets this promotion and finds himself in front of a new class of students who all know that he's completely hopeless.'

Two problems immediately became apparent. Firstly, the new guard were quite clearly not of the same ilk as their predecessors. Domenech's initial centre-back paring of Gaël Givet and Sébastien Squillaci had done well at AS Monaco and helped the team reach the 2004 Champions League final, but they were never going to meet the lofty standards set by Desailly and Blanc. Likewise, central midfielders Rio Mavuba and Benoît Pedretti looked to be a pale imitation of Deschamps and Emmanuel Petit.

The second concern was Domenech's lack of top-level managerial experience. A former France defender who won league titles with Strasbourg and Bordeaux in his playing days, Domenech's only tangible success in the dugout came in 1989 when he guided Lyon to the second division title. Would he command the respect of a dressing room that included a handful of strong-minded, proven winners like Fabien Barthez, William Gallas, Thierry Henry, Patrick Vieira and Robert Pirès?

Domenech soon discovered that the methods he had employed with the France under-21s were less effective with established, millionaire footballers. After an opening 1–1 draw with Bosnia-Herzegovina, the coach kept his players back in the dressing room and asked each and every one of them to offer their thoughts on the performance. A series of long silences ensued. 'The older players had one thing on their mind: they wanted to get home as soon as the game had finished,' Domenech wrote in his book *Tout Seul*. 'Unsettled by the reticence of their elders, the younger ones didn't know what to do. But I didn't back down and the debriefing went on until after midnight.'

This inauspicious start was confounded by the rising tensions at Clairefontaine. For Domenech, ill-discipline was the main reason for France's recent failures. He looked to rectify this by laying down clear ground rules: players should meet for breakfast at 8.30 a.m., be on time for every meeting, put away their telephones during massage and physio sessions, and wear their shin pads during training. 'I made it clear that the players would not be dictating their conditions to the technical staff, as certain individuals wanted to,' he explained. 'I took it upon myself to clean up a harmful situation for the good of the team.'

The requests seemed reasonable, but France's mollycoddled players had grown accustomed to calling all the shots. According to Domenech, the captain Vieira was particularly reluctant to give up on his morning lie-ins. With two other senior figures, Pirès and Henry, backing their clubmate, an impasse that the media referred to as *'le problème Arsenal'* developed. Domenech travelled to London to try to clear the air. 'We met up in Arsène Wenger's office and I was ready to listen to their recriminations,' Domenech revealed in his book. 'But I didn't understand them. When they started talking about their desire not to wear shin pads and to get up late in the morning, I asked myself what I was doing there.'

If Henry had carried over a healthy relationship with Domenech from his time with *Les Espoirs* (the name for the French under-21 team), and if Vieira's stance softened after Zidane's return, Pirès never saw eye to eye with the coach. The former Metz and Marseille and Arsenal playmaker adopts a serious tone as soon as the subject is broached. 'Domenech didn't like my game and he didn't like my face,' Pirès says. 'From that first game, it was very tense between him and me. I don't know why. But he clearly wanted to punish me for something. I was at war with Domenech. And when you go to war with the national team coach you always lose.'

With the relationship close to breaking point, Domenech pushed Pirès over the edge by subbing him at half-time during a World Cup qualifier in Cyprus and sending on Daniel Moreira, a relative novice, in his place. Domenech claims Pirès spent the second half in the car park, showing no interest in the match.

Domenech refused to pick Pirès again, but the Arsenal star continued to haunt the coach, who felt sure he was bad-mouthing him to the press. 'Robert was popular with the media and I was able to see that by the lies and false information that came out following his exclusion,' Domenech noted.

Even today, Pirès seems genuinely perplexed by Domenech's stance. However, he was not the only top player left in the cold by Domenech: Barcelona winger Ludovic Giuly also failed to make the World Cup squad. Like Pirès, Giuly knew Domenech's TV presenter girlfriend Estelle Denis, and the media was rife with reports that the coach had allowed personal matters to influence his choices. In his book, Domenech admitted feeling relieved when Arsenal's goalkeeper Jens Lehmann was sent off in the eighteenth minute of the 2006 Champions League final against Barcelona. The decision denied Giuly a goal – he would have scored had the referee played advantage – and led to Pirès being substituted off. 'Leaving those two out of my squad could've brought a hellish pressure on us,' reasoned Domenech. 'But now we'll be left in peace. Thank you, mister referee.'

Domenech's relationship with the media became a major issue. Most journalists were initially pleased about his appointment because they had enjoyed working with him when he was the under-21 coach. Domenech would feed reporters colourful stories and offer them the kind of inside information that sat well with their editors. His strategy changed radically, though. Convinced that the media had been harmful during France's last two campaigns, he made a conscious decision to stop playing the game. He no longer wanted details of tactics and line-ups getting leaked, and did everything possible to starve the press of information. 'Between certain journalists and me, the climate became aggressive,' observed Domenech. 'I didn't care and that was a fatal error. The power of the media is far greater than one can ever imagine. If the media aren't with you, they are against you.'

Press conferences were tense, unpleasant affairs. They felt like point-scoring exercises between Domenech and senior reporters. Rather than answering questions seriously, Domenech invariably looked to respond with witty one-liners. He has a passion for theatre, and that penchant for acting in front of an audience was often evident.

On one occasion, fed up with persistent questions surrounding the omission of Manchester United defender Mikaël Silvestre, Domenech suggested that star signs were now an important criterion. 'When I have got a Leo in defence, I've always got my gun ready, as I know he's going to want to show off at one moment or another and cost us,' quipped the superstitious coach. As a result of Domenech's intransigence, the newspapers were unforgiving. When the coach made an unguarded comment – stating, for example, that he had to 'rummage about in the back of the drawers' to find enough players for his latest squad – the media jumped at the chance to criticise him.

This meant that even the victories were hollow. *Les Bleus* took a giant stride towards World Cup qualification by winning 1–0 away to Ireland in September 2005, Henry curling a sublime winner into the top corner from long range. But Domenech left Dublin with a sour taste in his mouth having been duped by a radio show. Before the game he had received a phone call from a comedian impersonating Jacques Chirac. The French President was unwell in hospital at the time, so when the voice asked Domenech if he would get his players to put their hands on their hearts when singing *La Marseillaise* before kick-off, he did not dare question the caller's sincerity and informed the squad to do so.

Domenech was left fuming when he discovered it was a prank, not just because he and his team had been made to look foolish, but also because he had actually enjoyed this stirring, emotion-filled moment. 'For once our team adopted the kind of patriotic attitude that our detractors had been calling for,' he said. 'But ultimately one of the strongest communal moments we had experienced was hijacked by a troublemaker looking to enhance his own personal glory.'

Domenech could do no right. He insisted he was thrilled when, in August 2005, Zidane announced that he was coming out of international retirement along with Lilian Thuram and Claude Makélélé. Domenech explained in his book that he had been campaigning for it, and even travelled to Madrid for talks with Zidane and to Turin to meet Thuram. For the media, however, this was another example of Domenech being weak, effectively admitting that his initial plan of building a team around the new generation had failed.

Stories emerged claiming that Zidane had only agreed to return under certain conditions. Would Domenech have to consult Zidane on team selection and tactics? The coach gave short shrift to such suggestions, but he did soften the rules in order to keep Zidane happy. 'I made a slight adjustment to my behaviour,' he admitted. 'For example, I stopped insisting on them wearing shin pads in training. If Zidane reacted badly to one of my decisions all the young players would've imitated him.'

The upturn in results that followed was largely attributed to Zidane's presence. For many, France reached the 2006 World Cup final thanks to Zidane and in spite of Domenech. Yet those inside the camp dispute the theory that Domenech was merely a puppet. 'It's pure fantasy,' Thuram states dismissively. 'Our run was down to Domenech and all of the players. How many coaches have reached a World Cup final? You must be very careful what you write. Domenech is the one who chose the tactics and who put the players out on the pitch. Never underestimate the role of the coach.'

Dhorasoo, for his part, unquestionably suffered from Zidane's presence. He made late substitute appearances in the first two matches of the 2006 World Cup campaign, but was then confined to a watching brief. The midfielder occupied himself by filming passages inside the team hotel, and later released a documentary called *The Substitute*. It is fair to say Zidane does not have the starring role in Dhorasoo's film. 'In the collective conscience, Zidane came back and he saved French football,' Dhorasoo says. 'But people forget certain facts. First of all, with Zidane, we only just qualified. We qualified because Alexander Frei missed a one-on-one for Switzerland in the last minute against Ireland. That was thanks to Shay Given, not Zidane. Then at the World Cup we were laborious in our three group games. We drew the first two and then we won the third [against Togo] when Zidane was suspended. We reached the World Cup final thanks to Zidane but also thanks to a lot of other players. And thanks to Domenech.' Dhorasoo subsequently quit international football but did not make a public statement because, as he dryly notes, 'nobody cared'.

Zidane's definitive retirement following his red card in the 2006 World Cup final had a far bigger impact. *Les Bleus* needed to pick themselves up from the crushing disappointment of losing to Italy on penalties in Berlin, but without Zidane's discreet yet immense presence, they lacked leadership both on and off the pitch. Domenech convinced his defensive linchpin Thuram, who was then thirty-four, to continue through to Euro 2008, but the hierarchy within the squad was about to be shaken up.

If Henry, Thuram and Vieira looked like they were obvious leaders from the outside, the likes of Franck Ribéry, Florent Malouda and Éric Abidal wanted more appreciation after impressing at the World Cup, while new kids Samir Nasri and Karim Benzema arrived with a self-assurance that unnerved some of the older players. There was an almighty scramble for power, and over the next two years Domenech spent most of his time trying to put out the fires that flared up within the camp.

'When I think about what it was like, I can honestly say I

wasn't surprised by what happened in South Africa two years later,' reflects Thuram. 'The way the players were acting, only worrying about themselves, I knew we were in trouble. I'd sit with Patrick Vieira at mealtimes and talk about this. I tried to warn people. I remember taking one of the younger players to the side and telling him: "Be careful! You're going to be a key player in the coming years and your behaviour is going to set the tone for the rest. You will determine which direction this team moves in, so be very careful." Did he listen to me? I don't know.'

Thuram refuses to answer when asked if the individual concerned was Nasri, but the Marseille youngster had become a considerable source of tension within the group. Nasri was hyped up as being the next Zidane by the French media, and not just because he came from Marseille and had Algerian roots. Voted best young player in Ligue 1 in the 2006/07 season, he was one of the most gifted and coveted talents in Europe, and Arsenal felt they had pulled off shrewd business when they signed him for €17 million in the summer of 2008.

Le Petit Prince, as Nasri was known, perhaps bought into the hype too much. Although he was just twenty at the time, he felt that he deserved as much consideration as any player, and was not prepared to sit quietly in the background waiting for his turn. It was an ominous sign of what was to come from France's latest wave of ambitious yet impatient youngsters.

During a training camp in Tignes before Euro 2008, Domenech had to inform seven of his thirty players that they would not be partaking in the tournament – a task that he was dreading. He asked his players to wait in their bedrooms so that he could address the 'eliminated' ones individually. Domenech could not get over the fact that one player thought it was amusing to go knocking on doors pretending to be the coach. He was convinced that he had identified who the culprit was too. 'I later discovered that Samir Nasri had played this joke of astounding intelligence and class,' Domenech wrote in his book. 'What a disappointment. If I'd heard about this before [naming the squad], I'd have fired him instantly. Impossible to rely on a player capable of acting this way.'

Unsurprisingly, Domenech opted to put Nasri on the bench for France's opening game at Euro 2008 in Switzerland, a mind-numbing goalless draw against Romania. But the midfielder continued to make waves off the pitch. In his autobiography, William Gallas told the story of a player referred to as 'S' taking Thierry Henry's seat on the team bus and refusing to budge when asked to by France's star striker.

A squabble over seats on the bus may seem trivial, but certain codes matter in the everyday life of a footballer and respecting your elders is one of them. 'When I was a young player in the France squad, I didn't sit down at the table before the others,' Thuram describes. 'I waited to see where there might be a spare seat. Why? Not because I was afraid of my elders, but because I thought it was respectful.' Dhorasoo is of the same view. 'When I was at AC Milan,' he recalls, 'I'd never just get on the bus and sit down. I waited for everyone else to get on first. There was no way I wanted Paolo Maldini or Clarence Seedorf to come on and say, "Hey, this is my place."'

Les Bleus appeared more interested in their petty squabbles than in making things work on the pitch. 'Their attitude after the Romania match shocked me,' Domenech revealed. 'They seemed almost satisfied. The only player acting appropriately was Claude Makélélé whose face was 6ft long.' On the train back to their base camp, Domenech put a video of the 0–0 draw on the television hoping his players would watch and try to understand how they could improve. The majority continued playing their card games.

Domenech had run out of ideas. He was tired of fighting with the press and striving to find the right words for his pampered, underperforming players. His biggest satisfaction in the build-up to the second game against the Netherlands stemmed from fooling the media by switching the location of a training session at the last moment without any warning. It was hardly surprising when the young legs of Robin van Persie, Wesley Sneijder, Rafael van der Vaart and Arjen Robben ran amok against the French side, roaring to a 4–1 win that all but ended the nation's chances in the competition.

A pitiful campaign was rounded off by a limp 2–0 defeat to Italy. *Les Bleus* found themselves a goal down inside twenty-five minutes having lost Ribéry to injury and Abidal to a red card, and they never recovered. 'After Abidal's sending off, I sacrificed an attacking player, Nasri, for a defender [Jean-Alain] Boumsong. Of course, Nasri didn't understand and he sulked, as if his case was more important than the team's,' noted Domenech.

What happens in a dressing room at such times is telling. While certain players prepared for their showers as normal, perhaps thinking about their forthcoming holidays, Thuram burst into tears. France's record appearance-maker with 142 caps knew that a compelling chapter in his life had just come to a sorry end, and he could not keep his emotions inside. But he did manage to pull himself together enough to deliver an important speech. 'I said that I wanted to thank everybody,' Thuram remembers. 'I wanted to thank all the players that I'd played with during my time with the national team. I made it clear that without them I could not have won everything that I won. By speaking like this, I was trying to pass on a message: "You cannot achieve anything without the others. Be careful. Without the others you do not exist."'

Domenech feared Thuram's message fell on deaf ears. 'I believe some of the young players he was addressing couldn't have cared less,' he wrote. 'But I found his words just and touching, an expression of true grandeur. Knowing what he really thought about certain players, part of me worried he might explode into a rant. At the same time, I hoped he would. It would've saved me from doing it myself one day, something I felt would be inevitable if I stayed on.'

That Domenech was even considering continuing at this point is surprising. He may have been rewarded for reaching the 2006 World Cup final with a four-year contract, but it was glaringly obvious that he had lost any lingering respect in the dressing room and his players were not responding to his instructions.

If further evidence of Domenech's inability to think clearly was required, he provided it during a post-match interview with the television network M6. Domenech's long-time girlfriend Estelle Denis worked for the channel and was preparing to host a show when the coach decided to propose via her colleague who was conducting the interview with him. He described this moment of madness as being part of a need 'to cling on to the people I love' at such a difficult time and insisted that it was merely an 'ill-judged impulse'. The French public saw it differently – as did Denis, who was furious; she turned the proposal down, and reportedly took several months to forgive him. He also looked to be heading for a messy divorce with *Les Bleus* too. As the fans and newspapers called vehemently for Domenech's head, the bookmakers slashed the odds on him holding on to his job.

Incredibly, though, during this stormy, troubled time, the FFF showed itself to be even weaker than the national team. '[FFF president] Jean-Pierre Escalettes knew that if he sacked Domenech, he'd have to go as well,' journalist Daniel Riolo explains. 'Domenech is a canny politician and he got the important people – guys like Gérard Houllier – on his side. But because of these pathetic games, France was left in a state of inertia. Nobody wanted to move. So they stuck with Domenech and things got worse, far worse.'

During their qualifying campaign for the 2010 World Cup, *Les Bleus* struggled in what should have been a straightforward group. Collectively, they were a rabble. But every time Domenech's sacking looked like it was inevitable, he was saved by some individual brilliance. Following a dismal opening 3–1 defeat in Austria, for example, Henry and Anelka dug Domenech out against Serbia four days later. Two goals down in Romania, Yoann Gourcuff's stunning thirty-metre strike brought France back to 2–2. Ribéry's goals home and away against Lithuania earned them six vital, if somewhat miraculous, points.

The players knew they had the power and Domenech knew his fate was in their hands. By now, any attempts to impose his authority created fresh problems. On the way back from the Saturday night loss in Austria, Domenech told his squad that as punishment for their abysmal performance, they would not be afforded their usual Sunday off. They would have to stay at Clairefontaine and focus on the upcoming game against Serbia. Domenech claimed that the players were furious, and revealed that Gallas even threatened to underperform against Serbia if he refused to change his stance. 'If that's the way it is, then you'll see on Wednesday...' Domenech quoted Gallas as saying. The coach thought he must have misunderstood and so he asked Gallas to confirm the threat, which he did. 'My coaching team and I just looked at each in stupefaction,' Domenech wrote.

In September 2009 reports emerged of a player mutiny led by Thierry Henry. According to *Le Parisien*, the day before hosting Romania, the Barcelona forward stopped a training session and issued a damning assessment of the players' feelings towards Domenech. 'Coach, we've got something we want to say,' Henry reportedly declared. 'I'm talking on behalf of the group here. We are also dissatisfied. We are bored during your training sessions. I've been in the France team for twelve years and never found myself in this situation. We don't know how to play, where to position ourselves, how to set up. We don't know what to do. We have no style, no plan, no identity. It's not good enough.'

Although Henry appeared on TF1's evening news programme to claim that his words had been 'distorted', it was obvious that *Les Bleus* were now sailing a rudderless ship.

After finishing as section runners-up behind Serbia, the team faced a severe examination: a two-legged World Cup playoff against the Republic of Ireland. Nicolas Anelka's strike sealed a 1–0 win in the first leg at Croke Park in Dublin, but the return provided a night of pure theatre. Robbie Keane's goal gave the Irish real hope and left the France players paralysed with fear. The tension inside the Stade de France was palpable, so when Gallas nodded home a winner in extra-time the outpouring of relief proved immense.

The Irish players protested furiously, and understandably so. Replays showed that Henry had used his arm to control the ball before crossing to Gallas. Yet the goal stood and Domenech, once again, was off the hook. France were heading to South Africa, but their popularity, both at home and abroad, had plunged to new depths.

President Nicolas Sarkozy issued an apology to the Irish Prime Minister Brian Cowen, and FIFA handed Ireland €5 million in compensation. Painfully aware that he was being cast as a cheat, Henry suggested replaying the game, but the idea was rejected by FIFA. Domenech, however, refused any concession. 'I don't understand why we're being presented as guilty,' he railed. 'Nobody apologised when the referee wrongly sent off our goalkeeper against Serbia. Nobody apologised when a Dutchman prevented us from equalising at Euro 2008 by using his hand. I don't get all this moralising.'

Unlike Diego Maradona, who was deified in Argentina following his 'Hand of God' goal against England at the 1986 World Cup, Henry was cast as a villain by the French people. The public had by now fallen out of love with their national team and they felt ashamed by the inglorious way in which the side had qualified for the competition. The FFF offered no support at all to France's record goal scorer, and only two players, Bacary Sagna and Florent Malouda, spoke out with any sympathy for the striker. 'The lynching [of Henry] was unfair and it hurt me,' Sagna told *Le Figaro* newspaper. 'Certain French people treated him like dirt. After everything he has done ... it's a shame.' Henry's standing suffered, and the aura, respect and influence he had once exerted within the France squad had disappeared for ever.

One man who was hoping to take Henry's place in the 2010 World Cup, and perhaps even displace him in the record books further down the line, was the prodigiously talented Karim Benzema. But the former Lyon striker had just endured a difficult first season at Real Madrid and, according to Domenech, was 'carrying too many kilos'. Benzema's faint World Cup chances were not helped when he was one of four French internationals named in an underage prostitute scandal in April 2010. Hatem Ben Arfa's name was quickly cleared, but Sidney Govou, Ribéry and Benzema were all called in for questioning. *L'Affaire Zahia*, as it became known, had just begun, and it was under this ominously dark raincloud that a beleaguered, exhausted Raymond Domenech set about picking his 23-man squad to travel to South Africa.

CHAPTER 10

LA CATASTROPHE!

Time has passed and I still don't know how we got to that. I don't know how football and surrounding events led to my three-year-old son going up to his father, the day after he returned from the World Cup in South Africa, and asking: 'Daddy, are you going to prison?' I often wanted to scream: 'It's football, it's only football!' But I couldn't because I knew it wasn't only football. It was something else as well.

It is with these deeply troubled words that Raymond Domenech started his book *Tout Seul*, a blow-by-blow account of his time in charge of the *Les Bleus*, which ended so disastrously in the summer of 2010. Reading them, you almost feel sorry for the maligned coach. Then you remember that much of what happened was the consequence of his own poor management and catastrophic decisions.

On 20 June 2010, French football hit an all-time low. The training session that had been scheduled to take place on the inaptly named 'Field of Dreams' on that cool Sunday afternoon in Knysna in South Africa represented an opportunity for *Les Bleus* to rescue a slither of dignity. It was a chance for them to meet and greet children from the local township, to show that there was still a modicum of unity within the team, and to earn some much-needed positive publicity.

Three days after surrendering pitifully in their second group match against Mexico in Polokwane, the 2006 finalists were on the brink of elimination from the World Cup. To make matters worse, details about a half-time altercation between Domenech and Nicolas Anelka had been published in the press, and a decision was taken to send the disgraced striker home.

The world's media travelled to Knysna, a small town 500km east of Cape Town, sensing that another big news story might be about to break around this mutinous team. They would not be disappointed. After getting off the bus to greet the children, the players walked straight back onto it. France's fitness coach Robert Duverne was seen remonstrating with the captain Patrice Évra; after being ushered away by Domenech, Duverne then hurled his stopwatch into the bushes in disgust. Évra and the team had decided to go on strike. They would not go ahead with the training session. In an astonishingly misguided show of support for Anelka, a group of millionaire footballers sat obstinately on their bus, curtains drawn, sulking like a group of spoilt children.

In the space of a decade, *Les Bleus* had gone from being world and European champions, footballing pioneers, and an inspiration to millions, to a national embarrassment and global laughing stock. As Domenech stood pathetically in front of the team bus and began to read out a letter that had been penned by his absent players, it was hard to believe what was unfolding was actually real.

● ● ●

To get to the bottom of understanding how and why the national team reached this low point is no simple task. Even today, the players who were involved refuse to speak about the events that led up to the strike, as if some kind of unofficial pact has been agreed. Maybe they are too ashamed. Maybe they know that any attempt at an explanation would be met with utter scorn. Or maybe they simply don't understand how it happened themselves.

What is clear is that Domenech travelled to South Africa as an alienated figure, exhausted by six years of fighting with his players and the media, devoid of ideas and totally incapable of commanding a group of headstrong footballers. His already tenuous position was undermined further when the FFF tactlessly let it slip that Laurent Blanc would be replacing him after the tournament, regardless of how the team performed in South Africa.

Domenech was a sitting duck, but he still had a sly streak. In the May before the competition, he vowed to deliver a surprise when unveiling his World Cup squad live on television. More than 12 million people tuned in, looking forward to discovering which new talent might get the chance to play the role that Franck Ribéry had performed so brilliantly four years earlier when he made his senior tournament debut. There were no unexpected selections, however. The surprise, to everybody's disappointment, was that Domenech had decided to name an enlarged squad of thirty.

The coach had wanted to give two injured defenders – Éric Abidal and William Gallas – more time to prove their fitness. But the main reason for the delay seemed to stem from Domenech's fear of telling Thierry Henry that he had not been selected. Then aged thirty-two, Henry was slowing down and had played only a minor role at Barcelona that season, scoring just four goals. Knowing he would not be his first-choice striker, Domenech doubted that the nation's record goal scorer would be happy to sit on the bench.

Tellingly, though, he could not bring himself to inform Henry about his omission from the squad. He admitted to suffering sleepless nights over it. When Domenech finally arrived at Henry's Barcelona home for the dreaded face-to-face chat, he caved and allowed the forward to talk him into changing his mind. Henry was duly picked for his fourth World Cup, a first for a France player, but Domenech regretted the decision as soon as they arrived in South Africa.

The circus surrounding Henry was a perfect example of the extent to which Domenech's judgement had been clouded. But it also illustrated the way the players were now calling the shots, and were often putting their own interests ahead of the collective cause.

In the months preceding the World Cup, Domenech accumulated thousands of airmiles, jetting around Europe essentially pandering to the whims of his rogue players.

In early 2010, Domenech travelled to London to meet Nicolas Anelka. The idea of the rendezvous, it seems, was to clarify Anelka's role in the team in South Africa, but there are conflicting reports as to what was actually said. In his book, the coach claims he told Anelka that he wanted him to be the side's centre-forward and insisted that he would have to operate as an orthodox number nine. When Anelka responded by asking to be afforded a free role – dropping off into midfield when he wished, as he was doing to good effect with Chelsea that season – Domenech declined. The 58-year-old says that he explained to Anelka that such a system could not work without the presence of another out-and-out striker, as was the case at Chelsea with Didier Drogba. Yet, when I contacted a source close to Anelka, they dismissed this version of events and told me that in reality Domenech had arrived unannounced at Anelka's home and had simply asked him what role he would like to perform at the World Cup.

Sensing that Domenech had lost control, the players tried to seize power. The atmosphere was toxic by the time they arrived at their luxurious coastal hotel in Knysna. The fractures in the team that had been expanding over the past months were by now gaping cracks. Domenech claimed that Florent Malouda was jealous when he discovered that the coach had flown out to Munich to holds talks with Franck Ribéry. Malouda knew that Ribéry wanted to play on the left flank, where he had excelled for Bayern Munich over the past three seasons, but the Chelsea left-footer felt that this position should be his own. Malouda refused to defend in training after being re-positioned in a midfield three, according to Domenech.

In his 2012 book Domenech pulled no punches with regards to Malouda's behaviour. The coach claimed that in the final training match before the opener against Uruguay, Malouda ran about and intentionally clattered into Abou Diaby and Mathieu Valbuena, who were now rivals for his place in the team. For his part, Anelka supposedly continued to drop off and complain that nobody was making forward runs. 'I'm sick of it,' Domenech wrote in his diary that night. 'My team-talk for tomorrow is ready: "Go fuck yourselves!" is what I should say.'

Ribéry also appeared to have issues. Domenech wanted the exceptionally talented Yoann Gourcuff to be his playmaker. The Ligue 1 player of the season at Bordeaux in 2008/09, Gourcuff was the closest imitation of Zidane that France had produced since he had retired: balanced, two-footed and capable of dictating play with his visionary passes; he was a wonderfully elegant footballer who also happened to be blessed with boyish good looks. He was very different to the other players. Gourcuff, whose father Christian is a respected coach, enjoyed a middle-class upbringing in Brittany. He is a reserved character, likes to play tennis in his spare time, and while his teammates enjoyed card games on the bus, he read books.

Gourcuff was not popular within the squad, and as the tournament progressed rumours of a rift between him and Ribéry gathered pace. Domenech recalled the moment he told Gourcuff he wanted him to be the team's creative fulcrum against Uruguay. 'I looked at Ribéry and I saw the hate, contempt and jealousy in his eyes,' the coach noted.

In such a toxic environment, Gourcuff did not have the strength of character to impose himself and he received no support from other senior figures. Évra and Abidal were both close to Ribéry. Henry had reportedly made a clear decision to move to the periphery of the group as soon as he realised he was no longer a starter. And William Gallas was, according to Domenech, sulking ever since he discovered he would not be captain. 'The real problem in 2010 was the leadership,' explains L'Équipe's chief football writer Vincent Duluc. 'Domenech was worn out. It was one fight too many for him and he'd lost control. He thought Évra could cope with the captaincy. He made Ribéry and Abidal part of his leadership group. In this respect, he made some terrible choices.'

In these circumstances it was somewhat surprising that France got a point against Uruguay in Cape Town during their first group-stage match, playing out a goalless draw that was devoid of chances and link-up play in attack. Combative midfield displays from Jérémy Toulalan and Abou Diaby, who had replaced a disgruntled Malouda, papered over the cracks, but Gourcuff's horribly timid display was an area of major concern.

Observing the players during the warm-up, it was obvious that Gourcuff had been snubbed by his attacking partners. While groups of players passed to each other in triangles, Gourcuff cut a sad figure as he strolled about the pitch alone, occasionally juggling the ball. Once the action commenced, Anelka and Ribéry appeared intent on ignoring him. At times, the Bordeaux playmaker would be glaringly free, yet his petulant teammates went out of their way to find a more complex passing option. Anelka, in particular, frustrated Domenech by dropping back into Gourcuff's zone, reducing the 23-year-old's influence further and leaving Les Bleus without a striker.

Domenech took Gourcuff to one side for a pep talk after the match and urged him to show more gumption. 'Listen to me well, Yoann,' he said. 'I've played with Platini and I've worked with Zidane. When you didn't pass them the ball, they let you know about it. They insulted the others, they frightened the life out of them. Instead you sulk, you don't say a word. They were bosses. You're not. If you want to become one, you have to impose yourself because no one is going to do it for you. If you think I'm going to tell the others to pass you the ball, to be nice to you, you're dreaming!'

With hindsight, Domenech admitted that this forthright approach, as detailed in his book, was not the right one. Gourcuff had not been able to impose himself in a star-filled dressing room, and he needed more protection from his manager. When he joined AC Milan at the age of twenty back in 2006, he failed to cope. He even angered the club's legendary skipper Paolo Maldini, who argued that he had behaved like a loner. 'He got everything 100 per cent wrong,' Maldini said of Gourcuff's two disappointing seasons at San Siro. 'He failed to integrate because of his behaviour. He didn't study Italian, he didn't adapt to our way of working and living, and he was never on time. It's a shame because nobody ever questioned his talent.'

Gourcuff was aloof in the dressing room, but he did enjoy speaking to the media. Furthermore, he analysed the game in an intelligent and lucid manner that sounded very similar to his father – the former Rennes, Lorient and Algeria manager – but contrasted sharply with some of his less educated teammates. His interviews invariably grated with Ribéry, who allegedly thought that he was arrogant and felt he was speaking out of place. Indeed, after his own terrible display against Uruguay, Gourcuff told TF1's cult television show *Téléfoot* – nicknamed 'the great Sunday Mass', as it has become so enshrined in French culture – that France's problems had stemmed from the back-four. 'Our defensive block didn't push up quickly enough,' he argued. 'They didn't provide us with any solutions.'

Already disliked by his attacking colleagues, France's mercurial talent had now successfully alienated the defenders.

Domenech accepted Gourcuff's position in the side had become untenable, and he brought Malouda in for the crunch game with Mexico.

In Polokwane, *Les Bleus* proved to be no better without Gourcuff. While the Mexicans displayed verve and desire, Domenech's side resembled a uninterested, unmotivated mob of individuals. The tournament was only a week old, yet France looked ready to go home. 'I realised very early on we would never score a goal against Mexico,' Domenech wrote in his book. 'I understood this after the first action of the game, when Ribéry picked up possession and Anelka, who was ten metres away, didn't even move, didn't try to create anything, didn't even ask for a ball in behind.'

Anelka was so ineffective in the first half that Domenech's decision to replace him with André-Pierre Gignac did not seem strange in the least. But after seeing his team lose 2–0 to second-half goals from Javier Hernández and a 37-year-old Cuauhtémoc Blanco, the coach looked white as a sheet at the final whistle. It was clear that on top of the dreadful performance, something else had happened away from the pitch.

My strongest personal memory of France's 2010 World Cup meltdown is Domenech's press conference after that Mexico defeat. Until then, even during the toughest moments, he had remained combative. This time, there was nothing left. In my role as a reporter for the *Irish Times*, I thought about asking him if he believed the Republic of Ireland would have put up a better fight than his French side. Probably wisely, I decided not to. Adding Henry's handball to the cocktail of negative thoughts that were swirling about in his mind could well have pushed Domenech over the edge. 'At that moment, I just felt sadness. Disorder,' he later wrote. 'I think I was already somewhere else. In that press room, I looked at my own face on the television screen from time to time. It felt like I was looking at somebody else, somebody who was a long way from the match.'

On the occasions that I got to interview Domenech during his time as France manager, he was always engaging and happy to discuss football. As a member of the foreign press, I sensed he was relieved to get away from the endless mind games he played with his compatriots. He could relax and talk about the sport he loves without worrying about any malicious headlines that might emerge. Once, before France's game against the Netherlands at Euro 2008, he spoke to me in animated fashion about how the Ajax side featuring Johan Cruyff had ignited his love for coaching in the 1970s. He talked passionately about a European tie he had played in with Strasbourg against Ajax. It was fascinating and showed me a different side to his personality. He was completely unrecognisable from the cagey, unfriendly, arrogant figure that confronted the French press.

After the Mexico loss, Domenech looked like the last place he wanted to be was in South Africa talking to French journalists. But he had to stay. His team had not been eliminated yet. They still had a very slim chance of squeezing through.

Anelka, on the other hand, would soon be on his way home. The next day, Domenech informed his bosses that there had been a clash between himself and the striker at half-time. According to the coach, he had asked the striker to provide more movement, only for Anelka to accuse Domenech of persistently picking on him. When Domenech insisted he do as he say, the forward lost his cool. 'Forget it, make your shitty team without me, I quit,' Domenech claimed Anelka said, before continuing to insult him under his breath.

Internal discussions opened with a view to expelling Anelka, but the situation became a whole lot worse the next day when *L'Équipe* newspaper made the dressing room spat public. France's biggest selling newspaper not only claimed to know what Anelka had said, but splashed his alleged expletive-filled rant in large letters across the front page: '*Va te faire enculer, sale fils du pute*' ('Go fuck yourself, dirty son of a whore'), read the alarming headline. 'I felt the shock of that front page and the story itself with an unspeakable violence,' Domenech revealed in his book. 'But I quickly realised that the players were less affected by the scandal than by the fact it had been leaked. Within the squad, a question kept on resurfacing: who is the mole? In the eyes of certain players, this dressing room affair – which should never have come out – became a grave topic that put the honour and solidarity which links them in jeopardy.'

Domenech is right: for footballers, the dressing room is sacrosanct. But the fact that 'finding the mole' suddenly became the priority of the French players shows just how blinkered they were. The reputation of *Les Bleus* back home was already rotten. Before the tournament, a poll carried out by *Le Parisien* newspaper revealed that 46 per cent of French people no longer even liked the team. No sooner had they arrived in South Africa than the players were under attack from the Secretary of State for Sports, Rama Yade, who accused them of 'showing a lack of decency at this difficult economic time' by staying in the Pezula Hotel, a luxury five-star retreat with stunning ocean views. 'I'd rather they blew us away with their results than with their flashy hotels,' Yade declared.

Inside that hotel, which was totally cut off from the world by a series of security checkpoints that lined the narrow, winding private road leading up to it, *Les Bleus* went stir crazy. Évra's furious rant in the press conference the day that *L'Équipe* published their story demonstrated their misplaced siege mentality. 'The problem with the France team isn't Anelka,' the captain fumed. 'The problem is the traitor who, let's face it, is here within our ranks. How could something like this come out? The players and the coaching staff are the only ones who knew. We need to eliminate the traitor from the group.'

Speculation was suddenly rife. Reports claimed that Ribéry and Gourcuff had come to blows on the flight back from Polokwane. Could the ostracised, unhappy Gourcuff be the mole?

Domenech claimed in his book that certain players suspected Thierry Henry, albeit only briefly.

Yet, ultimately, finding the mole would prove to be an impossible task, essentially because the leak emanated from several sources. Despite the lucrative nature of modern football, there remains a genuine proximity between French players and French journalists. It is one of the most appealing aspects of working in the French media: unlike in the Premier League, where the clubs have more or less succeeded in cutting off all direct contact between players and the English press, French journalists are still able to develop relationships with international footballers. In turn, the players are treated like adults and are deemed to be capable of deciding whom they should talk to.

This endearing, human side to the French game does not always sit well with the coaches. On many a morning, Domenech must have choked on his croissant upon discovering that one of his new tactics or team selections had been revealed to the press.

Such revelations meant that any number of individuals could have let slip that the contretemps between Domenech and Anelka occurred during the Mexico game. Then, once a journalist has got the scent of a story, they go digging for the details. 'There wasn't just one mole,' *L'Équipe* journalist Vincent Duluc explains. 'There must have been forty people in that dressing room. If each one of them speaks secretly to one source, and then those sources tell three more people, within an hour you have 120 more people who know what happened. By the end of the day 500 people know. If, as a journalist, you can't get hold of at least three people out of 500, then you're not doing your job properly.'

Anelka was told he could stay in South Africa if he apologised publicly to the players and the coaching staff. He was prepared to offer an apology, but not in public, so the FFF booked him onto a flight home the next day. His teammates were furious that the decision had been taken without their consultation. They held a secret meeting late that evening and it was then that they decided to boycott training the following day.

Back home, the French public was left saddened and bewildered by the collective suicide taking place 9,500km away, but they never imagined how bad things would get the next day. On Sunday morning, the latest edition of *Téléfoot* – which was being filmed from the players' training base in South Africa – took an unexpected turn when Ribéry walked into the studio unannounced during the live transmission still wearing his flip-flops. Emotional and struggling to hold back the tears, he denied having a problem with Gourcuff, then asked the public to forgive the players for their poor performance. Duluc, who was a guest on the show that morning, remembers: 'When I saw the state Ribéry was in, I almost found him sincere. I almost found him touching. I thought, "Maybe they are affected by this." Then, three hours later, they went on strike.'

Ribéry's unplanned intervention, and the comically terrified look on Domenech's face when the winger turned up on the set, was further proof – if any was needed – that the team was out of control. When news of the player strike reached France, the country's highest authority demanded action. Over the phone, President Nicolas Sarkozy instructed his Minister for Health and Sports, Roselyne Bachelot, who was already in South Africa, to 'go and see the players and yell at them'.

Bachelot reported back to the National Assembly with the following observation: 'I can only confirm the disastrous state of the French national team where immature ringleaders are bossing frightened kids, where the coach is distressed and without authority, and where the federation is on the verge of collapse.'

Much like when Sarkozy had employed the word '*racaille*' (scum) to describe young people in *les banlieues* in 2005, Bachelot's use of '*caïds*' (ringleaders or gang-leaders) seemed to have been carefully chosen. 'By using this term, Bachelot made it sound like these guys were hardened drug-dealers,' describes Joachim Barbier, author of the book *Ce Pays Qui N'aime pas le Foot* (*This Country That Doesn't Like Football*). Barbier shakes his head in disgust. He has no doubt that the politicians seized on the football team's failings in 2010 as an opportunity to cast aspersions on France's immigrant communities. 'There was a clear attempt by the politicians to link the players to unruly youths in the suburbs. They wanted us to believe that this had happened because of the blacks and the Arabs. Évra and Anelka were at the heart of everything, and in the eyes of many people Ribéry was even worse. He was a white guy from Boulogne-sur-Mer, but he talked like them, dressed like them, and to cap it all off he'd converted to Islam. It was unquestionably a racist reaction.'

Ribéry had gone full circle in four years. Welcomed like a breath of fresh air in 2006, this simple, wholehearted kid from an extremely poor background was initially applauded for having triumphed against the odds. Few footballers had overcome as much adversity as him. From the car accident he suffered as a two-year-old that left his face badly scarred, to his difficult childhood in northern France that included getting expelled from Lille's youth academy for bad behaviour, life had been one long battle.

During those early months with *Les Bleus*, the public admired Ribéry's commitment to childhood sweetheart Wahiba, a local girl of Algerian origin for whom Ribéry converted to Islam in order to marry. But the Bayern Munich star's attitude changed along with his status. The exuberance that was once his trademark had been replaced by petulance, and his involvement in *L'Affaire Zahia* turned the public against him once and for all. 'There was a very negative image being created,' Duluc states. 'People talked about Ribéry as this scummy individual, and, what's more, a converted Muslim, bullying a shy white boy from Brittany [Gourcuff]. This was supposed to be a reflection of the problems in modern-day France, but it had nothing to do with French society. It was simply a case of the eternal laws of the dressing room being applied: in a football dressing room, only the strongest survive, and Gourcuff was very fragile.'

Yet, the make-up of France's dressing room was evolving from a sociological viewpoint. In 1998, Aimé Jacquet had drawn his squad from all corners of the country. Bixente Lizarazu and Didier Deschamps were from Basque country, Emmanuel Petit from Normandy, Robert Pirès from Reims in France's Grand Est, Youri Djorkaeff from Lyon, Laurent Blanc from the Cévennes, Frank Lebœuf and Zidane from Marseille. The core of the squad had middle-class backgrounds, and there were no extreme differences between the players.

By 2010, this had changed. Gourcuff was not the only middle-class member of Domenech's squad – Hugo Lloris, Anthony Réveillère and Jérémy Toulalan were also from affluent backgrounds – but he was in a minority. Most of the team had emerged from tough, working-class suburbs. And crucially, the squad leaders – Évra, Abidal and Ribéry – were all from *les quartiers* surrounding Paris, Lyon and Boulogne. 'From a sociological viewpoint, the 2010 team was different to the previous sides,' says Daniel Riolo, author of *Racaille Football Club* (*Scum Football Club*).

'The past teams had many immigrants, but the guys who played with Platini in the '80s and Zidane in the '90s were looked at in a favourable way. They were seen as "happy labourers", a by-product of *Les Trente Glorieuses* (the period of economic boom after the Second World War), which saw immigrants coming over to help France's economy. That wasn't the case in 2010 with the players from *les banlieues*.

'Don't forget,' Riolo continues, 'France had been through a prolonged period of economic and social strife. Many of the problems are perceived to come from the suburbs, so when your average France fan sits down on his sofa to watch *Les Bleus*, he makes the link. That's fine if the team's winning. But when they aren't – and when they're a mess and the players are misbehaving – the negative reaction is multiplied. People think, "Not only are you the cause of my country's problems, now you've gangrened my football team and ruined the one moment I have to relax when I get home from work."'

Anelka's presence at the heart of the scandal in 2010 was equally significant. A wonderfully talented player from the Paris suburb of Trappes, Anelka was a fast, powerful and technical forward and something of a pioneer when he emerged at Paris Saint-Germain in the late 1990s. He epitomised the 'bling' culture that would sweep through French football and trigger a disconnect with the public. He also possessed a dark, surly demeanour and, like so many kids in the suburbs, he identified closely with rap culture.

As he jumped from one top club to another, he became an idol for France's immigrant youth. But the way in which his brothers appeared to turn his career into a money-making exercise – engineering transfers from PSG to Arsenal to Real Madrid back to PSG to Liverpool to Manchester City, all before he was aged twenty-four – distanced Anelka further from the wider public. 'Anelka was a strong symbol for *les banlieues*,' Riolo states. 'He represented them with a style and a swagger that young people could identify with. But the average French guy in front of his TV no longer felt represented. When he looked at these players, with their headphones and their baseball caps, it just reminded him of those kids who were always causing problems at the bottom of his building.'

The media was merciless in its treatment of the disgraced players in the wake of the World Cup in South Africa. Indeed, the stigmatisation of young black and Maghrebi footballers became so relentless that certain stereotypes have remained ingrained in the national psyche. Samir Nasri, Karim Benzema and Hatem Ben Arfa often hear their names being discussed in

debates about the 2010 debacle. None of them were even selected. 'There was a general lie that was being told and it seemed to
stick,' asserts Riolo. 'People wanted to believe it was the blacks
and the Arabs. Nobody wanted to hear that Jérémy Toulalan
was involved.'

Toulalan, however, did play a part. The mild-mannered,
well-spoken, impeccably behaved white man from Nantes was,
to the public's general surprise, involved in writing the letter
that Domenech read out to the media when he announced the
strike.

Toulalan had been so shocked by the number of grammat-
ical errors and spelling mistakes on the initial draft, that he
called his adviser and asked him to re-write it. Later he was
among those to get suspended. While Anelka was banned for
eighteen games, Évra five and Ribéry three, Toulalan received
a one-game suspension. But nobody in France talked much
about that. Toulalan's part in the crime did not seem to fit in
with the story that had been so carefully scripted by France's
mainstream media and politicians.

For the record, *Les Bleus* lost their final game 2–1 against
South Africa, and Domenech disgraced himself one last time
by refusing to shake the hand of his opposite number Carlos
Alberto Parreira after the game. It felt like a suitable way for the
darkest chapter in France's footballing history to close.

CHAPTER 11

L'AFFAIRE DES QUOTAS

In May 2011 the news agency *Agence France-Presse* sent journalists to Bondy to report on the latest scandal to hit French football. The controversy known as *L'Affaire des Quotas* erupted after it was revealed that several high-level figures within the FFF had been discussing the possibility of introducing a quota system, based on race, in an attempt to limit the number of dual-nationality children selected for the federal academies.

On the *Agence France-Presse* video report, youngsters of various backgrounds are seen running about on a dusty Bondy pitch. Two kids of North African origin are interviewed. 'This is racism,' insists the first. 'If you take away the blacks and Arabs, the France team is finished,' adds the second. Then a twelve-year-old boy sporting an AC Milan shirt with Robinho on the back steps up to the camera. 'If you look back through history, the best [French] players have always been blacks and Arabs,' he states. 'Apart from Platini, Cantona and those guys.'

That third boy is Kylian Mbappé. Even at twelve, he is composed in front of the camera, adept at expressing himself clearly, and able to offer context to a difficult subject. Mbappé, like most people in France, was shocked by the thought that race might be taken into account when selecting the nation's best twelve-year-old footballers. Given that he himself was in the process of carrying out tests to enter Clairefontaine's famed academy at the time, the scandal must have felt very relevant.

The man that sparked the controversy was Mohamed Belkacemi. As the FFF's technical adviser for football in the community, Belkacemi was concerned that casual racism had become embedded in the federation. In November 2010, he secretly recorded a meeting in which France manager Laurent Blanc, FFF technical director François Blaquart and several other national-level coaches discussed the criteria used to select kids for the FFF academies. Belkacemi handed his recording on to his superior, expecting the matter to be addressed internally. Five months later, the transcript was published by Mediapart, an investigative website. It is still not known who leaked it. 'For those operating at the highest level of French football, it has been decided: there are too many blacks and Arabs, and not enough white players on the pitches,' Mediapart announced.

Certain remarks made by Blanc and Blaquart were deeply shocking. While discussing the high number of dual-nationality players that come through the French system – and can potentially go on to represent another nation – the idea of limiting the intake of black and Maghrebi players to 30 per cent was raised. 'Yes, we need some form of quota, but this isn't something that can be said,' Blaquart is heard saying on the tape.

'Personally, I'm in favour [of a quota system],' Blanc said. 'Honestly, the current situation disturbs me a lot. I believe we must try to eradicate this problem. And this belief has no racist connotation.' Blanc and Blaquart were responding to a claim made in the meeting by Erick Mombaerts, the France under-21 coach. Mombaerts stated that out of the most recent thirty players to gain international status after coming through the French federal system, only four were playing for France. Twenty-six, he said, were representing other nations.

This struck a chord with Blanc, who had previously expressed frustration at the fact that Lille striker Moussa Sow had slipped through the net. Sow, a French-born forward who represented France at under-19 and under-21 levels and finished as Ligue 1's top scorer in the 2010/11 season, had opted to represent Senegal at senior level.

But on top of the very clear issue of dual nationality, a second, more complex issue was added to the discussion. When he took charge of *Les Bleus* in 2010, Blanc made it clear that he wanted the French national team to move away from a playing style that was defined by strong, physical, athletic footballers, and towards the kind of technical, intelligent game that Spain, at the time, were practising to such devastating effect. There was a feeling that France's youth system, which continued to follow the guidelines laid out at Clairefontaine, was favouring big, powerful kids and all too often neglecting the smaller ones, some of whom possessed the potential and game intelligence to become fine footballers.

In the meeting, Blanc expressed concerns that France was now developing too many of the same profile of footballer be-cause too much emphasis was being placed on size when select-ing 12-year-old boys for the academies. Critically, he linked this trend to the high number of black children being drafted. 'We don't want to eliminate the foreigners, not at all,' Blanc started. 'We want to ensure that the federal academies define their crite-ria better so that we attract different people, because if we keep the same criteria, we will always get the same people. I go out on the pitches [to watch games] every Saturday, I see the acad-emies: one has the impression we're producing the same pro-totype of player: big, strong and powerful. Which players are big, strong and powerful at the moment? Black players. That's the way it is. It is a fact at the moment. God knows that in the academies, in the football schools, well, there are a lot of them. I think we need to balance it out, especially for the boys aged thirteen to fourteen, twelve to thirteen, to have other criteria that is [better] adapted to our own culture. Take the Spanish:

they don't have these problems. They have a very precise play-ing style criteria for twelve to thirteen year olds.'

At this point Mombaerts interjected to concur with Blanc and said, 'This is the project'. The France manager then came back in with a particularly crude comment: 'The Spanish said to me: "We don't have a problem here. We don't have any blacks."'

The discussion had started with two legitimate concerns being raised: France was losing a lot of the players it trained to other African (and sometimes even European) nations, and the academy system was no longer producing the variety of foot-balling profiles that was desired. Both matters were potentially harming the national team's development. However, the discus-sions overlapped, the talk became loose, and certain remarks – not least the outrageous suggestion that a quota system be introduced – quite rightly sparked a huge uproar.

The issue of dual nationality has always been a thorn in the FFF's side. The majority of twelve-year-olds that are chosen to attend Clairefontaine each year have the option of playing for more than one country: many are born in France but can also represent the nations of their parents. Through the years, the authorities have been forced to accept that they will spend time developing young footballers who may ultimately play for Alge-ria, Morocco, Tunisia, Mali, Côte d'Ivoire, Senegal, Cameroon or even Portugal.

In 2002, when Senegal stunned France in the opening game of the World Cup, twenty-one members of their twenty-three-man squad were on the books of French clubs, and fourteen had benefited from youth training in France.

When I raise the thorny issue with Gérard Houllier in his Paris office late in 2019, the man responsible for instigating the *préformation* system at Clairefontaine back in 1990 still finds it hard to accept that France loses so much of its talent to other countries. 'We recruit boys from the Paris region,' begins Houllier. 'We teach them and we develop them. We do this with taxpayer money because our academies are financed by the state. If, at the end of his training, when he has learned everything he needs, he decides he doesn't fancy France, and actually he'd rather play for another country, this makes me uncomfortable.

'I wasn't happy about that,' Houllier insists. 'I wondered if we could do something about it. For example, could we tell the player that if he comes to train with us, he has to commit to France? But that was not legal.'

Houllier points out that France could have lost Mbappé to Cameroon or Algeria. But then, as if trying to reassure himself, he adds: 'We haven't lost any players that we regret. The best kids always choose to play for *Les Bleus*.' In terms of players who attended FFF academies, Houllier is right. Former Bayern Munich defender Mehdi Benatia (Morocco) and Borussia Dortmund left-back Raphaël Guerreiro (Portugal), both of whom attended Clairefontaine, are arguably the biggest losses. But *Les Bleus* would surely have liked to draw on the talents of Pierre-Emerick Aubameyang (who plays for Gabon), Kalidou Koulibaly (who plays for Senegal), Nicolas Pépé (who plays for Côte d'Ivoire) and Riyad Mahrez (who plays for Algeria), all of whom were born in France and honed their skills in the French system. Even Ivorian striker Didier Drogba, who moved to France aged five, could have pulled on the blue shirt.

The current FFF technical director, Hubert Fournier, assures me the dual nationality issue does not even get mentioned at federation headquarters these days. *Au contraire*. 'We're very happy when we see any of our players thriving at international level,' Fournier states emphatically. 'When Algeria won the Africa Cup of Nations [in 2019] with a number of French-trained players, it was a great source of pride for us.' Lessons, it seems, have been learned.

Algeria's title-winning squad contained fourteen French-born players. Yet France, it should be said, do not only give. They also take. Patrick Vieira was born in Senegal and Marcel Desailly in Ghana. When, in 2019, Angolan-born midfielder Eduardo Camavinga broke into the Rennes side aged sixteen and received rave reviews, his application for French citizenship appeared to suddenly accelerate.

In 2006, Domenech – in typically provocative fashion – named Gonzalo Higuaín in his squad to play Greece after being made aware that the uncapped Argentinian striker was born in Brest. Higuaín turned down the chance to play for *Les Bleus*, saying that this was 'a choice from my heart' and that he could only ever imagine playing for Argentina.

And therein lies a key point. Many of the youngsters being trained at France's academies feel a strong connection to the countries that they or their families are from. Such players may be born in France, but grow up in immigrant communities and are raised in the traditions of their African roots. Ricardo Faty is a good example: the midfielder was born in the Paris suburbs and came through the French system, attending Clairefontaine before representing France at youth level. He was even voted best player of the Toulon Tournament for under-20s that France won in 2006. But Faty – like his older brother Jacques – later opted to play for Senegal, which is the country of his father.

The tall, rangy midfielder, who now plays in Turkey, pauses and takes a deep breath when I ask him about his national allegiances. It feels like this is a subject he has already devoted a good deal of thought to in his life. 'In France, there is a little problem with identity,' describes the former FC Nantes and AS Roma player. 'People are always asking "Where are you from?" For me, playing for Senegal is a way of getting closer to my origins. I am French and I like France. I grew up loving the France teams of Henry, Zidane and Vieira. But at the same time, I was surrounded by an African culture at home. The pull can be very strong. I believe it's a legitimate question that we should be allowed to ask ourselves.' Faty comes across as a loyal man and the nationality issue has evidently weighed heavily on him. After opting for Senegal, he and his father travelled to Claire-fontaine to apologise in person to the academy's technical staff.

In the wake of France's South African disaster, *Les Bleus* dropped to twenty-first in the FIFA rankings. But their popularity levels plunged even lower. The question of whether the shamed World Cup players – and in particular those from immigrant backgrounds – genuinely wanted to don the French national shirt surged to the surface. The image of certain players not singing the national anthem before games further fuelled the heated debate. Many fans felt that the players did not care enough about the national team simply because they did not feel French enough. 'The dual-nationality players nearly all support their country of origin,' the journalist Daniel Riolo states. 'When France played against Algeria, Morocco and Tunisia, on every occasion the fans booed the French anthem. There is a form of rejection from the North African communities towards their host country.'

Again, it is important to stress that none of Karim Benzema, Samir Nasri and Hatem Ben Arfa were present in South Africa in 2010. However, the 'national identity' debate often focuses on these three talented footballers, who are of Maghrebi descent. Benzema is repeatedly reminded of a radio interview he gave as a teenager in which he talked about his fondness of Algeria. 'It's my parents' country and it's in my heart,' he told RMC. 'But I'll play for France.' Riolo believes the Real Madrid striker should be commended for his honesty rather than derided: 'Benzema was just expressing the same feeling that most kids from the suburbs have. He loves Algeria but decided to play for France because he knew it'd give him more exposure and generate more interest.'

Several years later, another gifted Lyon forward, Nabil Fekir, hesitated over the decision of what country he should play for.

Fekir eventually chose *Les Bleus* ahead of Algeria. But when he made his international debut against Brazil in 2015, he was whistled by sections of the Stade de France. 'Fekir had always wanted to play for Algeria,' Riolo claims. 'But his agent at the time, Jean-Pierre Bernès, who also happens to be [the current France coach] Didier Deschamps's agent, explained to him that his future contracts would be more lucrative if he played for France.'

The idea that players might be hesitating before committing to *Les Bleus* did not sit well with the French public. 'If you have guys who are openly saying, "I'm playing for France because it's in my own personal interests, but actually my heart is elsewhere," well it's normal that this unsettles people,' Riolo argues.

Gérard Houllier has a very different theory as to why France's players appeared to be less committed to the team's cause than their predecessors. He believes the French system failed to move with the times. France, according to the former technical director, remained good at developing individual talents in the 2000s but had begun neglecting the very essence of football itself: a collective identity. 'We were developing football players, but not football teams,' Houllier states, banging his pen on the table to emphasise the difference.

In the years that followed Houllier's departure in 1998, Clairefontaine continued to develop strong, technical footballers at an impressive rate. Indeed, the flow of French talent to Europe's major leagues even accelerated. French players had become ideal 'commodities' that could be sold to foreign clubs at a young age because they had a solid grounding and were able to adapt quickly to new surroundings having already lived away from home.

But such youngsters who had been through the French training system often had a far more individualistic mindset. Many had represented half a dozen different teams by the time they reached the age of eighteen. The notion of club loyalty no longer appeared to count. For the generations who came through federal and club academies in the 2000s, the idea of success was increasingly driven by their capacity to seal a transfer to a bigger club, to earn more money and fame, and, in the case of some, to gain more kudos on social media.

For Houllier, the way children were being taught to play the game in France contributed to the emergence of this self-centred mindset. 'We spent too much time working individually with players on their technique, and not enough time looking at the bigger picture,' he argues. 'I went to Spain to see how they were working. They'd copied everything that we had done in the 1990s. But they added the collective element. When they work on technique, the exercises they do are always applied in the interest of the team.' Is that why Spain developed players like Xavi Hernández, while France was producing players like Hatem Ben Arfa? 'You could put it like that, yes,' Houllier smiles.

The mention of Ben Arfa, a player Houllier managed at Lyon, brings the former coach seamlessly onto another issue: 'There was also a problem with mentality in France. In Spain, if a player caused a problem, they didn't pick him. If Barcelona see a kid who is really talented but always shouting at his teammates, throwing his arms up in the air, or not defending when he loses the ball, they don't even look at him. We tended to favour the individual, technical side of a player. But football is so demanding at the highest level, you have to have eleven players who are fighters for the team.'

France had got complacent and they were paying the price. When *Les Bleus* won the World Cup in 1998, Aimé Jacquet became a national treasure. The manager stepped down but was rewarded with the prestigious position of technical director of the FFF, which had been made vacant by Houllier's switch to Liverpool. For many experts, this was a calamitous appointment for French football. *L'Équipe* journalist Vincent Duluc describes

Jacquet as 'the worst technical director in history'. He held the position for nine years despite no longer having an appetite for football after achieving the ultimate dream of winning the World Cup. 'His legacy was a disaster and he's responsible for a lot of the problems we encountered,' Duluc states. 'Ask Jacquet what he did during his time as technical director and he has absolutely nothing to show. He did nothing.'

When Houllier returned for his second stint as technical director, succeeding Jacquet in 2007, he had it all to do again. Not that he blames his good friend for effectively squandering France's advantage. 'Look, when things are working people don't change them,' Houllier says. 'There was a sense of: "We won like that, so let's keep on winning like that." But as soon as you start to stand still, you are in danger of getting overtaken.'

Jacquet had merely looked to reinforce the methods that had taken *Les Bleus* to the top. His World Cup-winning unit was founded on power, speed and an exceptional defence, and that team became the blueprint for French football. Academies were encouraged to find and develop athletic footballers, and an obsession to unearth the next Vieira or Desailly emerged. Under Jacquet's watch, aspiring coaches were taught about organisation and tactical discipline when they attended the classes at Clairefontaine, which were compulsory in order to obtain the coaching badges. Many of today's Ligue 1 trainers have sat in one of those Clairefontaine classrooms listening to the likes of Domenech stress the importance of playing two defensive midfielders who never leave their zone.

Labelled as Jacquet's favourite son, Domenech was caution personified during his time in charge of *Les Bleus*, always insisting on a pair of holding midfielders. Arsène Wenger once suggested putting Samir Nasri in the middle, and the press frequently urged Domenech to revert to one defensive midfielder when playing against smaller nations. He never budged. In August 2009, Domenech's decision to include both Jérémy

Toulalan and Lassana Diarra against the Faroe Islands, while Franck Ribéry and Karim Benzema sat on the bench, left the nation perplexed. France laboured to a 1–0 win.

This safety-first approach trickled down from the national team to the club game. 'From a philosophical point of view, 1998 hurt us a lot,' Duluc explains. 'Our domestic league is still suffering. We have the league that produces the fewest goals and the least excitement. Why? Because all of the coaches who have emerged since 1998 are disciples of Jacquet. They have all been taught in Jacquet's way.'

Ligue 1 suffered badly from the ultra-cautious approach of the coaches, with most teams setting out to defend, packing the midfield, and hoping the solitary forward would nick a goal on the counterattack. For a commentator, injecting life and interest into such games could be challenging. Players often kicked the ball straight into touch from kick-off. There would then be what the French like to call *un rond d'observation* (an observation round) as teams tentatively stood off and observed each other's tactics. Contests were frequently goalless at half-time, at which point one player from each side would be interviewed pitchside and express satisfaction that his team is *bien en place* (in position or defensively solid).

It felt like a different sport to the one being played on the other side of the Channel. 'Teams in Ligue 1 were well organised but they weren't playing to win,' Houllier observes. 'In England a draw is like a defeat, whereas here a draw felt like a win. Players in England fight throughout a game. We don't have that culture. But the Ligue 1 coaches who preach caution are wrong. You have to take risks in football.'

Not only was Ligue 1 losing its best players, but its teams were also failing to entertain. In the 2005/06 season, with the league averaging fewer than two goals a game – compared to more than three goals a game in the Premier League – the authorities commissioned ex-France coach Michel Hidalgo, who won the European Championship in 1984, to find ways of changing the mindset. Hidalgo suggested offering two points for a score draw, four points for a win and five points for a win by a two-goal margin. His proposals were given serious consideration but in the end none were implemented.

Ultimately, the problem ran far deeper. Altering the points system was never going to change a flawed philosophy. Most players coming through the youth structures were now tall, athletic individuals capable of playing a destructive role on the pitch, but far less geared towards creating. 'Our methods were based purely on a defensive, physical style of football,' says Riolo. 'If you went to see any junior team play, you could be sure they'd have a big kid in central defence, another in central midfield, and another in attack. The coaches thought that size was a guarantee for future success.'

Claude Puel is well placed to judge the mentalities in France compared to England. The experienced coach, who returned to Ligue 1 with Saint-Étienne in 2019 after spells at Southampton and Leicester City, believes France is still today guilty of developing big, strong, powerful footballers at the expense of smaller, more skilful ones. 'The priority is being given to physical players who can penetrate but are not creative,' Puel told *Le Monde* newspaper. 'This is the main problem. The lack of fluidity in Ligue 1 is the result of the structural choices being made by recruiters at youth level. They are drawn to the big strong players who make a physical impact because there is a fear of bad results. They want to be solid first and foremost. Football comes after. Many intelligent footballers are being cast aside. I feel like we want to reassure ourselves by choosing the big guys, thinking we can maybe teach them technical skills. But it's too late for them!'

Former FC Nantes manager Raynald Denoueix, who is regarded as a pioneer in youth development, agrees with Puel. 'I heard that some clubs were refusing to take kids for their academy if they were under 6ft,' Denoueix says, shaking his head at the thought of such a notion. 'That might explain what happened. The trouble is that kids who rely on their physicality to dominate in junior football don't develop other aspects of their game. So, when the others finish growing, they lose their advantage. When a player realises at the age of twenty that, in fact, he doesn't know how to play football, it's very hard for him to deal with.'

Denoueix's theory is supported by the marked difference in France's record at junior level compared to the under-21 age group. In modern times, France has excelled internationally from under-15 level up to the under-20s. Yet the under-21s have failed categorically. Indeed, *Les Espoirs* did not qualify for a single European Championship between 2006 and 2019, an appalling record for a nation that prides itself on youth development.

In this context it is understandable that Laurent Blanc was questioning France's methods and particularly its obsession with player size. Even before the quota scandal, Blanc had voiced concerns. In 2010, after Spain had won the World Cup with Barcelona's pocket-sized duo Xavi and Andrés Iniesta at the heart of their team, the newly appointed France boss suggested that those two midfield maestros might not even have turned professional had they grown up in France and been exposed to the French system.

France's smaller kids were having to find alternative routes into the game. Diminutive playmaker Mathieu Valbuena was released by Bordeaux's academy due to his stature. Thankfully for Valbuena, what he lacks in size he makes up for in determination, and he battled his way up through lower leagues to the national team, winning fifty-two caps. Antoine Griezmann was consistently told he was too small by youth coaches in France, so he jumped at the chance to move to Spain aged fourteen when Real Sociedad recognised his abilities. As France's most creative talent since Zidane, Griezmann's vision, technique and intelligence unquestionably benefited from crossing the Pyrenees.

Two other internationals, Kévin Gameiro and Marvin Martin, who are 5ft 8in and 5ft 7in respectively, attended trials at Clairefontaine only to be rejected for being too small. Indeed, Martin passed every test bar one; the results of a wrist x-ray that predicted his future growth did not meet the required criteria.

Houllier made sure Clairefontaine's out-dated methods were replaced when he returned to the FFF in 2007. There would be no more wrist x-rays. No more fixation with size. And no more endlessly repetitive drills designed to make technique second nature. From now on, the players would be expected to think for themselves both on and off the pitch.

François Blaquart, the former youth coach who had been employed by the FFF since 1999, became Houllier's number two and was charged with the task of carrying out the reforms. 'We've changed the way we get our message across,' Blaquart told *Vestiaires* magazine in 2010. 'The "explain everything" approach brought some great moments, but we've seen its limits. Players need to learn how to solve a problem themselves. Too much emphasis was put on physique and technique. Now we take the person into account, his spirit, his footballing intelligence – qualities that were ignored in the past.'

●　●　●

When I meet André Merelle in the gardens of a restaurant in the leafy town of Rambouillet, just up to the road from Clairefontaine, the retired coach is friendly and talkative. But it is impossible not to notice the hint of sadness lurking behind his jovial exterior. The man who committed thirty years of his life to working for the FFF, and was instrumental in developing players like Thierry Henry, Nicolas Anelka and Blaise Matuidi, found himself unceremoniously sacked in 2010. He knows that, inevitably, I will be wanting to ask about that, and about the quota scandal that cast a horribly dark shadow over Clairefontaine six months later.

The wound is still raw. Merelle is convinced that Houllier and Blaquart needed to find a scapegoat for *Les Bleus'* shortcomings and unfairly pointed the finger at Clairefontaine's old guard. 'I remember when we had meetings to discuss modern trends in football,' Merelle begins. 'I'd always mention the importance of technique, and I'd see them rolling their eyes. [France under-21 coach] Erick Mombaerts would tell me that technique is only secondary. Apparently mentality is more important now. But who are Blaquart and Mombaerts? What have they done in their careers? I heard Blaquart say we should stop hyping up individuals and start focusing more on the collective. But don't we need talented individuals too? Perhaps he wants France to have a team without talent because he didn't have any and he's jealous of those who do.'

Merelle was not surprised by the quota scandal. He says he had sensed for some time that the FFF wanted to reduce the intake of children from immigrant backgrounds, something he steadfastly refused to adhere to. 'Our job was to pick the best kids from the Paris region,' he insists. 'The fact is the majority of the kids who play football in these areas are black, and more often than not they are the best players.'

It is easy to feel sorry for the former Bordeaux and Rouen defender. When France won the 1998 World Cup, he and his colleague Claude Dusseau were hailed for their roles in developing so much exceptional talent. A decade later, despite having continued to work in the same, diligent manner, they were blamed for French football's woes. Not only were their training methods being described as archaic, they were also accused of contributing to the brat culture that was plaguing the national team.

By putting children on a pedestal at such a young, impressionable age, Clairefontaine was creating egos and raising individuals in a bubble that bore no resemblance to real life. 'The kids did sense that they're part of an elite, and the environment makes them very sure of themselves,' Merelle concedes. 'But we're not the ones giving them big heads. You see twelve-year-old kids arrive. They have an agent, their parents are telling them they're going to be stars, and some of them have already signed pre-contracts with professional clubs. It's not easy to keep them grounded in those circumstances.'

Merelle, however, insists the problem with player behaviour that came to the surface so noticeably in South Africa is a general one that the modern game must deal with. When he hears people linking the 2010 player strike to *les banlieues*, he explains how this reinforces his feeling that racist attitudes are widespread. 'There seemed to be this message that was being put out there: "The blacks and the Arabs from the suburbs are dragging the team down." I wasn't happy about that because it's absolute rubbish. And it's probably the real reason why they started talking about quotas at the federation.'

When the saga erupted, Blanc initially denied any wrongdoing, claiming that he had not heard any talk of a quota system being introduced. But after Mediapart published the entire transcript of the meeting, he was forced to apologise and to participate in the FFF's internal investigation. Blaquart was suspended, but the coach survived. Blanc's role in the affair sparked much debate, and for the first time, cracks started to appear in France's World Cup-winning squad. The 1998 side had often been hailed as a beacon for unity, but thirteen years on it became clear that they were not all best friends.

The initial reaction was a supportive one. Christophe Dugarry, Marcel Desailly and Bixente Lizarazu offered Blanc their public backing, as did the most influential figure of all, Zinédine Zidane, who told *L'Équipe*: 'Of course he is not racist.'

Not everybody agreed, though. Patrick Vieira described Blanc's comments as 'scandalous', and Lilian Thuram questioned the FFF's decision to keep him on. 'It's clear that we are at the heart of a scandal,' Thuram said. 'In light of what happened, his apologies are not sufficient.'

The public bickering that followed did little to lift French football out of the gutter. As well as accusing Thuram of 'acting like he's the judge in a Supreme Court', Dugarry claimed the defender had been guilty of a racist act himself in the dressing room after the 1998 win. 'I heard Thuram say: "Come on, let's get a photo with all the blacks together." I wasn't the only one,' Dugarry said. 'Frank Lebœuf heard it as well.' Later, Emmanuel Petit claimed the story about posing for the photo was true. 'It did more than just annoy me,' Petit wrote in his book *Mon Dictionnaire Passionné de L'Équipe de France* (*My Passionate Dictionary of the France Team*). 'I was hurt by it.'

The public had just about come to terms with the infighting that had ravaged France's 2010 World Cup campaign. Now they were having to take on board the fact that even the 1998 side that they so loved and cherished was being divided by racial tensions.

Today Thuram insists he still has a good relationship with Petit, Dugarry and Blanc. But the anti-discrimination activist states that he was not prepared to sit in silence when *L'Affaire des Quotas* first broke. 'I was hurt, I was very hurt. It hit me hard,' says Thuram gravely, looking me in the eye with a penetrating glare. 'For some people, the big number is scary. They think: "It's OK to have a few, but not too many. We need to make sure there's enough room for us."'

For Thuram, the quota scandal was clear evidence of the existence of racism in French society. The FFF had been accused of discriminating against blacks and Arabs, but Thuram turns the equation around: he believes Blanc and Blaquart – perhaps without even realising it – were trying to protect their own kind. 'Racism is about people wanting to conserve their advantage,' Thuram explains. 'The quota scandal was not about discriminating against certain people. It was about favouring certain people. It was about protecting the people who are like them: their children, their cousins, their friends.'

This is an alternative view and one that few people in football are prepared to consider. But how many black or Maghrebi coaches have been given a chance with French clubs? How many non-white faces are there in positions of responsibility in French football? The answer is not very many at all. It may sound far-fetched, but Thuram is as well informed on the roots of racism as anybody in the world of football, and his theory might just carry more weight than those running the game in France would care to admit.

CHAPTER 12

LA GÉNÉRATION '87

Samir Nasri is about to play in the first final of his career. The sixteen-year-old from Marseille appears to be in relaxed, confident mood. Laughing and joking with his France teammates as they gather in the rustic tunnel of Stade Gaston-Petit in Châteauroux, Nasri even takes a moment to playfully tease his opposite number, a small Catalan boy with a mullet and the name 'Cesc' on the back of his shirt. 'We're going to win this,' Nasri tells Spain's number eight, pointing at the trophy. 'Look at that cup, it's ours.'

It is 15 May 2004 and the hosts are facing Spain to decide who wins the European Under-17 Championship. Spain have clinched the continental prize six times in the past – unlike France who have never won it – and Juan Santisteban's tyros boast a strong side that includes two exceptional products from Barcelona's academy: Gerard Piqué, the centre-back who is on the verge of joining Manchester United, and the highly promising midfielder Cesc Fàbregas, now at Arsenal. Fàbregas – who went on to be voted player of the tournament – netted a late penalty to knock out England in the semis following a foul by Mark Noble.

Nasri, though, is not worried about Spain's talent. France had already beaten them in the group stage and a supreme confidence reigns among Philippe Bergeroo's side. They have team spirit, the home advantage and, above all, a huge amount of attacking ability. Indeed, until now, nobody has been able to live with France's skilful, direct, pacy front four; Nasri, Hatem Ben Arfa, Jérémy Ménez and Karim Benzema are simply a cut above.

This was France's Golden Generation. Portugal had Luís Figo, Fernando Couto, Paulo Sousa, Rui Costa and João Pinto. England had Steven Gerrard, Rio Ferdinand, Frank Lampard, David Beckham, Paul Scholes and Wayne Rooney. France had this group: *La Génération '87*, a glittering cohort of virtuoso footballers all born in 1987. 'We stood out from the rest,' Ménez later commented. 'That's always the way with great players.'

The self-belief of France's attackers rubbed off on the other members of the team. 'We were so laid-back,' Pierre Ducasse, the midfielder who would go on to play for Bordeaux, told *So Foot* magazine. 'It was unthinkable we could lose.' In the semi-finals against Portugal, France were trailing at the interval. Steven Thicot, the future Hibernian midfielder, admitted he was fearing the worst. 'Then Nasri came up to me and said: "Stop sulking! I've sworn on the life of my twin brothers that I'll win this tournament for you. We'll beat Portugal."' Nasri duly equalised before Ménez and Ben Arfa sealed a 3–1 triumph.

It took France all of eleven seconds to break through in the final. Ménez sliced open the Spain defence with a powerful run, cut the ball back from the right, and Kévin Constant volleyed home. Complacency may then have crept in, and Piqué was able to equalise from a corner in the second half. But Nasri delivered on his promise and surged forward to fire in a precise low shot from twenty metres in the last minute.

That night, Bergeroo's ecstatic title-winners wanted to celebrate in a Châteauroux nightclub, but for the first time – and sadly not the last – their fame caught up with them. They were the talk of the town, and of course nobody will fall for a fake ID when you've just been crowned under-17 champions. Despite the setback, defender Thomas Mangani later confirmed a fun night was had by all in the local kebab restaurant.

When I catch up with Samir Nasri in his hometown of Marseille several years later, and ask him about those 2004 exploits, his eyes light up. 'It's my best football memory,' the former Arsenal and Manchester City playmaker remarks. 'It was a period of pure happiness and insouciance. We just were mates, playing football together and having fun. And we were brilliant! Honestly, we used to be able to pass to each other with our eyes closed. As a group, we really clicked on and off the pitch. Nobody could stop us.'

But sadly, for many players in that France team, Châteauroux would prove to be the pinnacle.

Sixteen years on, six of the eighteen squad members have already quit football, and now even the bigger names from that group are wilting. Indeed, at the start of the 2019/20 season, a 32-year-old Ben Arfa – regarded by many as the best of the lot – did not even have a club. Likewise, Ménez was struggling for employment after returning from a stint in Mexico. In September, Ménez eventually agreed a deal with Ligue 2 basement side Paris FC. As for Nasri, after a year out due to a doping ban and poor spells at Antalyaspor and West Ham, the man once labelled Zinédine Zidane's successor is playing in Belgium.

Ultimately, just one member of the squad has truly excelled: Benzema may have only been sitting on the bench for the 2004 final, but he went on to be Real Madrid's striker for more than a decade, winning four Champions League trophies. That said, even Benzema's career will be looked upon in a mixed light after the Lyon-born forward dropped out of the France fold aged just twenty-seven in the wake of a series of off-field controversies.

For their parts, Nasri, Ben Arfa and Ménez enjoyed varying degrees of success. Yet none came close to hitting the heights they had seemed destined for.

To understand why *La Génération '87* failed to deliver on

its immense promise, it is important to acknowledge the role of the media. *Les Bleus* had conquered the world in 1998 and Europe in 2000, and this fantastic new generation looked well-equipped to step into the shoes of Thierry Henry, David Trezeguet and Zinédine Zidane. Never before had a group of young French footballers been hyped up and exposed to such an extent so soon, and the pressure on their shoulders was immense from an early stage.

Jean-Christophe Cesto, who played midfield in that same under-17 team and now works as a video analyst at FC Nantes, was struck by the attention that they were already attracting back in 2004. 'I remember the way people looked at as,' Cesto told *So Foot* magazine. 'It was like we were stars already. There would always be a crowd following the team. People would ask for autographs, and girls used to hang around us too.'

Ben Arfa was a household name even before his Châteauroux exploits. Between the ages twelve and fifteen, he starred in Bruno Sevaistre's documentary series *À la Clairefontaine*, which followed an intake of boys during their time at the academy. Over the course of the sixteen episodes, a cheeky, affable Hatem assumes an increasingly central role, and the left-footer's extraordinary skills begin to draw comparisons with Diego Maradona no less.

Ricardo Faty was in the same year at Clairefontaine and witnessed Ben Arfa's magic at close quarters. 'I don't think there's another person or player like him,' Faty remarks. 'Hatem was an artist. What he could do with a football at the age of thirteen was phenomenal.'

Ben Arfa grew up in the Paris suburb of Clamart. But upon graduating from Clairefontaine, he opted to join French champions Lyon after the club's long-serving President Jean-Michel Aulas – one of the most influential figures in the French game – travelled to the capital in person to convince the fifteen-year-old and his parents to join the club. Already being tipped as a future Ballon d'Or winner, the prodigious attacker was a celebrity, and the status went to his head. He behaved like a star and by all accounts was afforded special treatment by the staff at Lyon's academy.

'I remember at one stage, when he was sixteen, his coach decided he'd had enough,' *L'Équipe*'s chief football writer Vincent Duluc recalls. 'He was always late, he was nonchalant and pretty much out of control, so the coach decided to suspend him. The club didn't support the suggestion, though. They said it was out of the question to suspend a boy who was worth €20 million already.'

Lyon thrust Ben Arfa into the spotlight at seventeen, blooding him in Ligue 1 and even in the Champions League for a game against Manchester United. But the teenager's brashness did not sit easily with his older teammates. According to multiple reports, he also had a problem with authority, which was almost certainly exacerbated by his early fame. The winger came to blows with Lyon's international defender Sébastien Squillaci during one training session, then later clashed with the club's Brazilian stalwarts Cris and Cláudio Caçapa over a spilt water bottle.

When Ben Arfa quit Lyon for Marseille, aged twenty-one, he left under a cloud, taking the club to court and verbally attacking Aulas over the alleged non-payment of a bonus. 'People were scared of Aulas because he was powerful, and a member of the [disciplinary] commission,' he told the magazine *Les Inrockuptibles*. 'But I didn't care a damn. I was just thinking: "It's a good job we're not animals, otherwise I'd have killed him."'

Ben Arfa was gaining little public sympathy – especially when it was later reported that a cheque for €90,000, which matched the missing bonus, had been found in his otherwise empty locker at Lyon's training ground. His attitude shocked many, but it is important to acknowledge that he was still a young man for whom everything had happened too quickly.

Ben Arfa was not getting the advice or protection he needed from his entourage. His first agent Frédéric Guerra believes the considerable influence of Ben Arfa's adviser Michel Ouazine, a former neighbour from Clamart, became his biggest problem. Ben Arfa's father claims Ouazine, who continues to represent the winger today, has a 'harmful relationship' with his son. Kamel Ben Arfa reportedly had a fight with Ouazine outside the FFF headquarters in 2012. Hatem is no longer thought to be in contact with his dad.

Behind the scenes, Ben Arfa's career became a sorry state of affairs. But it was becoming common for elite youngsters to mix in unhelpful, sometimes unsavoury circles.

Nasri certainly had questionable off-field allies. After moving from Marseille to Arsenal in 2008, the playmaker reportedly developed a friendship with Farouk Achoui, who, through his cousin, the lawyer Karim Achoui, is alleged to have links to the mafia in France, as detailed in the 2018 book *Les Parrains du Foot* (*The Godfathers of Football*). Nasri and Farouk Achoui, who in the past has been accused of a long list of criminal offences, were photographed together on holiday. The pair invested in a shisha lounge in Paris, and Nasri would reportedly travel over to the establishment from London at every opportunity. That same summer, Nasri made enemies within the France squad after being selected for Euro 2008 by Raymond Domenech. Although aged just twenty-one, his sense of self-worth seemed to be high.

Like Zidane, Nasri had grown up in a tough northern suburb of Marseille, and from the age of twelve he was consistently likened to the France legend. Whether those early comparisons went to his head, or whether he was born with a disconcerting sense of self-assurance, some of France's senior players had trouble accepting him. William Gallas expressed his disdain after Nasri took Thierry Henry's seat on the team bus, and the defender developed a poisonous relationship with his Arsenal teammate. In 2009, after Gallas and Nasri had clashed again, the former claimed on RMC Sport TV to have been accosted and threatened by a group of Nasri's friends while having dinner with his family in a Paris hotel. Gallas even said they were armed with tasers. It is claimed in *Les Parrains du Foot* that Farouk Achoui was among those present.

Ménez's story is rather tame in comparison. However, the dynamic teenager, who was invited to Manchester United by Sir Alex Ferguson aged fifteen and could have joined the English club, has not come near to fulfilling his potential either. Ménez followed up his under-17 triumph by exploding onto the Ligue 1 scene at Sochaux. The quick, powerful, two-footed attacker set two records when he scored a magnificent seven-minute hat-trick against Bordeaux, aged seventeen and eight months, becoming the youngest man to score three goals in a Ligue 1 fixture as well as registering the fastest top-flight treble.

However, like Ben Arfa and Nasri, Ménez's individualistic style prevented him from succeeding at a top club. Monaco, AS Roma, PSG and AC Milan all tried to coax the talent out of him, but all ended up frustrated. 'I know I have a nonchalant side out on the pitch,' Ménez told beIN Sports. 'It's just something I have in me. I don't do it on purpose.'

Gérard Houllier, who coached Ben Arfa for two seasons at Lyon, believes the difficulties encountered by players from *La Génération '87* are partly a consequence of France's youth training methods. 'I do feel like we are a bit responsible,' Houllier explains. 'We did too much technique with them. We needed to adjust our training methods, become more like the Spanish by focusing more on collective training exercises and collective play.'

For Faty, Ben Arfa could have played for any one of Europe's biggest teams had he been programmed slightly differently. 'He finds it hard to be part of a collective,' the former Clairefontaine student begins. 'He's a sensational talent and can win matches on his own. But when he has to fit into a manager's plans, when he has to be part of a team, it's much harder. That's why a

Barcelona or a Bayern Munich never went for him. They knew that for all his individual talent, he couldn't easily integrate in a collective.'

It is easy to find dazzling YouTube compilations featuring France's supposed Golden Generation. Watch Nasri's mesmerising dribble for Arsenal against FC Porto, Ménez's crazy run and back-heel goal for Milan against Parma, or Ben Arfa's Maradona-esque strike for Newcastle against Blackburn, and it is easy to believe you are looking at three of the world's best players. Sadly, that is nowhere near being the case.

Nasri briefly hit the heights with Arsenal, and did so again with Manchester City in 2013/14, contributing seven goals and seven assists in their title-winning campaign. But more often than not he flattered to deceive. Meanwhile, Ben Arfa (with Lyon and Marseille) and Ménez (with PSG) only played peripheral roles in their clubs' title wins. Looking back, Ben Arfa believes those thrilling beginnings, which culminated in the victory in Châteauroux, ultimately worked against him and his teammates. They had been put on a pedestal by the media and were unfairly judged as a result.

'I feel like we became easy targets,' Ben Arfa told Canal Plus. 'I don't want to sound like a cry-baby, but people used to hammer us for even the slightest thing. I don't know why. Maybe because we were the first generation to be hyped up like that, so young. Everyone thought we'd set the example, but you mustn't forget we were only seventeen or eighteen. We couldn't assume the status of a 25- or 26-year-old man, who already has children and a family. We didn't even have driving licences. We couldn't do it.'

When Laurent Blanc took charge of France in the summer of 2010, replacing Domenech, a door opened for *La Génération '87*. Benzema, Ben Arfa, Nasri and Ménez all had one considerable advantage over the competition: none of them had been part of the South African debacle and therefore none of them had seen their reputations tarnished. They were also nearing their playing prime and they all played for top European clubs.

Furthermore, *Les Bleus* now had a coach who encouraged attacking, possession-based football and had a penchant for gifted individuals. After naming the mercurial attackers in his first squad, Blanc insisted he had no qualms about selecting all four. 'They have one quality in common: talent,' he quipped. 'We're lucky to have these players and it'd be wrong to say I've chosen too many talented players.'

In truth, Blanc had needed to dig deep to find twenty-three men for that opening friendly in Norway. On top of the bans handed out to Nicolas Anelka, Patrice Évra, Éric Abidal and Jérémy Toulalan, the FFF suspended every other member of the 2010 World Cup squad for one game. This blanket ban was unprecedented, but it was hardly a severe punishment. Indeed, most players were perfectly happy to miss an early-season friendly, especially when – a month later – they were recalled for Blanc's first competitive game.

By imposing such a light sentence, and offering such a quick reprieve, the FFF and Blanc missed an opportunity to stamp their authority on France's capricious players. 'Blanc was a symbol of the good, well-liked, well-behaved France teams from the past, so a lot of people thought he'd bring some order,' the journalist Daniel Riolo states. 'But suspending them for a meaningless friendly, then recalling them straight away was like saying: "You can keep on doing what you want." When a new manager takes charge he has to assert his authority. Otherwise he won't be respected.'

Yet Blanc did manage to trigger a significant improvement on the pitch. The aura he possessed in his playing days had been enhanced by a successful managerial stint with Bordeaux, where he won the league title in the 2008/09 season, and at first France's players, media and public all seemed happy with this alternative to Domenech.

After an early hiccup against Belarus, Blanc's side roared through Euro 2012 qualifying, embarking on a 21-match unbeaten run that included wins over Brazil, England and Germany. They travelled to the finals in confident mood, even if the new FFF president Noël Le Graët – who was appointed in 2011 and had begun imposing some much-needed rigour to the management of football in France – urged caution. Le Graët said reaching the quarter-finals would be a success, but only if the team behaved itself on and off the pitch. 'This must be a fresh start,' he stressed. 'I want them to win back the public. I want French people to be proud again. I'm confident these players can make that happen by creating a positive image of themselves.'

The stage was set for Nasri and Benzema, in particular. This was their time. Blanc was showing considerable faith in Nasri, who became France's youngest captain in over a century when he wore the armband in a qualifier against Luxembourg. He would be afforded the central playmaker role that he craved in the opening game in the group stages in Ukraine against England. Benzema, meanwhile, had just netted thirty-two goals for the newly crowned Spanish champions Real Madrid and was expected to make his mark on the international scene.

The competition started well for Nasri. The 24-year-old was France's best player against Roy Hodgson's team, cancelling out Joleon Lescott's opener with a superb low strike to seal a 1–1 draw. Unfortunately, though, there would be more talk about his goal celebration than his performance. Nasri felt he had been victimised by the French media, and in particular by *L'Équipe* newspaper, which had been critical of his performances in the lead-up to the tournament. After firing the ball past Joe Hart, he turned towards the media stand in Donetsk, put a finger over his mouth and screamed: 'Shut your mouth!'

Nasri explained that his angry reaction had been aimed at a specific *L'Équipe* journalist whose criticism of him had upset his sick mother. 'It doesn't unsettle me because I don't read the press,' he told journalists after collecting his Man of the Match award from UEFA. 'But my mother's unwell, and when she reads in her bed that her son is "useless", well it's awkward.' For the French public, the wounds of Knysna were still fresh. France's campaign was just a game old, and yet another public spat between a key player and the country's biggest selling newspaper had erupted.

L'Équipe, it should be said, wields considerable power in the French game. Many players claim that they pay no attention to the sports daily, but the marks out of ten that are allocated to every player after every game are often the subject of heated debate in the dressing room and can even prompt players to call up journalists for an explanation.

From that day on, Nasri's relationship with the media only deteriorated. 'He attacked the one institution you mustn't attack: the press,' said Blanc in a documentary produced by the television channel *La Chaîne L'Équipe* called: *Nasri, la Mauvaise Réputation* (*Nasri, the Bad Reputation*). 'If you speak your mind [to journalists], it might relieve you, you might enjoy it, but you'll have to pay the consequences.'

For the rest of the tournament, the papers were unforgiving. Nasri's celebration was seen as proof of the existence of a brat culture within the team. 'But what did he actually do?' Nasri's father asked in the same documentary. 'Did he kill someone, rob someone? He just told a journalist to be quiet, and the media jumped all over him. "He's no good, he's uneducated, he's badly raised." Badly raised?! My boy? It killed me when I heard that.'

Almost certainly affected by the furore, Nasri had a quiet game in the second fixture against Ukraine. But two of his peers stepped up: Benzema picked out Ménez to open the scoring, then notched a second assist for Yohan Cabaye to seal a 2–0 triumph.

Les Bleus had a chance to claim top spot by beating Sweden in Kiev, but they crumbled to a 2–0 loss and again made the headlines for the wrong reasons. Reports emerged of an angry altercation between Nasri and fellow midfielder Alou Diarra in the dressing room at half-time. Then, after the game, Blanc was stunned to see Ben Arfa looking down at his telephone as the manager addressed his players. 'Hatem, why don't you call your family while you're at it,' shouted a furious Blanc. Rather than apologising, or just keeping quiet, Ben Arfa used the moment to tell the manager he thought he had been substituted too early. 'There were guys even more rubbish than me,' he is reported to have said.

In 2010, the players did not respect Domenech at all, but Blanc was hardly having more luck. The problem, it seems, ran deep. In his book, Domenech admitted to feeling relieved by the ongoing breaches of discipline after he had been replaced. 'It did appease me,' he wrote. 'That tournament showed that French football was capable of running into problems without me. Just as I had before, Blanc was facing the sporting and behavioural limits of his squad.'

Indeed, with Nasri, Ménez and Ben Arfa by now confined to the bench, France were outplayed by world champions Spain in the quarter-finals, exiting 2–0 without so much as a whimper. Benzema failed to score for a fourth game running, but he did at least avoid controversy. Ménez, on the other hand, left his mark during a dreadful twenty-six-minute cameo. Not only did he make no positive contribution, the winger distinguished himself by shouting abuse at the referee, then swearing at his own captain Hugo Lloris after the goalkeeper reprimanded him for failing to track back. Another player, Yann M'Vila, added to the malaise by refusing to acknowledge either Blanc or Olivier Giroud when the manager sent the striker on in his place.

Giroud, who was playing in his first major tournament, had to make do with just a handful of minutes on the pitch in Ukraine. Looking back, the striker thinks France may have paid a price for picking too many individual talents. 'On paper, France had an unbelievable team,' Giroud begins. 'But football isn't about piling up talents. It's not about trying to get as many talented players onto the pitch as possible. The most important thing is collective strength. You need players who are ready to go that extra yard, attackers who are prepared to run back and tackle, players you can count on in the difficult moments. It's easier to do it when you are really together and united.'

A tournament that was supposed to be the launching pad for their international careers had turned into a disaster for *La Génération '87*. Yet the grand finale was still to come. In the mixed zone of the Donbass Arena in Donetsk – a tight, cordoned-off area next to the tunnel, where journalists can speak to the players – Nasri momentarily lost the plot.

For journalists, trying to obtain interviews in this area after matches is generally an unpleasant, unforgiving business. Dozens of tired reporters jostle for position, and when a player finally emerges, they fight for his attention, knowing full well that the chances he will stop to talk are slim. Especially when his team has just lost and suffered elimination from the Euros. When players continually shun the media, as was the case with much of the French team at Euro 2012, tensions run high and arguments often break out between reporters who are under pressure to secure reactions for their employers. It is unusual, however, that players get dragged into the mire.

On this occasion, the relationship between certain members of *Les Bleus* and the national press was at breaking point. So, when an *Agence France-Presse* journalist standing next to me asked Nasri for a few words, and the request was waved away, the reporter reacted badly. '*Casse-toi alors*,' he muttered under his breath but loudly enough for Nasri hear. Those words, loosely translated as 'Piss off then', prompted Nasri to turn around and walk purposefully back towards the journalist. 'What did you just say? You guys say I have no manners and yet you talk to me like that,' Nasri shouted menacingly, his face reddening as the anger boiled over. He then began to insult the reporter using a tirade of expletives and invited him outside for a fight.

It was a surreal moment. Seeing this baby-faced footballer, who stands at barely 5ft 9in tall, acting the hard man like a playground bully beggared belief. Much like Éric Cantona or Nicolas Anelka before him, Nasri had been driven to this state of self-destruction by being part of the French national team and the circus that surrounds it. Above all, though, it felt like a desperately sad way for a tournament that had promised so much for Nasri and for France to end.

Nasri had erred and he had done so at a time when the French public was fed up with overpaid, underperforming and unruly footballers. Again, the media reaction was disproportionate to the crime. L'Équipe reported that Nasri was facing a two-year ban for his behaviour, but this felt more like the newspaper's wish rather than the reality. Nasri eventually got a three-match suspension. Ménez was banned for one match. Ben Arfa and M'Vila escaped with slaps on the wrist.

The damage, however, had been done. Ménez would win just eight more caps; Ben Arfa, two. As for Nasri, he played six times under Blanc's successor Didier Deschamps before infuriating the coach with his attitude after being dropped to the bench for France's World Cup play-off second leg against Ukraine. Deschamps left him out of his 2014 World Cup squad, prompting Nasri to announce his international retirement at twenty-seven.

Tellingly, Nasri appeared to blame the whole world for the situation, apart from himself. 'The French national team doesn't make me happy,' he told The Guardian newspaper. 'Every time I go there, there's just more trouble. I face accusations about me, and my family suffers ... It's not just him [Deschamps]. It's everything. It is not him who talks in the press, it is the press who say things about me, and the players as well. Why do you want me to be in the squad with some players who can't even be true in front of me and tell me that they have a problem? I don't want to be there. I am not happy.'

In France, few people felt that Nasri had been wronged or treated unfairly. Indeed, FFF president Le Graët delivered a damning assessment of the former France player. 'A great player needs to be complete,' he told *La Chaîne L'Équipe*. 'He needs to like his teammates more, and like himself a bit less. He needs to be a bit more of a team player, and maybe more respectful too.' An international career that had promised so much on that sunny day in Châteauroux in 2004 ended with forty-one caps, five goals, and a distinctly bitter taste. France's Golden Generation was in fact made of lead, and it sank without trace.

CHAPTER 13

LES ENTRAÎNEURS

Throughout the past two decades a common theme has emerged. Whether it be Éric Cantona, David Ginola, Nicolas Anelka, Hatem Ben Arfa, Samir Nasri, Jérémy Ménez or Karim Benzema, French football has had great difficulty accommodating colourful characters. The message appears to be: if you are different, if you do not conform to the behaviour expected of a prototypal French footballer, you will not be picked. Regardless of how talented you are.

Cantona was always ahead of his time. In 1988, when he likened the France coach Henri Michel to 'a bag of shit', he was merely paving the way for his fellow rebels. Ginola's spat with Gérard Houllier – which started in 1993 when the manager accused the winger of costing *Les Bleus* their place at the World Cup – continues to this day.

In 2003, after falling out with Jacques Santini, Anelka told the press he would only consider returning if the France manager 'got down on his knees and apologised' to him. Raymond Domenech was on the receiving end of some far more scathing abuse from the former Chelsea man. And, of course, *La Génération '87* had huge difficulty expressing itself within the constraints of the deeply conservative French system.

These days there is a distinct difference in social backgrounds between players and coaches. While an increasing number of footballers are emerging from humble, immigrant communities, French coaching has maintained a status quo. In the professional game, coaches are predominantly white, middle-class, middle-aged men. There is no suggestion that they harbour any kind of racist attitudes. However, when it comes to understanding the mentality of a headstrong, self-assured kid from *les banlieues*, they may be less well equipped than the hundreds of black and Maghrebi coaches operating at amateur levels.

For France's ethnic minorities, the world of professional coaching remains largely out of reach. At the start of the 2019/20 season, OGC Nice's Patrick Vieira was the only non-white coach in Ligue 1. In recent times, two other former greats from the modern era have broken through in coaching. Yet, Thierry Henry was afforded just three months at AS Monaco, and Claude Makélélé got a meagre six months to try to turn around SC Bastia's fortunes. Their appointments appear to be exceptions rather than an indication of changing patterns.

Historically there have been only two black coaches who have withstood the test of time. The former FC Nantes and PSG defender from New Caledonia, Antoine Kombouaré, has enjoyed managerial spells at seven different Ligue 1 clubs. But it should be noted that Kombouaré was sacked by PSG in December 2011 despite his team sitting top of the table. His replacement, Carlo Ancelotti, failed to win the league that season.

Jean Tigana, one of France's greatest midfielders, had spells coaching Lyon, Monaco (where he won the title in 1997) and Bordeaux. Tigana was in the running for the France job in 2004. After losing out to Raymond Domenech, he accused the FFF of racism. 'I was overlooked because of the court case I was involved in with [then Fulham owner Mohamed] Al-Fayed, and also, from what I've been told, because of the colour of my skin,' he said. In an interview with *France Football* magazine, the ex-Fulham manager even claimed the principal objector to his appointment was FFF president Claude Simonet: 'He told a very important figure in French football, somebody I have known for thirty years: "There are too many black players in the France team now, we can't have a black coach as well."'

Whether subconscious or otherwise, there was – and probably still is – a feeling within the French football authorities that black footballers are fast and physical, but do not possess the tactical intelligence required to make key decisions on the pitch and to become managers later on. This shocking stereotype manifested itself in the 2011 'quota scandal' and reappeared in 2014 when the Bordeaux coach Willy Sagnol was explaining to the press why he did not want to pick too many African players. 'The advantage of the African player is he isn't expensive, generally he's ready to fight, and he's powerful on the pitch. But football isn't only about that,' stated Sagnol, who had previously coached France's under-21s. 'It's also about technique, intelligence and discipline.'

French football was blessed with scores of brilliant black and Maghrebi footballers in the 1990s and 2000s, yet precious few have gone on to coach in the professional game. Algerian trainer Kader Firoud was an exception, overseeing 782 top-flight games. But when Firoud left his final Ligue 1 role at Montpellier in 1982 there was a thirty-four-year gap until another manager of North African origin secured a head coaching position in France's elite league. Even then, the Franco-Algerian trainer Mohamed Bradja was only placed in temporary charge of relegation-bound Troyes along with two other coaches. Sabri Lamouchi, a former French international with Tunisian parents, briefly coached Rennes in 2017/18, and he has admitted that he is concerned about the lack of diversity. 'It is clear that we have much greater diversity on the pitch than we have in the dugouts,' Lamouchi stated in Nicolas Vilas's book *Enquête sur le Racisme dans le Football* (*Investigation into Racism in Football*). 'Football is influenced by the outside world, and we have a right to ask the question.'

World Cup-winning goalkeeper Bernard Lama, who grew

up in French Guiana, struggles to hide his frustration. 'Maybe club owners are scared of me,' the former Paris Saint-Germain star told *L'Équipe* newspaper. 'When you've played at the top level for twenty years, representing six or seven French clubs, when you've achieved what I achieved, and you don't even get an offer to work as a goalkeeping coach, nothing at all ... Well, it means what it means. France is still scared of offering positions of responsibility to black people.'

In this respect, French football could be described as a mirror for society. The French game's governing bodies are made up almost entirely of white people. Yet the same observation can be made at international level with UEFA and FIFA, both of whom claim that ridding football of racism is among their priorities. It is astounding that an individual like Lilian Thuram, who achieved so much in the game, is respected and renowned around the world and possesses such a deep understanding of discrimination, has not even been asked to contribute to football's fight against racism.

When I ask Thuram if he is surprised that neither FIFA nor UEFA have approached him to ask for help, he shrugs and insists he is happy working for his association, educating young people on the subject of discrimination. It feels like he is resigned to never receiving a call. Inevitably, though, Thuram has his own carefully considered theory for the absence of black faces in positions of responsibility: 'The answer isn't simple,' he begins. 'You must consider one of the most damaging effects of racism: when you are discriminated against, your self-esteem goes down. You end up thinking that there are certain places you don't belong. You don't see black people in certain spheres because they've been told this isn't for them. They are made to believe that even if they try to succeed, they won't make it. When you are told you can't do something, you have to be very, very courageous and sturdy to go against it. In life, people tend to go towards things they think are possible for them.'

The world of coaching in French football is almost a closed shop. But the issue goes beyond skin colour. There is a French ethos that people within the game seem determined to protect. When the FFF set up the National Football Institute at Clairefontaine in 1988, Gérard Houllier made French coaching methods central to the strategy. Heavy emphasis was placed on the schooling that all trainers went through to attain their badges. There was a cautious, conservative mould that aspiring coaches had to fit into. Over the past twenty years, Ligue 1's coaching positions have been mainly occupied by the same select band of trainers, making it extremely difficult for 'outsiders' to break in.

Ligue 1 is packed full of French Harry Redknapps and Sam Allardyces, old-school coaches who are seen as experienced and reliable and move from one club to another. The likes of René Girard, Élie Baup, Rolland Courbis, Alain Casanova, Christian Gourcuff, Guy Lacombe, Antoine Kombouaré, Frédéric Antonetti, Claude Puel, Christophe Galtier and Michel Der Zakarian have dominated the Ligue 1 scene in the twenty-first century.

For fifteen years, Joël Müller, another veteran of Ligue 1 dugouts having worked with FC Metz and RC Lens, held the important, strategic position of president of the French coaches' union. When he stepped down in 2016, he was replaced by none other than Raymond Domenech. The symbol of France's biggest failure, the man who categorically failed to earn the respect of his players, the epitome of the negative mindset that has plagued the domestic game for so long, Domenech is now effectively in charge of determining the direction taken by French coaching.

Domenech defends the national coaching philosophy as ferociously as his mentor Aimé Jacquet used to. He invariably expresses disapproval if a club dares introduce a new coach. In 2019, when Olympique Lyonnais replaced their solid

French manager Bruno Génésio with Sylvinho, a highly rated, if novice, Brazilian coach, Domenech was extremely vocal in his criticism. Every time Lyon lost, the ex-France boss took to social media to ridicule the appointment. Three months in, Sylvinho was sacked and the former Lille OSC and Olympique de Marseille boss Rudi Garcia – who is considered to be a far safer pair of hands – stepped in.

In France, coaches are expected to coach in a certain way: the way that has been preached through the years in those Clairefontaine classrooms by the likes of Houllier, Jacquet and Domenech. But with Ligue 1 continuing to suffer badly from the cautious, negative mindset imbued in so many of their coaches, it is clear that a shake-up is desperately required. Gone are the days when Europe's leading clubs would come to France to hire a progressive, innovative manager. At the time of writing, Zinédine Zidane is the only Frenchman coaching in one of Europe's big four leagues outside of France; and that is just one of the statistics which should set alarm bells ringing in those Clairefontaine corridors.

CHAPTER 14

KYLIAN, L'ENFANT TERRIBLE?

When you watch Kylian Mbappé today it is difficult to imagine that any coach in the world would envisage leaving him out of his team. However, as a boy Kylian was cast aside, and this occurred on more than one occasion. His strong personality did not sit easily with certain trainers.

Kylian was freakishly good as a boy. His ability always stood out. But his high levels of self-confidence, his single-mindedness, and his occasional reluctance to work hard in the interest of the team, created friction and conflict both at Monaco and within France's junior sides. Like Cantona, Anelka or Ben Arfa before him, Mbappé has the kind of non-conformist, strong-willed character that is frowned upon in French football circles.

In September 2011, a twelve-year-old Kylian moved out of his home for the first time, trading the dusty pitches and high-rise concrete towers of Bondy for the peace, quiet and lush green grass of Clairefontaine. The decision to send Kylian to the national academy eight years after his step-brother Jirès had attended was not straightforward. Clairefontaine's reputation had suffered along with the French national team's demise, and clubs were now offering excellent *préformation* courses themselves. Indeed, with Ligue 1 and Ligue 2 sides increasingly anxious to secure the best talent as early as possible, the FFF agreed to reduce Clairefontaine's *préformation* training scheme from three years to two in 2010.

RC Lens came agonisingly close to securing Kylian's signature before he went to Clairefontaine. Their head of youth recruitment, Marc Westerloppe, alerted Lens to Kylian's talent in June 2010, and they had more or less convinced Fayza and Wilfrid to send their boy to the northern club that had recently developed Raphaël Varane and Serge Aurier. However, Lens were relegated to Ligue 2 at the end of the 2010/11 season, and Kylian opted instead to attend Clairefontaine from 2011 until 2013.

For this ambitious, determined kid, it was the perfect time for a change of scenery. Kylian had grown bored of life at his Catholic school and was getting in more and more trouble. Living at Clairefontaine during the week, along with twenty-two other talented, likeminded boys in a football-obsessed environment, proved just the antidote.

At 8 a.m. every morning, the boys would take the bus to the *Collège Catherine de Vivonne* in nearby Rambouillet where they had lessons until 3 p.m. Upon returning, they would have a snack, attend a meeting with the coaching staff, then train for two hours between 4.30 p.m. and 6.30 p.m. The evenings were set aside for homework, although on Champions League nights first-year students were allowed to watch the first half of a game, while second-year students could watch until the end.

Kylian decorated his room with posters, mainly of Cristiano Ronaldo, and spent his spare time either watching football clips on his phone (kids were allowed their phones for forty-five minutes a day), kicking a ball about in the corridors or playing on his games console. His roommate in the first year, Armand Laurienté, spent many an hour playing FIFA with France's future sensation. 'He used to take Real Madrid and I'd be Barcelona,' Laurienté, an attacker who later joined Rennes, told *France Football* magazine. 'Kylian would choose to play as Ronaldo and he was very good.' Kylian's second-year roommate Khamis Digol confirms both his FIFA skills and his passion for CR7. 'He was a funny boy, a real joker. And he was always talking about his idol Ronaldo,' Digol said.

On the training ground, Kylian also tried to impersonate the Portuguese forward. But it was not always easy for him. Most of his classmates were more advanced physically, particularly during the first year, and Kylian did not necessarily stand out. 'He wasn't the best player,' said goalkeeper Allan Momège, who has since given up professional football. 'You could see he had something, but he hadn't yet made the step up physically.' Also speaking to *France Football* magazine, Loreintz Rosier, a midfielder who went on to join Vitoria Guimarães in Portugal and plays for the reserve side, claimed: 'Arnaud Nordin was the best player. He was faster and more robust than Kylian.'

Nordin is also making a name for himself in the professional game these days, but his progress has been more gradual and far less eye-catching. After breaking into the Saint-Étienne first team in 2016/17, aged eighteen, and even scoring a couple of Ligue 1 goals, he was used mainly as a substitute over the next two seasons. But at Clairefontaine, Nordin was the main man. He played as centre-forward, with Kylian confined to the wing. The two got on well, but Kylian did not enjoy playing second fiddle to anybody and his frustration often boiled over. Indeed, during that first year he earned the nickname Mbébé (M-baby) because of his small frame and his penchant for sulking when he did not get his own way.

Right-back Marvin Plantier used to enjoy winding the forward up. 'When Kylian was having trouble getting past me, he used to sulk and he'd curse to himself a bit,' recalled Plantier, who now works as a carpenter. 'That's where the Mbébé nickname came from.'

Kylian's bad moods never lasted long, though. 'He was a competitor, and when he lost any game or training exercise, he'd sulk or ask to have another go straight away,' Nordin said in Arnaud Hermant's book *Mbappé: Le Phénomène*. 'He didn't like losing. But he was still a joy to be around. He had this *joie de vivre* and he was always nice. He did take the piss a bit, but always in a fun way. He especially enjoyed making fun of you out on the pitch. He'd dribble past you then turn around and say: "Did you see how I did that?"'

Kylian's diminutive stature actually aided his football development. Pitting himself against bigger boys at Clairefontaine – and also in Bondy where he continued to play with older age-groups at weekends – forced him to find alternative ways to gain an advantage. 'He had to adapt his game because he could not compete with the others physically,' the head of the Clairefontaine academy at the time Jean-Claude Lafargue explained in Hermant's book. 'He made sure he stayed clear of the opposition defenders, and his first touch would always be accompanied by a movement to unsettle them.'

At the ages of twelve and thirteen, Kylian did not dominate opponents. But he was already obsessed with statistics and used to count the number of goals and assists he notched up in training. Lafargue describes his time at Clairefontaine as 'inconsistent' and remembers a boy who 'used to shirk defensive work'. But there was already a ruthlessness in front of goal that set him apart. 'He wouldn't see a lot of the ball, but when he did he always made it count,' stated Lafargue. 'He was explosive over ten or twenty metres. He was remarkably efficient and had this confidence that he'd succeed.'

At the start of his second year, Kylian had a growth spurt and everything became much easier. 'He just exploded in those last six months [at Clairefontaine],' Lafargue, the academy director, remarked. 'He really worked on his play with his back to goal, off the ball, and his runs in behind. He was intellectually sharp and had good tactical awareness. He was starting to realise how good he could be. He consistently showed variety in his play, and he understood the importance of using both feet. He just took off.'

Real Madrid would happily have taken him following his trial in December 2012, but Kylian's parents were not chasing short-term glory. They already had a meticulous career plan mapped out for their son and felt sure that he needed to stay in France to finish his education both as a footballer and as a man. France's biggest clubs started to circle, hoping to sign the fourteen-year-old for their academy when he graduated from Clairefontaine in 2013. Yet it was a modest provincial club, Stade Malherbe Caen, that very nearly hit the jackpot after convincing Wilfrid and Fayza to send Kylian to Normandy.

Caen's head of youth recruitment Laurent Glaize was alerted to Mbappé's extraordinary talent when the boy was twelve. 'I sent my assistant David Lasry to go and watch him,' Glaize told the newspaper *Sud-Ouest*. 'David doesn't usually get carried away, but this time when he called me he was crazy. He said: "Laurent, I've seen a future Ballon d'Or." I went to see him for myself. Technically, he could do everything. His dribbling was unbelievable, and what's more he did it all at incredible pace. He was barely twelve but had the intelligence of a fifteen- or sixteen-year-old. In all my career, I'd never seen anything like it.'

When Glaize contacted Kylian's father to inform him of Caen's interest, Wilfrid was initially surprised. He even mocked them a little. 'Caen? Really? You're trying to catch a whale with a fishing rod,' he reportedly said. The top clubs were queuing up, but Wilfrid listened to Caen's proposal, discussed the project with his wife, and they agreed to a meeting. 'They wanted us to lay out a precise career plan,' Glaize recalled. 'It had to include details of future contracts and the academic programme he'd follow at school. They were calm, thoughtful, and they took their time.'

Soon after Kylian had started Clairefontaine, he went to Caen with his parents for another meeting. At the time, the club was coached by the charismatic Franck Dumas, a former AS Monaco and Newcastle defender. 'Franck put on a real show,' Glaize described. 'He made it clear the club really wanted Kylian and insisted he'd be playing in the first team at sixteen. Everything was agreed contractually. The parents wanted to sign straight away, but the rules didn't allow a boy of his age to sign for a club situated more than 50km from home. We asked the FFF to make an exception, but they refused.'

Caen's chance to sign the country's most exciting youngster had gone. The club was relegated from Ligue 1 in 2012, and suddenly became a less attractive proposition. Caen continued to court the Mbappés, and it was even agreed that Kylian would sign for the team if they bounced straight back up. But they did not, and the door opened for Monaco.

• • •

The summer of 2013 was an exciting one for AS Monaco fans. Thanks to Claudio Ranieri's shrewd management the principality club had won promotion back to the top tier. With their Russian billionaire owner Dimitry Rybolovlev now loosening his purse strings, a number of big-name signings arrived: Radamel Falcao, James Rodríguez, João Moutinho, Jérémy Toulalan, Éric Abidal and Ricardo Carvalho were all paraded on the majestic port in front of a gaggle of stunning yachts. PSG, it seemed, had a domestic rival.

Yet arguably the biggest signing of all went under the radar. When a fourteen-year-old Paris-born youngster penned a three-year trainee contract in a non-descript office inside the

Stade Louis II, Monaco and Kylian Mbappé commenced a relationship that would reap huge rewards for both parties. Like
Caen, Monaco assured Kylian's parents that his schooling would
be taken seriously. The fact that schoolteachers were employed
by the club and lessons took place inside the multipurpose
Stade Louis II – which also includes dormitories for academy
kids – particularly impressed Fayza. They were assured that
Kylian would be fast-tracked into Monaco's under-17 side in his
first year.

Two other factors played in Monaco's favour. Firstly, the club
has a sensational track record in youth development, having
brought through the likes of Thierry Henry, Lilian Thuram,
David Trezeguet and Emmanuel Petit. Secondly, the location
is one of the most beautiful and tranquil in the world. Indeed,
in this stunning corner of Europe, wedged between Italy and
France, there is little to do other than admire the sea views and
concentrate on football. Especially if you are not old enough to
get into the casinos.

Wilfrid highlighted his devotion by taking a year off from his
coaching work in Bondy in order to live with Kylian in south-
east France, renting a small flat in Cap-d'Ail, a gorgeous village
situated between the principality and the club's training ground
at La Turbie. Fayza stayed in Bondy to look after Kylian's seven-
year-old brother Ethan, but the conditions for a determined
youngster desperate to make that final step up to the professional game seemed to be absolutely perfect.

Things did not go according to plan, however. In the first
year, the coach of Monaco's under-17s, Bruno Irles, did not
think Kylian was ready to play at such a high level. He told
the boy that his attitude needed to improve and he should
put more effort into tracking back. Irles refused to pick him,
sending him instead to play in the *Division d'Honneur* amateur
league. 'I wanted to show him what he was lacking,' Irles later

told *L'Équipe* magazine. 'I wanted him to understand what his strengths were, but also understand what he needed to develop in order to play at the top level. I didn't feel he was receptive to these remarks, even though they would have been constructive for him.'

Wilfrid attended every training session and was sometimes joined by his brother Pierre Mbappé. They both felt the ex-Monaco defender Irles was picking on Kylian and trying to assert his authority by unfairly making an example of the cock-sure youngster. 'This isn't Real Madrid here,' was one the barbs Irles allegedly used to direct at Kylian.

Wilfrid demanded an explanation from Irles. Exchanges became more and more heated, and on one occasion Pierre nearly came to blows with the Monaco youth coach. 'I've also been a youth coach and I've been a sporting director,' Pierre Mbappé stated in *L'Équipe* magazine. 'We do the same job. We can discuss things. When I see my nephew is unhappy, and my brother is unhappy, I intervene. I'd never intervene just to ask a coach why he's not picking my nephew. That's his choice. But when you are a youth coach you have a duty to accompany the boy. You have to explain things.'

Blessed with supreme assurance and surrounded by family members who knew the game and told him he was being un-fairly treated, Kylian lost respect for his coach. Irles stuck to his guns, but by taking on one of the club's most valued assets, he was fighting a losing battle. 'Kylian gets told all the time: "That's good, that's good,"' Irles remarked. 'But at some point, he needs to be told what isn't good, what he can improve on if he works at it. The relationship was a bit strained because of that.'

The conflict was taken to a higher level. Wilfrid and Pierre were afforded a hearing with Monaco's top brass, and Irles was subsequently instructed to stop sending Kylian to play in the amateur leagues. They could not, however, force the coach to pick him for the under-17s. With Monaco's blessing, Kylian trained alone for the final weeks of the season.

In the summer of 2014, Irles moved to one of Monaco's partner clubs, Arles-Avignon. It is not clear if this was a consequence of his frosty relationship with the Mbappé family, but with Irles no longer around, the second year went far better for Kylian. The club asked one of its reliable youth stalwarts, the local-born trainer Frédéric Barilaro, to take Kylian under his wing. Barilaro kept a close eye on his performances both with the under-17s and under-18s, before deciding to blood him with the under-19s in the UEFA Youth League. Despite being three years younger than most of his teammates, he looked totally at home.

Kylian commenced the third and final year of his trainee contract in Barilaro's under-19 team, but this kid was in a hurry and already had his sights set on Leonardo Jardim's first-team squad. He may have been only sixteen years and eight months old at the start of the 2015/16 campaign, but there was no doubt in his eager mind that he was good enough to train alongside Radamel Falcao, Bernardo Silva and Fabinho. Those urges became stronger when he netted ten goals in his first five matches with the under-19s. Kylian left observers open-mouthed in one of those games, away to Toulouse, when he gave Issa Diop a torrid afternoon. Diop was regarded as one of France's best young defensive prospects, yet he could not live with Monaco's electric sixteen-year-old.

Kylian waited for Jardim's call. But September came and went, as did October, and still nothing happened. The Mbappé family began scratching their heads once more. Again, Wilfrid spoke to influential figures at the club about his boy's frustrations. Finally, in November 2015, with a host of first-team regulars away on international duty, Kylian got the opportunity he had been craving: a chance to train with the senior squad.

Totally at ease in the adult world, he made a big impression.

'I remember Kylian's first training session with the pros very well,' Monaco's sporting director at the time Luís Campos told *L'Équipe* magazine. 'At the end of the session, Jardim called me over and said: "This boy must not go back to the reserves. He has to continue working with us. And when he has his chance, I think he'll do well."'

Jardim was right. On 2 December 2015, Kylian became Monaco's youngest ever player – beating Henry's long-standing record – when he was introduced in a Ligue 1 game against Caen aged sixteen and eleven months. He surpassed another of Henry's marks on 20 February 2016 when he established himself as the club's youngest ever goal scorer by netting against Troyes at the age of seventeen and two months. There was no explosion of joy from the forward when he swept in Helder Costa's cross with his left foot. It looked like he knew this was just the start – an impression confirmed by the man himself four years later. 'It was the first message that I sent,' Kylian told *France Football* magazine in January 2020. 'I knew it was just the start of the long story, the start of a great book.'

It quickly became obvious to even the casual observer that Monaco had a very special talent on their hands. But Kylian had still not signed a professional contract with them, and the problems he had previously encountered with Irles, coupled with Jardim's initial reluctance to promote him, had planted seeds of doubt. With the top clubs again circling, Monaco were in serious danger of losing their gem. Real Madrid made fresh enquiries, while Liverpool, Arsenal and Paris Saint-Germain joined the battle to secure his signature. Gunners boss Arsène Wenger even travelled down to his old stomping ground in Monaco for face-to-face talks with Kylian and his parents.

Ultimately, Campos found the right words to reassure the

teenager – or perhaps more importantly, to convince his mother. The former Real Madrid scout, who worked wonders during his three years in the principality, spent forty minutes talking to Fayza about the importance of Kylian starting out in the familiar, pressure-free surrounds of the French Riviera. 'I told her that the day he walks into a dressing room at a big club, he needs to hear the other players say: "Welcome, Kylian. We really like you,"' Campos explained. 'If he'd have left Monaco at that moment, he'd have gone into a big dressing room, full of big egos, as an unknown. They would have looked at him and said: "Who is this kid?"'

These words were echoed by Claude Makélélé, who briefly worked as Monaco's technical director between January and June 2016. The ex-France and Chelsea midfielder warned Mbappé that his playing time could well be limited if he joined PSG or one of the Premier League giants, and his words were heeded.

On 6 March 2016, Kylian signed his first professional deal. He could have earned more than the €20,000-a-week Monaco offered him by signing elsewhere. But for Kylian and his family, Monaco felt right. The reported €3 million signing-on fee probably helped as well. The money-making machine that is Kylian Mbappé was up and running.

•　•　•

Bruno Irles was not the only youth coach to take issue with Kylian's attitude during his childhood. The FFF-employed trainer Jean-Claude Giuntini also felt that the tyro from Bondy represented more trouble than he was worth. In the summer of 2015, Giuntini left the sixteen-year-old out of his squad for the under-17 European Championships in Bulgaria. PSG academy forward Odsonne Édouard – who would later join Celtic – led the France attack and finished as top scorer as Giuntini's side lifted the trophy.

From what he had seen, Giuntini felt Kylian was too inconsistent, too individualistic and reluctant to work hard for the team. The following year, after being placed in charge of the under-18s, the veteran trainer continued to ignore him.

Luckily for Kylian, he had a fan higher up the FFF tree. Ludovic Batelli was in charge of France's under-19s and had found himself short of a forward for the 2016 Under-19 Euros after another prodigious talent, Ousmane Dembélé, got fast-tracked to the under-21s. Batelli had kept Kylian in the back of his mind after having seen him play at Clairefontaine and decided to put some feelers out. 'I knew things weren't going well for him at Monaco,' Batelli tells me. 'When I asked around, I was told his behaviour and attitude weren't great. Apparently he could be a bit moody. I called Jean-Claude Giuntini, and he told me I could have him. He said he wouldn't be using him for the under-18s. I still had this image of a very fast kid, a boy who played with audacity and spontaneity. So I wanted to at least have a look. That's why I selected him for the elite round [qualifying] tournament in Serbia in March.'

Kylian was two years younger than many of his teammates but had no trouble fitting in. Indeed, the challenge of integrating with an older age group seemed to bring out the best in him. 'The Kylian I saw was nothing like the boy people had described to me,' the coach states emphatically. 'Socially, he fitted in well. He was polite, friendly, and he respected the rules. On the pitch, he carried out my instructions to the letter. He tracked back when we needed him to, and he scored the goal that qualified us in the final game against Serbia. At that moment, I had no doubt I was looking at a future star.'

Batelli did not hesitate in picking Kylian for the Under-19 Euros in Germany that summer. Starting on the left wing, he was simply sensational. The seventeen-year-old scored in the second game against Croatia, then added another two against the Netherlands. Batelli's charges fell behind in their semi-final against Portugal, but Kylian set up the leveller for Ludovic Blas before registering two more himself in the 3–1 triumph.

In the final against Italy in Sinsheim, Kylian had the chance to attract more personal glory by inspiring another victory and finishing as the tournament's top scorer. Going into the game, he was level with his teammate, PSG centre-forward Jean-Kévin Augustin, on five goals. Kylian failed to score in the 4–0 win. However, he was extremely effective, and the selfless nature of his performance was proof of a maturing attitude. 'Kylian showed real class in that final,' Batelli says. 'I know he wanted to finish top scorer, but he didn't make that an issue. He played superbly and was more than happy to set up his teammates. He shone for the team, not just for himself.'

Augustin ended up with six goals and the Golden Boot. But Mbappé had stolen the show. 'I still have vivid memories of the fourth goal,' Batelli interjects, laughing at the memory of Mbappé's audacity. 'We were in the dying seconds and Kylian did this amazing sombrero, flicking the ball over an Italian defender, and then helping to set up a goal for Issa Diop. It was so cheeky, so skilful. It was pure Kylian.'

Both his club and international careers were now up and running. In the spring of 2016, Kylian had won the Coupe Gambardella (the French Youth Cup) with Monaco, scoring two goals in the final against RC Lens, who must have been cursing their luck having come so close to signing him five years previously. Now, with a European title under his belt as well, he could start his senior career on a purely positive note. The past spats that he had endured with Irles and Giuntini could be confined to the past and forgotten. Or could they?

The fact is questions still get asked of Mbappé's attitude. His performances with Monaco, PSG and *Les Bleus* have been extraordinary, yet in France he gets accused of being selfish and too flashy. Rather than embracing this special talent, many in the media and within the French game seem intent on picking holes in it.

For Ilyes Ramdani, the editor-in-chief of Bondy Blog, the way Kylian is perceived reflects the conservative attitudes that have become embedded in the game in France. 'French football has never understood this guy,' argues an animated Ramdani, visibly annoyed by the negative comments. 'Don't forget, Kylian was ignored for three years by France's junior coaches. People say he's big-headed, but he isn't. He learned to be like that here [in Bondy]. You have to understand, Kylian grew up playing with older kids. He went to play away games in tough neighbourhoods, where he was threatened, insulted and intimidated. If he didn't have a strong character, he would've been eaten alive.'

This fearless mentality that is developed by so many of France's young footballers in their respective *quartiers* can be misinterpreted. 'It is not arrogance, it's personality,' stresses the journalist. 'The trouble is there is no room for personality in French football. If you have personality, French football is scared of you. Just look at Ben Arfa. He can't even find a club right now. He's a genius but he has too much personality.'

Luckily for Kylian, not every coach is afraid of characterful players. Batelli is one man prepared to show indulgence and perseverance with headstrong youngsters when the talent is clearly there. 'It's better to have characters who can win you a game than eleven players who do exactly what you ask of them but don't make the difference,' Batelli reasons. 'You need a balance. Sometimes coaches must accept that a player is different to the rest and won't always conform on the pitch.'

Didier Deschamps most definitely falls into the more traditional category of French coaches. The current France boss will always favour a reliable team player over a more talented, but less consistent rival. The continued selection of Moussa Sissoko, a robust, tactically disciplined right-winger, over mercurial talents like Ben Arfa and Nasri is testament to this mentality. Mbappé's style and his self-confidence were never going to sit easily with Deschamps. Yet the demanding ex-Monaco coach knew he could not ignore Mbappé's match-winning abilities. The way that the relationship between Deschamps and his young number ten evolved during the 2018 World Cup in Russia would prove to be one of the most fascinating – and important – sub-plots of France's fantastic story.

CHAPTER 15

LA RENAISSANCE

The appointment of Didier Deschamps in July 2012 proved to be a turning point in the French national team's modern history. It marked the start of a more serious, disciplined era and sparked an upsurge in results that culminated in the 2018 World Cup win.

Blessed with natural authority, a ferocious desire to win and – according to legend at least – a level of luck, or a golden touch, that has accompanied him throughout his career, France's 1998 World Cup-winning captain triggered the shift in mentality that *Les Bleus* so desperately needed. He transformed the team's image and helped the public to fall in love with its footballers once more. But most crucially, he got them winning again.

France's revival under Deschamps was far from straightforward. The coach was accused of racism and even received death threats, two of his senior players became entangled in a bribery case surrounding a sex-tape, and on one dreadful night a series of terrorist attacks were launched outside the Stade de France during an international match that had a profound effect on the players as well as the nation. The Deschamps era has been nothing if not eventful.

The truth is, France's rebirth very nearly did not happen at all. On 15 November 2013, *Les Bleus* were staring yet another inglorious failure in the face after losing the first leg of their

World Cup playoff 2–0 in Ukraine. The insipid, gutless performance was reminiscent of some of the worst capitulations under Raymond Domenech. The next day, as *L'Équipe* newspaper wondered if this France team was the worst ever, Deschamps's position was hanging by a thread.

Once again, the individual talent seemed to be there. But collectively the team was a rabble, and Mikhail Fomenko's well-drilled charges richly deserved their win.

At the time, Franck Ribéry was pushing Lionel Messi and Cristiano Ronaldo for the Ballon d'Or, yet the Bayern Munich winger disappeared without trace in Kiev's freezing Olympic Stadium. Samir Nasri, surprisingly preferred to one of Deschamps's favourites Mathieu Valbuena, was equally ineffective, and Olivier Giroud had one of those nights where every ball bounced off him. Giroud was not as bad as his Arsenal teammate Laurent Koscielny, though. Koscielny topped off a torrid night by clumsily conceding a penalty late on and then getting sent off for another reckless challenge.

The players returned to France with their tails between their legs. Back home there was no sense of outrage, but merely a sense of resignation as *Les Bleus* stumbled from one disaster to the next. This Ukraine side was solid. Unbeaten in twelve, they had kept eight clean sheets in a row. Furthermore, no European nation had ever overturned a 2–0 first-leg deficit to qualify for the World Cup, and Deschamps's bottlers hardly looked like potential record breakers. A poll in *Le Parisien* newspaper reflected the nation's downbeat mood, with 89.7 per cent of voters believing France's World Cup dream was already over.

Six years later, Guy Stéphan is bleary-eyed as he walks into the lounge of the chic La Maison Champs-Élysées Hotel in Paris. Deschamps's faithful assistant coach has had little sleep after driving to the capital from his home in Rennes, but he is in a good mood. Later today, Stéphan will go to the FFF headquarters to sign another contract extension that will keep both him and Deschamps in employment until 2022. Provided the contract is seen out, Deschamps will become the country's longest-serving coach, surpassing the much-loved Michel Hidalgo.

Sipping his coffee, Stéphan is proud and deeply satisfied as he takes stock of France's achievements. But the veteran trainer will not allow any complacency to creep in. Stéphan was Roger Lemerre's number two when *Les Bleus* won the European Championships in 2000 and then flunked so embarrassingly at the World Cup two years later. He knows just how easily the mighty can fall, and he knows that Deschamps's stint in charge might well have ended prematurely, in 2013. 'If we hadn't turned things around against Ukraine, we wouldn't be sitting here today,' he reflects. 'I wouldn't be here, Didier wouldn't here and nor would [FFF president] Noël Le Graët. That's football. It's about results and we simply had to qualify for that World Cup.'

Results are of course vital, but Deschamps and Stéphan had another clear objective when they took charge after a tumultuous Euro 2012. The image of the national team had been dragged through the mud for six years, and they desperately needed to restore pride in the blue shirt. 'The events of 2010, in particular, had left a deep mark,' Stéphan says. 'We have to be honest: when we arrived, the image was still not good.'

The players still seemed to be living on a different planet to the fans. They were unapproachable, aloof, and out of touch with reality. Most were millionaires, fighting for the Champions League year upon year with their big, glamorous European clubs, and it felt like playing for *Les Bleus* had become secondary to them. If the national side was to rise again, and if the people were to start liking this team again, attitudes had to change.

In that respect, Deschamps had the perfect profile. No French player has been more successful than the former midfielder in both club and international football, and nobody wore the blue shirt with as much passion and pride as the battler from Bay-onne. As Robert Pirès and Marcel Desailly told me, Deschamps was the leader and veritable motor of the France teams that they played in.

As a coach in club football, he carried that aura and determination into the dugout and achieved improbable results. Whether steering his AS Monaco side past Real Madrid and Chelsea to the 2004 Champions League final, or inspiring Marseille's first title triumph for eighteen years in 2010, Deschamps simply refused to accept defeat and was capable of transmitting his winning mentality to the players.

In his first press conference as France boss, he laid down the law in explicit fashion. 'The players will be expected to behave impeccably,' Deschamps declared. 'If any of them don't, they will not be picked. A national team coach must lay down ground rules. The clearer they are the better. In light of our recent history, of what happened in 2010 and in 2012, the players must be aware of the exemplarity that is required of them both on and off the pitch. Playing for France must be above anything else.'

Deschamps could count on a strong ally in Le Graët, who had been appointed FFF president in 2011. The former head of the *Ligue de Football Professionnel* is widely respected, and he brought some much-needed leadership to French football's governing body. Le Graët and Deschamps were obviously on the same wavelength.

In October 2012, when five members of France's under-21 side decided to have a night out together in Paris three days before a crucial match, Le Graët came down on them like a ton of bricks. Yann M'Vila, Antoine Griezmann, Wissam Ben Yedder and Chris Mavinga had all been involved in France's 1–0 home win over Norway in the first leg of the playoff for the 2013 European Under-21 Championships. Along with another squad member, M'Baye Niang, they then decided to let off some steam. After telling the coach Erick Mombaerts that they were going to visit a friend in Le Havre, where the team was based, the quintet hopped in a taxi and travelled 200km to a nightclub on the Champs-Élysées. Seventy-two hours later, *Les Espoirs* crashed to a terrible 5–3 loss in Norway.

When details of the jaunt emerged, the players were hung out to dry. M'Vila, who had already received a warning for his behaviour at Euro 2012, was banned from playing for all France teams for nineteen months until 30 June 2014, which meant that he could not feature at the World Cup. The other four were suspended for just over a year. 'The scale of the punishment was unbelievable,' the journalist Daniel Riolo remarks. 'The guys who embarrassed the country in front of the whole world in 2010 were given one match. These poor kids who had a night out were banned for years! It was totally out of proportion. But the federation felt they needed to make a statement.'

Deschamps did not aim to govern through fear alone. He wanted to create a happier and healthier environment around the team, notably by bringing the fans closer to their would-be heroes. As well as repairing a shattered image, the coach felt that regular contact with the supporters would help his players understand the immense privilege and responsibility that comes with representing your country.

A series of initiatives were introduced. At the start of every Clairefontaine gathering, an autograph session would take place with the fans. A group of twenty lucky school children would be invited to participate in 'a dream training session' alongside the France stars. The FFF also worked closely with the official France supporters' group, which has since taken off. 'Didier talked to the players about the importance of involving the fans, but he didn't have to impose anything,' Stéphan stresses. 'They were all happy to participate. A few started to put themselves forward to record little videos for the FFF website. Now they all go to salute the fans after matches. That's something which just happened naturally.'

The harmony that exists between France's players and fans today must have felt a long way off during the flight back from Kiev in 2013. The 2–0 loss in Ukraine had not been a major surprise. After all, Deschamps's first season in charge was extremely poor – the worst in terms of results for a new coach since the 1960s. There had been occasional signs of improvement: a 1–1 draw away to eventual group winners Spain, secured thanks to Giroud's late goal, and the 2–1 friendly triumph in Italy, suggested the team could compete with the best. But *Les Bleus* registered more defeats than victories, and the apathetic displays against Uruguay and Brazil during the tour to South America in the summer of 2013 showed motivation was still an issue.

France were even in danger of finishing third in their group and missing out on the playoffs when they started the 2013/14 season with a goalless draw against Georgia then found themselves 2–1 down in Belarus. Ironically, one of the men at the heart of the team's demise in South Africa emerged as France's saviour. As captain of the 2010 team that refused to get off the bus in Knysna, Patrice Évra was blamed and ridiculed by many people in France, notably by a host of influential media personalities. But Deschamps knew the feisty defender well from their time together at Monaco and the two had a good working relationship. Évra was captaining Manchester United on a regular basis at the time, and although Hugo Lloris continued to wear the armband for *Les Bleus*, the experienced left-back was very much Deschamps's leader in the dressing room.

Évra vented his fury at half-time in Belarus and demanded more fight, while reminding the players of their responsibilities. Ribéry, Nasri and Paul Pogba all scored in a vastly improved second period and *Les Bleus* won 4–2 to book a playoff position. Afterwards, all of the players spoke about how important Évra's talk had been. 'Pat's the boss in the dressing room,' stated Raphaël Varane. 'It's no coincidence he's captain of Manchester United.'

Until now, the national team's communication with the

outside world had been impeccably controlled. Only positive interviews and reports came out of the camp, and conflicts appearing in the media had become a thing of the past. Then, in October 2013, Évra decided to get a few things off his chest. Speaking to TF1's Sunday morning show *Téléfoot*, he began by confirming his status as a leader in the group. 'I feel like a soldier and a captain,' Évra said. 'You can't learn how to be a captain overnight. Sir Alex Ferguson appointed me for a reason.'

He then accused the French media of leading a witch-hunt and turning the public against him, singling out a series of high-profile individuals as 'tramps' and 'parasites'. 'What's his name? Michel Fernandel,' Évra started in reference to the former France and PSG midfielder Luis Fernandez. 'When he managed PSG, apart from sucking lollypops and dancing the *Macarena* on the touchline, what did he do?' Évra was only warming up. He launched a fierce attack on Bixente Lizarazu, the France legend who now works as a pundit for *Téléfoot*, threatened the journalist Pierre Ménès, and insulted the former manager Rolland Courbis, whom he called Rolland *Tournevis* (Screwdiver).

In the studio, Lizarazu responded with consternation. 'It's incomprehensible. Appalling,' the 1998 World Cup-winner said. 'He wanted us to show the entire interview, but the most vulgar passages have been cut out. It's ridiculous. We lost this guy in South Africa and now we've lost him again.'

This was hardly the publicity Deschamps needed before the Ukraine double-header, but the manager had little time to worry about such matters. He was far more concerned about matters on the pitch, and notably his problems in attack. When he took charge, Deschamps assured Karim Benzema he would spearhead France's attack. But the Real Madrid marksman was struggling to find the back of the net and had not scored in his first eleven appearances under the new coach. Factoring in the final games of Blanc's reign, Benzema had gone fifteen international appearances without scoring, for a total of 1,222 minutes on the pitch. The barren run finally ended when he notched the last goal in a 6–0 trouncing of Australia. But despite that strike, Deschamps had not felt that he could count on him for that ill-fated 2–0 first-leg loss in Ukraine, picking Giroud as his lone forward.

Who to play in attack was just one of the quandaries that Deschamps faced ahead of the second leg. But before contemplating the team selection for Tuesday's showdown at the Stade de France, he had to think up a way of injecting fresh belief into his depleted troops. And he had just three days in which to do it. The team returned to its base in Clairefontaine on the Saturday. Rather than waiting until the Sunday morning as usual, the coach addressed his players that evening. 'We've been slapped in the face but we're still standing,' Deschamps started, going on to deliver a rousing, ten-minute speech on the importance of showing a united front and fighting until the very last second.

'They were three very intense days,' Stéphan recalls. 'We had a number of team meetings. Didier and I had individual discussions with players as well. We showed them positive footage to remind them what they're capable of. We told them this is a moment they'll be telling their wife and children about in twenty years. We tried to make them feel responsible and you could see the penny was dropping. They had the opportunity to change the course of history and they were aware of that.'

The coaching staff were helped out by two other figures. Le Graët came to Clairefontaine on the Sunday and spoke passionately about the responsibility the players were taking on when they were wearing the blue shirt. Then, to relax, the team was treated to the screening of a film featuring the actor Jamel Debbouze. The choice of film was significant – and not just because Debbouze is popular among footballers. *La Marche* (*The Marchers*) tells the story of the 'March for Equality and Against Racism', a powerful anti-racism movement that took place in France in 1983. 'It's about a small group of people who start out in the countryside, and by the end there are tens of thousands of them marching through Paris,' Stéphan explains. 'It's shows what can be achieved through solidarity.'

Watching this collection of multi-ethnic French people pull together to achieve something against all of the odds, the players surely understood the symbolism. 'At times like these, the days can be long,' Stéphan says. 'You can't train or do video analysis all the time. The tension was mounting, which was a good sign. The players were focused. But you need to find a way to alleviate the stress as well. Enjoying a movie all together helped us to do that. The players seemed to enjoy it. It was a nice moment.'

Mamadou Sakho was put up for press conference duty on Sunday evening; a first indication that the Liverpool defender may have an important role to play. Rather than spouting the usual pre-match banalities, Sakho came out fighting. 'We have to give everything we've got to turn this around,' he said. 'Whoever plays on Tuesday, they need to go out there with a knife between their teeth. There's no other solution.'

Preparations continued on Monday with the team transferred to another hotel in Enghien-les-Bains, just north of the Stade de France. Deschamps informed his players of the starting eleven before the final training session at the stadium, and it raised more than a few eyebrows. He made five changes from the first leg, including a series of bold choices. A twenty-year-old Varane replaced the suspended Koscielny. But rather than opting for the experience of Éric Abidal alongside him, Deschamps went for the 23-year-old Sakho. In midfield, Yohan Cabaye was handed a pivotal, central role. Valbuena replaced Nasri, and against all expectations, the out-of-sorts Benzema returned to lead the attack. 'Didier certainly made some big calls,' Stéphan remarks.

For the most part, the players accepted those choices. Nasri, however, struggled to hide his disappointment, the Manchester City man making it clear he did not agree with the coach's decision to drop him. Deschamps was furious that a player could put his own personal situation ahead of the team's at such a critical moment, and he never forgave the midfielder. Some believe Deschamps is too prone to holding grudges. Others think he is just ruthless. Either way, Nasri did not play for France again.

The first indication that the tide might be turning came when the players stepped out of their hotel for the traditional morning walk on Tuesday. A cluster of around fifty fans had gathered in front of the entrance, and the cheering was raucous. It may not seem significant, but this reception reassured *Les Bleus* that the public was behind them.

They could not, however, have imagined the scenes that awaited them that evening. Deschamps's charges were greeted by a stunning sea of blue, white and red when they stepped onto the pitch at the Stade de France. Every supporter seemed to be equipped with a *Tricolore* flag and the noise was deafening. If the players were psyched up and ready for battle, so were the fans. 'The atmosphere was unbelievable,' Olivier Giroud tells me. 'We sensed instantly that the crowd was behind us. We were all focused on the same objective, the same dream. It was the first time I had truly felt that with France.'

As a rule, the Stade de France is not popular with the players. It is a cold stadium. The athletics track leaves the supporters a long way from the action. The 80,000-seat concrete bowl in the northern suburb of Saint-Denis lacks charm. It witnessed France's greatest moment when *Les Bleus* won the World Cup in 1998, but the team has experienced many more frustrating nights in the stadium than joyous ones.

Furthermore, the games attract a large number of what the French call *Footix*. This was the name of the mascot for the 1998 World Cup, an annoyingly cheery blue cockerel with a large red comb on its head. After that tournament, as football in France suddenly became popular and fashionable to the wider public, the new fans were dubbed *Footix*.

A *Footix* is even worse than a fair-weather or armchair fan. They are spectators who literally have no idea about football, but like everything else that comes with it, from the banter at work, to the light show before the game and the Mexican Wave during it. France, and Paris in particular, has a lot of *Footix*. During my early days in the country as an expat, I remember sitting in bewilderment as large sections of the Stade de France crowd started booing Thierry Henry and David Trezeguet after they missed a couple of chances in a game against Switzerland. For me, these were iconic players, World Cup-winning legends who were surely untouchable. Apparently not to the *Footix*.

Whether or not the *Footix* were present for that second leg against Ukraine, there was no booing. From the first minute, Deschamps's men displayed ferocious determination. Resembling caged tigers that had suddenly been released, they bit into challenges and attacked with vigour. From his position in front of the defence, Cabaye directed the tempo with the poise and class of the Italian master Andrea Pirlo. Whether playing short passes in to Pogba or Blaise Matuidi, or hitting long, penetrating balls for Benzema or Ribéry to run onto, the Newcastle midfielder got everything right and fully justified Deschamps's choice to place him at the heart of his revamped 4–3–3 formation.

Valbuena, another recalled player, buzzed about with menace and wreaked havoc with his set pieces. The Marseille playmaker was denied by a brilliant Andriy Pyatov save, then set up Pogba who headed over. As *Les Bleus* attacked in waves, a frenzied crowd roared its approval and the inevitable happened on twenty-two minutes. Valbuena's free-kick from the right was only half-cleared, Ribéry shot goalwards, and after Pyatov parried the strike, Sakho was on hand to score his first international goal from close range. The ex-PSG defender looked like a man possessed as he streamed wildly back up the pitch to celebrate with Deschamps and the substitutes.

Only a fraction of the job had been done – France needed to win by three clear goals – yet already there was a sense of euphoria and supreme confidence emanating from the players.

Benzema had a goal incorrectly disallowed for offside, yet nobody seemed too worried; a warped form of justice was done when he found the net again moments later. This time, France's striker was in an offside position when Valbuena chested the ball down to him, but the goal stood and *Les Bleus* led 2–0 after thirty-four minutes. Again, the celebrations were telling. Benzema, one of France's least expressive players, for once let himself go, tearing up the touchline and leaping into the arms of his rival Giroud before getting mobbed by the other substitutes.

It felt inevitable that the third goal would come in the second half, but the identity of France's hero was more unexpected. Before this game Sakho had managed just nine goals in nearly 300 games during his professional career. But the man who had broken the deadlock duly registered his first-ever double by turning in Ribéry's cross on seventy-two minutes. 'Mamadou was the man of the match,' recalls Stéphan. 'I still can't believe what he did. He was a defender and he hardly ever scored. It made me think of Lilian Thuram's two goals against Croatia in the 1998 World Cup semi-final. It's just one of those things you can't explain.'

For Sakho, the son of Senegalese parents who grew up in the immigrant neighbourhood of La Goutte-d'Or in northern Paris, it was a huge moment. Judging by his post-match comments, the muscular defensive unit had clearly heeded Deschamps's message. 'It was the biggest game of my life and the biggest day of my career so far,' Sakho told *The Guardian*. 'When you play for a club you know you're representing the supporters but when you are playing for an entire nation, the entire population, it is as big as it can get really.'

In case there was any doubt as to the significance of this rousing come-from-behind triumph, the wild scenes at the final whistle hammered the point home. Delirious players cavorted in front of the fans with *Tricolore* flags draped over their shoulders. Deschamps was ushered into the middle so that his players could give him the bumps.

Giroud then grabbed a microphone and started to sing *La Marseillaise*. Within seconds, several teammates and a few thousand fans joined in, and a hearty rendition of the national anthem was proudly bellowed out. 'It was one of the most beautiful moments I've had in a France shirt,' Giroud enthuses. 'Not many people believed in us before the game. But everybody in the stadium did, and their support gave us strength. The communion with the fans was unforgettable. It was a turning point for us, and a turning point for the fans too.'

Much like on 12 July 1998, *Les Bleus* had beaten a team in yellow shirts by scoring three goals and sent the country into a state of rapture. The Stade de France had not witnessed such euphoric scenes since that day in 1998. They may not have beaten Brazil this time, but they had qualified for a World Cup *in* Brazil. 'It was a special feeling,' Stéphan says of France's first major triumph of the Deschamps era. 'Playing a World Cup in Brazil is special. It's not the same as a World Cup in Russia. Everybody wanted to be there. Once the final whistle blew there was this huge outpouring of emotion. I did feel relieved, but I also felt that this was just the start of something special.'

A new team was born that day. Deschamps would show great faith in the players that had got him out of jail against Ukraine – ten of the starting eleven were picked for the first game of the World Cup against Honduras – and a new generation emerged. Varane and Pogba, both of whom made their France debuts in 2013, were about to become mainstays for the team. As was Antoine Griezmann, who slotted in seamlessly after Ribéry missed out on Brazil 2014 through injury. These were not only wonderful young footballers, they also carried a clean, positive image (Griezmann's involvement in the under-21 discrepancy had long been forgotten). This was a team the French people could get behind.

Indeed, the build-up to the tournament in Brazil had been so positive it felt strange. For the first time in a long time, there were no stories of infighting, no problems with authority, and no off-field scandals. *Les Bleus* looked like a happy bunch. 'There was more cohesion in the group and there were fewer problems,' Giroud explains. 'It's easier to work well when there are no off-field problems and the press aren't stirring things up. We had a good, young team. You could feel a certain freshness.'

They started in highly promising fashion too, scoring eight goals in their opening victories over Honduras and Switzerland. Benzema netted three of them and the 26-year-old looked ready, at last, to make his mark.

On the face of it everything appeared hunky dory. *Les Bleus* were creating positive vibes once again and the French press was full of praise for Deschamps and his players. Not everybody was buying into the fairytale, though. *L'Équipe*'s chief football writer Vincent Duluc insists that the transformation in France's image was a consequence of Deschamps's skills in PR rather than a true reflection of the reality. 'Deschamps wants to control everything,' Duluc claims. 'He has people he trusts in every media group and that's how he controls his image.'

Deschamps has been widely praised for picking *Les Bleus* up from the depths of despair in 2012 and taking them back to the summit. But Duluc insists Laurent Blanc deserves at least some of the credit. 'France's revival started with Blanc,' states the highly respected journalist. 'He had to build his team on ruins. Deschamps came in and he was able to build on what Blanc had put in place. Blanc didn't get the praise he deserves because he doesn't have the same influence as Deschamps in the media.'

Duluc cites a concrete example from the 2014 World Cup to illustrate Deschamps's power when it comes to communications. When the players' wives arrived in Rio de Janeiro one morning after a ten-hour flight, many of them accompanied by kids, their hotel rooms were not ready. They were not impressed with the four-star establishment booked by the FFF and began to kick up a fuss. 'They started phoning the players, some of them even called Deschamps,' Duluc explains. 'Suddenly everybody's phones are going off and there's a big hoo-ha. A crisis meeting is called, the FFF decide to change everything and they are moved to a more luxurious hotel. This made three lines in the paper the next day. Two years earlier, we'd have been talking about the return of the spoilt-brat culture. With Blanc, people were looking for problems. With Deschamps, they were telling a different story.'

On the pitch, the results were identical: just as Blanc's charges were knocked out of Euro 2012 by the eventual tournament winners in the quarter-finals, Deschamps's team would suffer the same fate in Brazil. Indeed, after an electric start, France's 2014 World Cup campaign petered out somewhat. A goalless draw with Ecuador was followed by an unconvincing 2–0 victory over Nigeria in the last sixteen courtesy of two late goals. Deschamps's men never looked capable of eliminating Germany in the quarter-finals. Mats Hummels took advantage of Varane's inexperience and beat the Real Madrid defender in the air to head past Lloris, and Joachim Löw's side saw the contest out.

Again, Benzema failed to score in the knockout stage. The striker had one difficult chance late on, but his shot from a tight angle was swatted away by Manuel Neuer. As had occurred against Spain two years previously, France came up well short against the very best. 'We did have some regrets because we lost to an innocuous free-kick, and it looked like Hummels gave Varane a little push,' Stéphan explains, miming the shove half-heartedly with his arms, as if he knows the argument is weak. 'Germany were strong. They scored seven goals against Brazil in the semis and then beat Argentina in the final. So we can't be too upset. We showed some good things and we learned from the experience.'

Above all, the team got through a tournament with their image and reputation intact. Perhaps even enhanced. 'The reality is that France has reconciled with its public,' enthused a satisfied FFF president Noël Le Graët. 'We're up to tenth in the FIFA rankings, and what's more I can feel affection for this team. That's the best news of all. Because when the players feel appreciated and liked, they play better.'

France's slate had almost been wiped clean. But to remind everybody just how fragile this state of calmness was, a story emerged after the tournament of a spat between Benzema's agent Karim Djaziri and three *L'Équipe* journalists. Djaziri was said to have been involved in a series of altercations with the reporters, one of whom he reportedly punched, insulted and threatened. The newspaper claimed it was ready to press charges. Just as *Les Bleus* had navigated a series of storms and was starting to sail on course, this story served as a timely warning: there were more choppy waters ahead.

CHAPTER 16

L'AFFAIRE DE LA SEX-TAPE

Atlético Madrid are 2–0 up and the vociferous Vicente Calderón crowd is baying for blood. It is May 2017 and defending European champions Real Madrid are up against it when Karim Benzema races onto a long throw-in from Cristiano Ronaldo close to the corner flag. The Frenchman is instantly closed down by Stefan Savić, and Atlético's two defensive units Diego Godín and José Giménez arrive just behind.

What followed was pure footballing genius. Benzema holds off Savić with his strength, twists, turns past the defender on the outside and darts towards the byline. Just as he is running out of space, the number ten opens up his body to invite all three opponents towards him. Then, with the drop of a shoulder and three delicate brushes of the ball – two with his right foot and one with his left – he flicks it inside, almost along the byline, and veers off the pitch to evade Savić's desperate lunge. Godín and Giménez, widely regarded as the best central defensive pairing in world football, are bamboozled by this space-defying dance.

Godín half-heartedly lifts his arm in some misguided hope that the ball had gone out of play, but it is too late. Benzema is away. He surges into the box, cuts a pass back to Toni Kroos, and after Jan Oblak saves his shot, Isco scores on the follow-up.

Thanks to the skills of their dazzling yet criminally underrated forward, Real Madrid have taken the wind out of their bitter rival's sails. They have wrested back control of this epic semi-final and are heading to yet another Champions League showpiece. 'I was pitchside and I didn't understand what he had done at first because it happened so quickly,' Real Madrid coach Zinédine Zidane says in the documentary *Le K Benzema.* 'Then I watched the footage back and I understood a bit better. It's an example of what Karim's capable of, besides scoring goals.'

Real Madrid president Florentino Pérez has treated Benzema like a son ever since he lured him over from Lyon for €35 million in 2009. Pérez said it was 'love at first sight' when he saw the forward play. 'I felt he was a mixture of the Brazilian Ronaldo and Zidane,' he enthused in the same documentary. 'Karim plays behind the forwards like Zidane and he scores goals like Ronaldo.' Cristiano Ronaldo is equally effusive. 'It's easy for me to play with Karim,' the Portuguese wizard said in *Le K Benzema.* 'I know his movements, when he plays first time, second time. I know what he's thinking because we played many years together. If you look at the statistics, we both scored many goals and got many assists.'

That Ronaldo revelled in playing alongside Benzema comes as no surprise. The two joined Real Madrid at the same time and became close friends. During their nine seasons together, Benzema was happy to shun the limelight and focus on serving his stats-obsessed mate. It is somewhat telling that his most-lauded moment in a Real Madrid shirt was neither a goal nor an assist, but this phenomenally skilful contribution against Atlético when his team needed it most.

Benzema's precise link-up play, intelligent runs off the ball, and selfless attitude played a major part in Ronaldo's success at Madrid. Indeed, if the former Manchester United man won four Ballon d'Or awards during his time at the Bernabéu, becoming the club's all-time record scorer, Benzema deserves a good deal of recognition.

No Frenchman in the history of the game has a more impressive list of club honours than the strong, technical striker from the Lyon suburb of Bron. He had already claimed four Ligue 1 titles and a Coupe de France when he left his hometown for Madrid, aged twenty-one. In his first ten years at the Bernabéu, Benzema surged beyond the 200-goal mark, claimed two more league titles and two Copa del Rey crowns, as well as four Champions League trophies, three European Super Cups and four Club World Cups. Yes, he struggled initially and suffered from the occasional goal drought. But by and large Benzema has been Real Madrid's first-choice striker for more than a decade and he is hugely respected within the club. His recognition has even increased, along with his strike rate, since Ronaldo left for Juventus; a move which allowed this self-effacing attacker to emerge from the shadows.

Yet for all Benzema's success in Spain, the French public has found it difficult to warm to him. As a boy he was quiet, but possessed the kind of steely self-assurance that typified the new generation of French footballers. Upon breaking into the Lyon first team aged seventeen, he had to sing an initiation song in front of the club's array of seasoned stars. As the likes of Juninho Pernambucano, Michael Essien, Sylvain Wiltord and Florent Malouda sniggered at Benzema's shyness, the teenager surprised everybody by issuing a stern warning shot: 'Laugh all you like, guys, I'm here to take your place.'

With people he doesn't know, Benzema is painfully shy. I remember interviewing him at Lyon's training ground in the spring of 2008, just days after he had scored a stunning goal against Manchester United in the Champions League. Totally at ease tormenting Rio Ferdinand and Patrice Évra on the pitch, he was a bundle of nerves in the press room and spent most of the discussion looking down, fiddling with his phone.

Much like Anelka, Benzema expresses little emotion and is often accused of being moody. The comparisons between the two don't end there either. Benzema is also a Muslim who grew up in a tough suburb, likes rap music and driving fast cars. Moreover, he appears to enjoy flaunting his wealth on social media. As Anelka discovered, some parts of French society have a problem with youngsters who have immigrant backgrounds showing off their success. Benzema has also been accused of damaging the image of the French national team. He has made mistakes. But in France it feels impossible to hold a balanced debate on Benzema's virtues as a person and a footballer without a racial undercurrent surging to the surface.

When *Les Bleus* flopped at Euro 2008, and details emerged of a clash between generations, Benzema was unfairly accused of being among the disruptive influences. In some respects, he has been a victim of *Les Bleus'* troubles. At a time when French people were struggling to identify with the national team, Benzema's laid-back, almost detached demeanour, and his refusal to sing *La Marseillaise* before matches, had many doubting his patriotism. The famous radio interview he had given, aged just eighteen, in which he spoke of his attachment to Algeria continually came back to haunt him.

Furthermore, Benzema's performances for his country were rarely as good as those with his club. He is far and away the highest-scoring Frenchman in the history of the Champions League having recorded sixty-four goals and counting – towering over second-placed Thierry Henry who scored fifty – yet Benzema has netted just half as many as the Arsenal legend in international football. In terms of ability alone, this is a player who should have written his name into France folklore.

But more than his lack of goals (Benzema has scored twenty-seven times in eighty-one France appearances) it is his attitude that has grated most. 'It felt like he enjoyed himself when he was with Real Madrid, but when he came back to play for France he didn't look happy and he wasn't good,' observes the journalist Daniel Riolo. 'Deschamps asked him to be the boss. He said: "At

Real, you're the man, so you need to step up now with France."
But he couldn't do that. And as people were looking for scape-
goats, blaming immigration and *les banlieues*, Benzema found
himself in the firing line.'

After an unhappy Euro 2008, Domenech left him out of the
2010 World Cup, and the striker struggled – along with many
others – at Euro 2012. Three goals in the group stage of the 2014
World Cup suggested his time was about to come, but he had
quiet games against both Nigeria and Germany, and overall the
press issued a harsh assessment of his performances in Brazil.
Indeed, Benzema's agent was so upset with his treatment from
L'Équipe he ended up confronting the journalists.

But those squabbles paled into insignificance following the
events of late 2015.

On the morning of 5 November, Karim Benzema found
himself in a holding cell in Versailles, having spent the night
in police custody. He had been asked to come in for questioning the previous day and was charged with 'complicity in an
attempted blackmail and participation in a criminal association
with a view to preparing an offence punishable by at least five
years' imprisonment'. The accusations related to the bribery of
Benzema's France teammate Mathieu Valbuena over a sex-tape.
Benzema was twenty-seven and just entering his playing prime.
He had just been named on a shortlist for the Ballon d'Or.

The case would damage his reputation beyond repair. It was
the start of a soap opera that hung menacingly over the French
national team for several years.

In 2014, two individuals named Mustapha Zouaoui – known
by his friends as Sata – and Axel Angot allegedly acquired a
video of a sexual nature featuring Valbuena and his long-term
partner. Sata and Angot were well known in football circles,
particularly at Olympique de Marseille. Regarded as two of
the best 'fixers' in the business, they prided themselves on providing footballers with everything they might need away from

the pitch: from clothes to houses, cars, telephones, multimedia appliances or luxury holidays; Sata and Angot could arrange anything for the right price.

They had an impressive client list that – according to a report in *Le Monde* – included a series of Marseille players from Bafétimbi Gomis to André Ayew, Jacques Faty, Samir Nasri, Djibril Cissé and Brice Dja Djédjé. Valbuena, who became a close acquaintance of the pair of fixers, was not the first footballer to be duped. Seven years previously, Cissé found himself on the receiving end of a similar blackmailing scam. Rather than risk the video being broadcast publicly, the ex-France and Liverpool striker agreed to pay up.

When questioned on his relationship with Valbuena, *Le Monde* reported that Angot told police: 'I buy things, I travel for him, I look after his computer. I found a buyer for his house in Aix [when he left Marseille for Dynamo Moscow in 2014]. I went out to his place in Moscow. My job included bringing him clothes.' It was during a meeting in Paris, in September 2014 – when Angot was asked to help Valbuena transfer his contacts from one of his telephones to another – that the police claim he obtained the video. According to his colleague Sata, it is not unusual to find explicit video content on footballers' phones.

In an in-depth investigation published by *Le Monde* in December 2015, it was alleged that Sata and Angot tried to find a middleman who knew Valbuena and could apply pressure on him to pay the ransom of more than €100,000 in order to assure the destruction of the sex-tape. Cissé was their first port of call in May 2015, but Valbuena's former Marseille teammate refused to help. Another fixer, Younes Houass, was reportedly mandated. On 3 June 2015, Valbuena was at Clairefontaine when Houass contacted him to discuss a deal. The newspaper explained how the France playmaker, who was preparing for a friendly against Belgium, kept Houass on the line long enough to find the security officer employed by *Les Bleus*. He put the phone on loudspeaker so the policeman could hear. Five days later, Valbuena pressed charges.

The police investigated Houass, but the problem did not go away. Valbuena started to receive anonymous, threatening text messages as his blackmailers upped the ante. It must have been incredibly difficult for him to focus on football. Yet remarkably, for a short period at least, Valbuena continued to thrive under Deschamps. The pair knew each other well from their time at Marseille, when Valbuena played a significant part in the club's 2010 title triumph, and Deschamps admired the midfielder's wholehearted attitude. Valbuena won forty of his fifty-two caps under Deschamps. When he scored the only goal of the contest against Portugal in a friendly in September 2015, he looked a sure-fire bet to feature at Euro 2016.

Four days after Valbuena's excellent display in Lisbon, Angot called Sata. On the police tapes, he is heard urging his friend to 'accelerate this thing' because Valbuena had now become 'the boss' of the France team. Sata prepared to take a more direct route to Valbuena. According to *Le Monde*, he contemplated using either Nasri or Benzema as a messenger. 'Nasri was an old acquaintance of Sata's, and he despised Valbuena,' the newspaper reported. 'If we are to believe the phone recordings, which were confirmed by the witnesses questioned, Nasri proposed his services as an intermediary. But Sata preferred the Benzema option as the forward was admired by Valbuena.'

Sata entered into contact with an individual named Karim Zenati, one of Benzema's friends who had been released from prison after serving time for armed robbery. Zenati and Benzema grew up together in Terraillon, a sensitive neighbourhood in Bron that suffered from high rates of delinquency. They would spend several hours together every day, playing football and hanging out, establishing a tight bond. 'He's my childhood friend,' Benzema said in an interview with TF1 in December 2015. 'He went to prison, but he came out two years ago. He's been reintegrated. He's done everything possible to be good because he is a good person. He got a second chance and he took it. He's like a brother to me.'

In many respects, Benzema paid a price for loyalty. Footballers are often accused of forgetting their roots when they become rich, but the Real Madrid star has remained faithful to many of his old mates. Benzema reportedly employed Zenati to look after some of his affairs, including the charity Partage 9 which supports underprivileged children growing up in troubled neighbourhoods. But it was during a lunch meeting involving Zenati and Sata that Benzema was allegedly informed about the existence of the sex-tape and asked to speak to Valbuena about it.

'Loyalty is a positive trait, but how far do you go?' muses *L'Équipe* journalist Vincent Duluc. 'Do you do stupid things for your mates, or do you settle for just helping them out when you can? There are lines you shouldn't cross and he let himself down. Benzema showed it is easy to leave *les banlieues*, but *les banlieues* never leave you.'

On 6 October 2015, France were training at Clairefontaine ahead of games against Armenia and Denmark when, according to *Le Parisien*, Benzema spoke to Valbuena about the sex-tape. Later that evening, Benzema called Zenati. 'He's not going to give anything, is he?' Zenati is heard saying. 'Yeah, yeah, he's not taking us seriously,' Benzema replied. 'I said to him: "I'm going to sort it out for you. You got to go see the guy. He'll come. He'll talk to you. I give you my word there isn't another copy [of the sex-tape]."'

Later in the twenty-minute conversation, Benzema says to Zenati: 'I tell him, "If you want the video to be destroyed, my friend comes up to see you in Lyon, you sort it out face to face with him."'

That taped conversation implicated Benzema in the affair. He was forbidden from entering into contact with Valbuena or any of the suspects involved in the blackmail. Benzema's lawyer Sylvain Cormier was furious that the media had apparently been forewarned about his client getting called in to the police station. The television cameras were waiting for the star when he arrived, hiding his face inside a big white hoodie, and Cormier complained the image of an innocent man had been unfairly and unnecessarily tarnished.

Over the course of the next weeks, the media had a field day. Just seven months before the nation was due to host the European Championship, two of *Les Bleus'* main players – and two good friends until this point – were involved in a mindboggling affair that had the potential to sell a lot of newspapers.

The radio station Europe 1 controversially broadcast recordings of certain key phone calls, then *L'Équipe* published the entire contents of the telephone conversation between Benzema and Zenati. With the country now captivated, sources informed *Agence France-Presse* that Benzema was changing his initial position to admit operating as an intermediary. Valbuena responded by offering his version of events to *Le Monde* newspaper, which later published comments that Benzema had made to the police. 'I think it's a big misunderstanding,' *Le Monde* revealed Benzema said during questioning. 'At the start, I wanted to let him [Valbuena] know about what was being said about him and I wanted to help him.'

Amid all of this, Deschamps had the small matter of preparing for games against Germany and England. When he named his squad for the November 2015 friendly games, neither Valbuena nor Benzema were selected. The latter was apparently carrying a hamstring problem, and therefore overlooked, but Deschamps justified Valbuena's absence by stating that he was not in a 'fit psychological state' to play. He arguably wouldn't be for the remainder of the season. Valbuena's form suffered a sudden dip, prompting him to lose his place in the Lyon side and then fall out of contention for Euro 2016.

Benzema, meanwhile, benefited from the unflinching support of Real Madrid. But his every move came under intense
scrutiny back home. When Zidane's charges played Barcelona
on 21 November, just eight days after a series of terrorist attacks
in Paris had left the nation stunned, *La Marseillaise* was played
as a tribute to the 130 victims. As ever, Benzema did not sing.
More troublingly in the eyes of certain observers, he chose to
spit on the ground afterwards. 'Benzema waited until the end of
the anthem before spitting on the pitch like footballers often do,'
read the in-depth analysis of on *Le Figaro* newspaper's website.

> On the video, from one-minute seventeen seconds, the
> Madrid player is careful to look up at the big screen to see
> if he is being filmed before discreetly turning. Right after,
> he looks at the screen again. Did he understand he had just
> committed something irreparable? His face, which falls at
> one-minute twenty-two seconds, suggests he did.

Again, the scathing media treatment seemed unnecessarily
harsh, but the sharks were now circling.

Initially, the French football authorities offered full support
to Benzema in the sex-tape affair, rightly insisting the presump-
tion of innocence be respected. However, with new revelations
emerging in the media on almost a daily basis, and the levels
of antagonism between the two players rising, the FFF decided
that firm action was required. 'Karim Benzema is no longer
available for selection,' FFF president Noël Le Graët declared
on 10 December 2015. 'Unless the situation evolves, that will
remain the case.' Deschamps reluctantly agreed. 'It's an affair
that bothers me,' the coach stated. 'It annoys me. It's something
I really could have done without six months before the Euros.'

Despite being placed under judicial supervision, Benzema
continued to excel in Spain. He crashed home twenty-eight
goals for Real Madrid that season, as well as winning the

Champions League. As the spectre of hosting Euro 2016 got nearer, the FFF stance seemed to be softening and there was a growing feeling that Benzema would be recalled. Indeed, with Deschamps offering a glowing appraisal of the striker in an interview with *L'Équipe* in March, it looked certain a way back was being paved. 'On a sporting level, I want to have my best players,' Deschamps declared. 'Benzema gets criticised for not scoring more with us. People think because he's a Real Madrid player he should score more. But it doesn't work like that. He contributes a lot to our build-up play. Every other country is jealous of us [for having him].'

The trouble was the case now went far beyond the realms of football. Benzema's situation was being discussed in the very highest offices, and the final decision may well have been taken out of Deschamps and Le Graët's hands. Prime Minister Manuel Valls made it clear that he did not want the Real Madrid striker playing for France. 'A great sportsman – and this includes Karim Benzema, as it includes others – must be exemplary,' Valls stressed. 'If he is not exemplary, he does not have a place in the France team.'

That Valls was born in Catalonia and is a Barcelona supporter led to many silly conspiracy theories. But his words were ominous for Benzema.

Elsewhere, France's extreme right jumped at the chance to attack the forward of Algerian origins. 'Benzema should never have been in the France team,' Front National leader Marine Le Pen told Europe 1 radio. 'He's expressed his contempt for France on a number of occasions. He behaves in a way that the French can no longer accept from people who earn astronomic sums and act like spoilt kids. He doesn't sing *La Marseillaise*, and in his interviews he expresses contempt for all forms of patriotism.'

Few felt as strongly as Le Pen and some pointed out that the legendary Michel Platini also refused to sing *La Marseillaise* during his playing days without attracting any negative comments. Nevertheless, a clear anti-Benzema sentiment was growing. In April 2016, a survey carried out for RTL radio revealed that 81 per cent of French people did not want Benzema to play in the Euros. The image of *Les Bleus* remained fragile and the disastrous events of recent years were still fresh in the mind of the public. Whether fair or not, Benzema's name was now associated with trouble.

His involvement in the sex-tape scandal came five years after *L'Affaire Zahia*, another long-running saga that saw Benzema and Ribéry charged as part of an investigation into an underage prostitution racket. From the start, Benzema denied having had a relationship with the escort girl Zahia Dehar, and he was acquitted of all charges in 2014. However, mud tends to stick and plenty was flung in Benzema's direction. Just days after Deschamps's positive interview in *L'Équipe*, his name came up yet again, this time in a money-laundering case reported by *Libération* newspaper. Again, Benzema did not appear to be guilty of anything, but Deschamps was furious that the striker had not mentioned anything to him and that he first heard about it when the article appeared in the press. It proved to be one scandal too many.

Minister of Urban Affairs, Youth Affairs and Sports, Patrick Kanner, called for Benzema to be overlooked for the tournament, and on 13 April 2016 a definitive decision was taken. The actual news of Benzema's omission did not come from Deschamps or Le Graët, however. Benzema got in there first, announcing the FFF decision on his own personal Twitter account.

With more than 40 million people following him on social media, Benzema has considerable clout online, and the tweet duly prompted outrage from his fans. Young people, in particular, flock to Benzema's Twitter and Instagram accounts. They love the photos and videos he posts of himself standing next to his latest sports car or hopping onto a private jet with his friend Booba, a hugely popular rap artist. Soon after Benzema's extraordinary run against Atlético in the Champions League, Booba posted a picture of the dribble on Instagram, except that the heads of Savić, Godín and Giménez had been edited out and replaced by those of Deschamps, Valls and Olivier Giroud. Benzema duly 'liked' the photo. When Deschamps was asked to comment, he looked stone-faced. 'I'll only say one word: it's pitiful,' the coach declared.

But in the spring of 2016, Deschamps, it seems, had been left with little choice. 'You can't build a team to try to win a tournament when your playmaker is pressing charges against your centre-forward,' Duluc states. 'Deschamps could have decided to go with only Valbuena, or only Benzema, but he'd have created a soap opera for the media and it certainly would've overshadowed the preparations. It's infuriating. A huge waste of talent. Benzema is the best striker France has had in recent years. But I can understand, and at the same time regret, Deschamps not picking him.'

In an official statement explaining the decision to exclude Benzema, the FFF stressed the importance of 'preserving unity' and of all players displaying 'exemplary behaviour'. It is still not clear as to whether Deschamps was pushed into making the decision. The Prime Minister had, after all, made a strong statement, and Deschamps always maintained that as an FFF employee he would have to respect the wishes of Le Graët.

Yet Deschamps's assistant coach assures me it was entirely the manager's call. 'Didier did not come under any external pressure,' Guy Stéphan explains. 'Of course, we'd have been far happier if the sex-tape affair hadn't happened. But it did happen and we have to live with it. Or rather they have to live with it.' More than three years have passed, but this clearly remains a sensitive topic. There is a lingering sense of sadness in Stéphan's voice when he talks about the player who could and should have become a France great. 'Didier rates Karim highly,' he says.

'Don't forget he picked him for eleven matches in a row despite the fact he didn't score a goal. It's just that the situation dictated the choice.'

Deschamps's decision may well have been influenced by the way his side performed without Benzema. In March, *Les Bleus* won 3–2 in the Netherlands and then beat Russia 4–2 at the Stade de France. The rapidly maturing Antoine Griezmann excelled in both games, operating just off Olivier Giroud in the first game and behind André-Pierre Gignac in the second. Dimitri Payet, Kingsley Coman and Anthony Martial also sparkled, and showed the coach that he possessed several good attacking options even without Benzema. Moreover, on top of the seven goals that they scored, the squad looked happy again. The scandal that had dominated national team affairs for months was fading into the background at last.

But any hopes Deschamps had of football taking centre stage once and for all disappeared a fortnight before the opening game. In an extraordinary interview with *The Guardian*, Éric Cantona accused France's manager of being racist. He suggested that Deschamps had overlooked both Benzema and Hatem Ben Arfa – who was enjoying the best season of his career with OGC Nice – because of their origins.

'Benzema is a great player. Ben Arfa is a great player,' Cantona began. 'But Deschamps, he has a really French name. Maybe he is the only one in France to have a truly French name. Nobody in his family mixed with anybody, you know. Like the Mormons in America. So I'm not surprised he used the situation of Benzema not to take him. Especially after Valls said he should not play for France. And Ben Arfa is maybe the best player in France today. But they have some origins. I am allowed to think about that.'

In France, nobody paid too much attention to Cantona's claims. It was widely known that he had a fractious relationship with Deschamps, whom he had labelled a 'water carrier' when the pair were France teammates, and the Manchester United legend did not command the same levels of respect on the French side of the Channel.

Five days later, however, the Spanish newspaper *Marca* published an interview with Benzema that would have far more serious consequences. 'Deschamps has bowed to racist pressure,' read the sensational quote splashed across the front page.

Reading the interview, it is clear Benzema does not accuse Deschamps of racism. In fact, when asked if he thinks whether Cantona's accusations have any accuracy, the striker replied: 'No, I don't think so. But [Deschamps] has bowed to pressure from a racist part of France. You have to know that an extremist party reached the second round in the last two elections in France. I don't know, therefore, if the decision was only Didier's because I have got on well with him and with the president [of the FFF].'

Benzema was not attacking Deschamps directly, yet the headline attracted a huge amount of negative publicity. Coming so soon after Cantona's claims, the notion that Deschamps might indeed be racist seemed to have become open to public debate. The situation then took a sinister twist. On 3 June, just one week before the opening fixture between *Les Bleus* and Romania, Deschamps's holiday home in Brittany was vandalised with the word 'racist' sprayed on the front wall.

Deschamps is an extremely robust character and has coped with a huge amount of pressure, but this was an act that affected his family and it upset the France manager deeply. 'I was worried about him, yes,' Stéphan tells me in a grave voice. 'He was receiving threats. It wasn't pleasant. Didier is a tough guy, but he's human and he has feelings like everyone else. It had become too much. I felt something had to be done.'

Stéphan decided to give an interview to *L'Équipe* with the aim of issuing a strong message to the nation. 'It's time to stop the lies, the insinuations, the gossip,' he declared. 'Didier's house has been graffitied. What's the next step? This is a time to come together. We can't deny there are problems with integration.

We can't deny that discrimination exists, or that economic problems are weighing this country down. But transferring these problems onto the French team, and in particular onto its coach, is intolerable, unacceptable and dishonest.'

Stéphan's words helped. He is a deeply respected figure among journalists and the former Lyon coach rarely speaks out. So the timing of this intervention, and the serious, forthright manner in which he spoke, had the desired effect. For the next few weeks at least, there were no more questions about racism and no more questions about Benzema. Deschamps, however, was left deeply scarred by the episode.

No sooner had Euro 2016 finished than the Benzema questions returned. In the 2016/17 campaign, the striker won the quadruple with Real Madrid. The following season, he lifted the Champions League for a third campaign running and the fourth time in five years, scoring and excelling in the final against Liverpool. In contrast, France's first-choice striker Olivier Giroud had been deemed surplus to requirements by Arsenal and, after joining Chelsea in January 2018, was struggling to impose himself in west London.

Each time Deschamps was asked about Giroud's situation and a possible return for Benzema – something that happened at every single press conference – he squirmed uncomfortably in his seat and insisted he would continue to make the right 'sporting decisions'. Deschamps says the door is not closed for any player, but it is highly unlikely he will ever forgive Benzema for bringing hurt to his family. 'Deschamps is the kind of person who will bear a grudge for next to nothing,' Duluc laughs. 'There's no chance he'll ever forgive Benzema for what he said.'

In January 2019, Deschamps dropped his strongest hint yet that the Real Madrid attacker would not return under his watch. Answering listeners' questions on Europe 1 radio, he was asked about the accusations of racism. 'We live with it,' Deschamps said, 'but I considered at that moment that the white line had been crossed. And when you cross the white line, there is a point of no return. I'll never forget that.'

Ten months later, FFF president Noël Le Graët went even further, telling RMC radio: 'Karim Benzema is a very good player. I've never doubted his qualities. With Real Madrid, he shows he's one of the best in the world in his position. But his time with France is over.'

Inevitably, Benzema reacted on social media, slamming Le Graët and leaving a tantalising message to his many supporters of Algerian origin. 'Noël, I thought you didn't interfere with the coach's decisions!' he wrote. 'Just remember that I am the only person who will be calling an end to my international career. If you think it's over for me, let me play for another country that I'm eligible to represent, and we'll see.'

Various media outlets quickly consulted FIFA regulations and concluded that there was only one way in which Benzema could be allowed to represent Algeria – or indeed Spain, where he had been residing for over a decade – having already played for *Les Bleus* multiple times in official competition. He would have to be stripped of his French nationality 'without his consent or against his will because of a governmental decision'.

Some members of France's government may even be willing to sanction such a step. But thankfully the voices of reason still outweigh the bigots. Benzema is French and always will be. As for the sex-tape affair, the case continues to rumble on. In 2017, the striker received encouragement when the Court of Cassation supported his legal team's claims that the police had acted dishonestly during their investigation. But a subsequent ruling more than two years later, in December 2019, judged that the methods used had in fact been within the law. There will surely be more twists to come in this sorry affair, but one thing is certain: Benzema's shortened career in a France shirt will for ever be tinged with regret, sadness and that painful unknowing sentiment of what might have been.

CHAPTER 17

L'EURO 2016
– VIVE LE FOOTBALL!

One man benefited from Benzema's absence at Euro 2016 more than any other. In his younger days, Olivier Giroud did not seem to be destined for a career at the very highest level. But the tall, strapping target-man has relentlessly defied his critics and battled through adversity to establish himself as Didier Deschamps's number one striker.

When Giroud scored his thirty-fifth international goal, against Iceland in March 2019, he moved ahead of David Trezeguet into third place on France's all-time list of scorers. Eight months later, he slotted home a penalty against Moldova, taking his tally to thirty-nine strikes, just two fewer than the legendary Michel Platini. France's record-holder Thierry Henry, who has fifty-one goals to his name, may soon need to start worrying.

Since Deschamps took charge in 2012, he has been blessed with a wonderful generation of talented players. Paul Pogba, Raphaël Varane, Blaise Matuidi, N'Golo Kanté and Antoine Griezmann would walk into most teams around the world. However, tellingly the player Deschamps has picked more often than any other is Olivier Giroud. Despite all of this, Giroud still has many detractors in France and his selection continues to divide opinion.

When we meet at Chelsea's training ground in Cobham to discuss his remarkable journey with the French national team, Giroud still seems to be humbled by his achievements. Kylian Mbappé may have grown up knowing that he would win trophies and play for France, but Giroud's childhood was very different and his dreams were far more modest.

'When I was a little boy, I never imagined I might play for *Les Bleus* one day,' he begins. 'I remember watching the 1998 World Cup. I was eleven and I was a passionate supporter. I watched with my cousin and we painted our faces blue, white and red. Of course, you dream and you think, "wouldn't it be amazing to do that". But even later on, when I signed my first contract with Grenoble, I felt like the French national team was light years away. It seemed inaccessible to me. My dream was to play in Ligue 1.'

In many ways, Giroud is the polar opposite to Benzema. The Real Madrid striker grew up in a deprived, urban environment and from a young age football was everything to him. He was a childhood prodigy – the best young talent Lyon had ever seen – and very quickly football was identified as an obvious and necessary route to a better life. Giroud's childhood was more comfortable. He was raised in the idyllic, rural surrounds of the French Alps. When he wasn't playing for his local team, Olympique Club de Froges, in the gorgeous valleys of the Isère region, he would be bombing down the mountains on a pair of skis.

Giroud was good at football but he was not exceptional. His older brother Romain was thought to be the best in the family. But after attending AJ Auxerre's youth academy in the 1990s, he failed to make the step up in the professional game. 'Romain was my hero,' Giroud says with an affectionate smile. 'He played against Titi [Henry], Anelka and Trezeguet in youth football. I wanted to follow his path.'

Yet Romain's struggles were a warning. So when Olivier signed his first professional contract with second-division side

Grenoble Foot 38, aged eighteen, he also registered at the town's university where he studied for three years with the aim of qualifying as a PE teacher. That was looking like a wise decision when Grenoble coach Mecha Baždarević told him, 'You're not good enough for Ligue 2, let alone Ligue 1', and sent the striker on loan to FC Istres in the third tier. At twenty-one, when Benzema was turning out for France at Euro 2008, Giroud was taking his final exams and at the same time negotiating a transfer to Ligue 2 side Tours FC.

Looking out of the window and seeing the lush training pitches of Cobham, those toils in the French lower leagues seem a long way away. But that period helped forge a steely resilience that Giroud has had to call on throughout his career. 'I realised from an early stage that I'd always have to prove myself, over and over,' he explains. 'People will always question me. That's been part of my career – I've had to build myself up through adversity. Thanks to my strength of character, and my belief in Jesus, I am able to turn criticism into positive energy. It's an engine for me. I don't let my head drop or feel sorry for myself. I want to prove to everyone that I can do the job on the pitch.'

Giroud certainly did the job at Montpellier HSC. After netting twelve goals in his debut top-flight campaign at the Stade de la Mosson, he registered twenty-one in the 2011/12 season, inspiring the southern club to its one and only Ligue 1 title. To pip PSG to the post was a stunning achievement and Giroud's exploits earned him a transfer to Arsenal.

In north London, he scored goals but he also missed chances, he could look slow and clumsy at times in the high-octane world of the Premier League, and continued to attract criticism from the media. Gunners legend Thierry Henry memorably said on Sky Sports that the club would never win the league so long as they had his compatriot in attack. Yet the Arsenal fans always seemed to like Giroud. They liked the way he fought for every ball, they liked his collective playing style, the way his hard work made his teammates look better, and they liked the passion he showed when he scored.

At times it feels as though this strong, bustling target-man – who could even be described as an old-fashioned English centre-forward – is more liked and respected by British football fans than by their French counterparts. I ask him if life might have been easier had he been born in England. 'It's true that I have quite English qualities,' he responds. 'I have a similar profile to Harry Kane: a big, powerful striker who fights for every ball. Maybe in France people prefer guys like Thierry Henry – and of course now Kylian Mbappé – players with incredible explosiveness and speed in everything they do. Maybe young people are more excited by a guy who pushes the ball and sprints at 37km/h. That's fine and I can understand it. Every profile has its own importance in the team.'

In the summer of 2016, as *Les Bleus* prepared to host the European Championships, few French fans were enthused by the idea of Giroud leading the country's attack.

On 30 May, two days after Benzema had won the Champions League with Real Madrid, Deschamps's team faced Cameroon in their penultimate warm-up game in Nantes. Giroud played well. He even scored a fine goal, meeting Pogba's fantastic curling pass with a precise volley. But when the maligned striker was substituted in the sixty-fifth minute, he was jeered off by sections of the Stade de la Beaujoire crowd. It was an extraordinary reaction and one that hurt the striker. 'I don't really understand the boos,' Giroud told the press after the game. 'It's a shame, but you know I've been through a lot of tough moments in my career. These things don't really affect me any more.'

The booing did not come totally out of the blue. There had been a smattering of whistles when Giroud came on against Russia at the Stade de France in March. But this was the first game he had played since Benzema's exclusion had been made official. It felt like the protests were as much about Benzema's absence as they were Giroud's inclusion.

'It was a strange context,' Giroud reflects four years on. 'Some people were blaming me for the fact that Karim wasn't there. There were pro-Karim fans and pro-Giroud fans. Some didn't want me in the team, and I sensed that. Then, the next day, my face was on the front page of *L'Équipe* with the headline "*Olivier Giroud, le mal-aimé*" [the unloved one]. Giroud smiles at the memory and then starts singing a song I have never heard of. 'You don't know it? It's '*Le Mal-Aimé*' by Claude François. After that headline in *L'Équipe*, my mates [Christophe] Jallet, [Benoît] Costil, [Laurent] Koscielny and [Hugo] Lloris kept on singing it to me. We were a really tight-knit group and we had a lot of laughs together.'

Giroud can laugh about it now, but other witnesses suggest that the Claude François tune and the situation with the fans did not amuse him in the least at the time. Having the responsibility of leading France's attack on home soil is a big challenge. Doing so knowing that certain people are willing you to fail must have been highly stressful. Some supporters simply wanted a more dynamic striker, but the anti-Giroud sentiment was clearly fuelled by more than just footballing matters.

'People looked at him as the guy who had taken Benzema's place, and there was a symbolic element to that: the white French guy had taken the place of the immigrant French guy,' argues the journalist Daniel Riolo. 'What's more, Giroud has this ungainly playing style, while Benzema is a purer, more technical player. Young people in *les banlieues* were naturally siding with Benzema.'

To Deschamps, the Giroud-Benzema debate was pointless and not especially helpful. But it did at least take French minds off a far more serious problem.

Seven months after a series of horrendous terrorist attacks had taken 130 lives in Paris and Saint-Denis, the country was still in a state of emergency and its grieving population continued to live with this deeply unpleasant, lingering sense of fear. The suicide bombings that subsequently accounted for thirty-two lives in Brussels airport and in a metro station in March only heightened concerns across Belgium's border.

On 6 June, four days before Euro 2016 kicked off, a French national was arrested in Ukraine accused of plotting fifteen separate attacks during the tournament. At the same time, US intelligence services issued a bleak warning to American fans planning to travel to France. 'Euro 2016 stadiums, fan zones and public places broadcasting games will all be potential targets,' it declared. There was unquestionably some scaremongering, and a good deal of paranoia, but the existence of a threat was real. France's President François Hollande looked to reassure the masses by declaring that 90,000 security officers would be deployed during the tournament to ensure fan safety. 'The threat of terror remains,' he stated, 'and sadly it will remain for a long time to come. So we must do everything in our power to make sure Euro 2016 is a success.'

The tragic events of 13 November 2015 will for ever be associated with the French national team. It was outside the Stade de France, soon after Les Bleus had kicked off against Germany, that the first in a series of bloody, coordinated attacks took place.

Three suicide bombers had planned to access the stadium, but thankfully they failed to get past security at the gates. The first nevertheless detonated his belt on Avenue Jules Rimet, the road lining the east side of the stadium, at 9.17 p.m., killing one other person. The second explosion followed in the same zone two minutes later, and its hollow, shuddering sound reverberated inside the stadium. Patrice Évra was in possession at the time, in front of the East Stand, and as he passed the ball backwards a look of fear briefly flashed across his face. Some supporters booed and there was an air of concern, but most believed – or least attempted to convince themselves – that the noises were the result of some harmless homemade pyrotechnics. They soon started singing again, and just before half-time Giroud gave the hosts the lead.

France's goal scorer had nevertheless sensed something was badly wrong. 'Out on the pitch, we heard the two explosions very clearly, especially the second one,' Giroud tells me. 'I remember seeing Pat Évra do this double-take. The noise was a pretty unbelievable. I jumped a bit as well. We knew something serious had happened.'

The third explosion took place during the interval, by which time the players were back in the dressing room. However, they were not informed about the attacks. 'The authorities decided to protect us from what was happening,' Giroud explains. 'All the information sources were cut off, including the social networks on our phones.'

Like the players, the majority of the 79,000 fans inside the stadium were unaware at this stage that several dreadful machine-gun attacks were unfolding simultaneously in cafés and restaurants in central Paris. The indiscriminate killings that took place in the normally calm, relaxed tenth and eleventh *arrondissements* of the capital accounted for thirty-nine lives. But the deadliest assault of all occurred in the Bataclan theatre, in the eleventh *arrondissement*, during an Eagles of Death Metal concert.

Three terrorists held several hundred people hostage, killing as many as ninety and injuring dozens more before blowing themselves up during the police raid three hours later. The so-called Islamic State would later claim responsibility, calling the attacks 'the first of the storm'.

Inside the Stade de France, with internet connections extremely limited, the oblivious supporters continued to focus on the game. Hollande was present, but the head of state left discreetly at half-time to attend a high-level security meeting.

A helicopter circled overhead for the entirety of the second half, which added to the sense of eerie confusion. By the time André-Pierre Gignac's goal sealed a 2–0 win on eighty-six minutes, the news had begun to spread and the celebrations in the stands were muted.

France's assistant coach Guy Stéphan was one of the few to be informed of what was happening at an early stage, and he found it hard to focus on the game. 'The staff were told at half-time that there had been some attacks,' he says sombrely. 'We weren't given details but we knew there had been shootings. It was hard to digest the information. At that point our job was to make sure the players carried on playing the game.' Indeed, for the security forces it was crucial everything continued as normal in order to avoid a sudden panic or an uncontrolled mass exodus. 'Pretending everything was OK for an hour was very difficult,' said Noël Le Graët, the FFF president. 'That second half was very, very long.'

At the final whistle, the players were quickly brought up to speed. French and German internationals initially gathered in front of television screens in the tunnel area where news channels relayed the latest information. Phones were checked. Loved ones were contacted. Opposition players mingled as the sporting rivalry that had separated them moments before disappeared. Raphaël Varane helped his Real Madrid club-mate Sami Khedira understand what was going on. 'There was a sense of togetherness because this was far bigger than football and everybody was concerned,' Stéphan describes. 'The German dressing room was next door to ours and we remained in constant communication. They were worried. They did not want to travel through Paris [to their hotel], so we offered for them to come back to Clairefontaine with us. I wouldn't say there was panic, but there was a lot of emotion. We were living a tragedy.'

Arrangements were made to accommodate the Germany

players at Clairefontaine, but they decided to wait in their Stade de France dressing room until the early hours of the morning. They were brought mattresses and food and drink, before leaving to catch a 7 a.m. flight home. 'We wanted to avoid any possible risk,' said the team manager Oliver Bierhoff. 'The players were shocked and very anxious.'

France's players left the stadium shortly before 3 a.m. By that point Antoine Griezmann had received the reassurances he had quite literally been praying for: his sister Maud, who had been held captive in the Bataclan for two terrible hours, emerged unscathed.

Lassana Diarra grew up in Belleville, a stone's throw away from the shootings in central Paris. He still has family who live in the area, and tragically his cousin Asta Diakité was among those to perish on Rue Bichat in the tenth *arrondissement*. The midfielder was distraught, but speaking from Clairefontaine the next day, he issued an admirable statement. 'She was an example and support to me, like a big sister,' Diarra began. 'In this climate of terror, it is important for all of us who are representatives of our country and its diversity to speak and remain united against a horror that has no colour, no religion.'

The remarkable strength and dignity demonstrated by Diarra was mirrored by the rest of the football community over the next few emotion-filled days.

The last thing Didier Deschamps's men wanted to do on that Saturday morning was prepare for another match. But a friendly against England at Wembley had been scheduled for Tuesday 17 November, and the FFF – after consultation with the French government – decided that they should play the game. 'The politicians told us it was important to carry on,' Stéphan recalls. 'The players didn't want to. They'd been seriously affected. The morning after the attacks, it was out of the question to go to England. But the message from the authorities was clear: we couldn't let the people who committed these attacks affect our lives. They couldn't get the better of us. That's what they want. The players understood and slowly they came around to the idea of playing.'

After travelling across the Channel, *Les Bleus* witnessed first-hand the love and empathy that France was receiving from its English friends. The day before the game, Deschamps was touched when English journalists presented him with a bouquet of flowers before his press conference. The next morning, the UK newspapers again struck a chord. 'Vive le football' was the headline on the sports section of *The Sun*. 'Song for France' read *The Times*. 'Sing up for France' came the *Daily Mirror*'s instructions. Every paper published the lyrics of the French national anthem to ensure English supporters could join in.

When the France team bus turned up Olympic Way and the players saw the magnificent Wembley stadium illuminated in blue, white and red, a poignant silence filled the air. An enormous *Tricolore* arch dominated the skyline and the words *Liberté, Égalité, Fraternité* were beamed onto the front façade of the stadium. The symbolism was incredibly powerful and the message hit home. 'The entente between the two countries has always been special,' Stéphan says. 'But the welcome we got that night was just amazing. You could sense this sincere friendship and togetherness between the nations.'

Of the 70,000 English fans present, it is safe to assume not many spoke French. But that did not stop them trying hard to sing *La Marseillaise* with the aid of subtitles on the big screens. Arm-in-arm the France players sung stoically, some like Pogba with his eyes shut, others like Diarra with his head bowed. Each and every one of them were overcome by emotion.

In a special interview with *L'Équipe* to mark 100 games as France boss, Deschamps stated that the match that evening was among his most memorable of all. 'To hear the English singing *La Marseillaise* was unbelievable,' Deschamps remarked. 'It went beyond the realm of sport. This was not a football match.

The players weren't there [thinking about football] and you couldn't expect them to be. At a moment like that, you realise the immensity of what it means to represent your country. You can never forget something like that. It marks you for life. Never again.'

This was a football team, and a country, that had been through an awful lot. The arrival of Euro 2016 was being greeted with apprehension in the streets rather than anticipation. To add to this sense of trepidation, Paris was hit by three days of extraordinary torrential rainstorms at the start of June. The River Seine flooded its banks, causing 15,000 homes to be evacuated and metro stations to close as central Paris came to a standstill. In all, the flooding caused more than €1 billion worth of damage. Furthermore, a national rail strike threatened to rumble on. It seemed like the last thing the country needed was a major international sport tournament.

Yet there was some relief when the football commenced on 10 June. First and foremost, because the evening's festivities at the Stade de France – and in the many fan parks around the country – proceeded smoothly without any security breaches. And secondly, because *Les Bleus* won their opening game. However, the 2–1 triumph over Romania was far from convincing. Giroud missed three clear chances before flattening goalkeeper Ciprian Tătăruşanu as he won an aerial duel to open the scoring. Then, after a distinctly average Romanian team had levelled from the penalty spot, Dimitri Payet secured the three points with a moment of individual brilliance on eighty-nine minutes.

Nobody was getting too excited by the disjointed display, however, and sadly the dark clouds returned the next day as the tournament was hit by scenes of extreme violence. There had been clashes between Russian and English supporters in the town of Marseille before the Group B game, but the attacks that took place inside the Stade Vélodrome were premeditated, organised and deeply shocking. Scores of balaclava-clad

Russian hooligans charged through a line of stewards to attack England supporters, causing many serious injuries. The fighting between the two sets of fans continued in the city long into the night. French people looked on, bewildered, no doubt wondering what more depressing, miserable scenes awaited their country in the coming weeks.

Then the Republic of Ireland and Northern Ireland arrived and everything changed. The Republic alone brought around 70,000 fans to France. The FA of Ireland say they received 275,000 requests for tickets in total. It is no exaggeration to suggest that their relentless singing, joking, warmth and friendliness towards their hosts helped transform the mood in France.

Indeed, the atmosphere on 13 June, the day the Republic of Ireland played Sweden at the Stade de France, was truly a breath of fresh air. Both sets of fans sang, drank and partied together throughout the capital. Videos of Irish fans serenading the French police, helping an elderly couple to change a tyre, singing lullabies to babies on the metro, offering wild ovations to dustmen on the Boulevard de Clichy, or dancing with bemused commuters went viral on social media. Entire neighbourhoods were transformed into merry, beer-fuelled seas of green. The Euro 2016 party could begin.

Supporters of Northern Ireland were not to be outdone. They were also present in their hordes, and the contagious chant of 'Will Grigg's on Fire!' (a tribute to their Wigan Athletic striker sung to the tune of 'Freed from Desire' by Gala) was soon being hummed unwittingly by fans of all nationality. Local journalists at the game between Michael O'Neill's side and Germany at the Parc des Princes in the capital were reminded of a time when PSG's old stadium was one of the noisiest around. 'Thanks to the Northern Irish, who turned this majestic stadium green and sang with heart and passion throughout the game, we witnessed an atmosphere that evoked fond memories of the 1990s,' reported *Le Parisien* newspaper.

Both sets of Irish supporters were rewarded by the mayor of Paris, Anne Hidalgo, who presented them with a Medal of the City. 'We have been charmed and impressed by their kindness, their chants and their good humour,' Hidalgo declared.

But they were not the only ones bringing joviality and passion. The French couple that got married in Bordeaux on 11 June are unlikely to forget the guard of honour they received from Wales fans outside the Hôtel de Ville. The enormous Turkish following was probably the most raucous of all, while Croatia, Romania, Poland and Belgium all brought over more than 20,000 fans respectively. Indeed, 10 per cent of Iceland's entire population travelled to France, displaying as much character, tenacity and facial hair as the battling Icelandic players who dumped England unceremoniously out of the tournament in Nice. With an estimated 1.5 million Portuguese migrants living in France, Cristiano Ronaldo and friends must have felt like they were playing at home, such was the size and fervour of their following.

During that wonderful month, I worked as a reporter for beIN Sports' English channel. My brief was to bring the colour and sense of excitement from France's towns and stadiums to living rooms around the world. The camaraderie between supporters of so many nationalities and the general feel-good factor that was sweeping through France ensured it was one of the most fun periods of my professional life. With its superb train network, its many stunning, historic towns, and an unrivalled love for food and drink, France is a fantastic tournament host. So many aspects of Euro 2016 reminded me of that magnificent summer of 1998; even the France football team, inspired by the fresh-faced Antoine Griezmann, was beginning to resemble the Zinédine Zidane vintage.

It took Deschamps time to find the right balance in his team. After the narrow win over Romania, *Les Bleus* needed late goals from Griezmann and Payet to beat Albania, then played out a goalless stalemate with Switzerland. Admittedly, the coach had not been helped by a spate of absences: Raphaël Varane was ruled out late on through injury, further weakening a defence already shorn of Mamadou Sakho – who had been suspended by UEFA after testing positive for a banned substance – Mathieu Debuchy, Jérémy Mathieu, Kurt Zouma and Benoît Trémoulinas. Add Benzema and the injured duo Lassana Diarra and Nabil Fekir to the list and Deschamps had a very depleted squad to play with.

Yet Deschamps still had an embarrassment of riches in certain areas. In N'Golo Kanté, Paul Pogba and Blaise Matuidi, for example, France boasted three world-class central midfielders. They should have been controlling matches from that area, but Deschamps's preferred 4–3–3 formation was disjointed and ineffective in the group stage.

Pogba, one of the tournament poster-boys, had been particularly disappointing in his position on the right of the three. In a bid to get the best from the Juventus man, the coach switched him to his preferred left-sided role against the Republic of Ireland in the round of sixteen fixture. Yet the move proved disastrous. Just a minute in, Pogba's clumsy lunge on Shane Long gifted the Irish a penalty and the opening goal. With the left-footed Matuidi looking all at sea on the right, the hosts could easily have fallen further behind in a woeful first half.

For his part, Kanté had won the Premier League with Leicester City that season and was emerging as one of the best destructive midfielders on the planet. But he was still finding his feet at international level, and after picking up a yellow card for a late challenge on James McClean, the holding midfielder was sacrificed at the break. Young winger Kingsley Coman came on, enabling France to switch to a 4–2–3–1, and *Les Bleus* were a team transformed. Pogba and Matuidi suddenly gelled as a duo and, crucially, Griezmann began excelling in a central attacking role behind Giroud.

The Atlético Madrid maestro levelled the game with an exquisite header on fifty-eight minutes, but it was the winning goal that best encapsulated his new-found partnership with Giroud. The Arsenal striker was proving a real handful for the Irish defenders, pulling them out of position and creating space for his quicker, more creative teammates. On sixty-one minutes, both Irish centre-backs followed his run to the right side of the box, so when Giroud flicked a header infield, Griezmann was presented with a clear run on goal. The sharpshooter finished with aplomb to seal the win. 'I have a great understanding with Olivier,' Griezmann commented in an interview after claiming his man-of-the-match prize. Deschamps duly took note; that particular partnership would be one of the cornerstones of France's success in the coming years.

The Griezmann–Giroud axis proved too much for Iceland in the quarter-finals as the hosts started to enjoy themselves. Giroud scored two and set up another for his irresistible partner-in-crime. *Les Bleus*, who were missing Kanté and Adil Rami to suspension, treated the Stade de France crowd to a stylish 5–2 triumph and the nation began to believe. 'In the end, the many absences aren't causing a problem in this funny tournament,' reported *Le Monde*. 'Quite the opposite in fact. Benzema's absence appears to have liberated everybody and facilitated the emergence of new talents.'

Germany were nevertheless strong favourites to defeat Deschamps's charges in a mouth-watering semi-final match-up. Two years previously, after beating *Les Bleus* in the quarter-finals, they had embarrassed World Cup hosts Brazil, putting seven goals past them. Moreover, France had not defeated Germany in a major tournament since 1958, memorably suffering one of their most painful, controversial and acrimonious losses against the West Germans in the 1982 World Cup semi-finals.

But on the night of 7 July, there was something special in the Marseille air. With 64,000 fans cheering on the hosts in the majestic, newly renovated Stade Vélodrome, Deschamps's team fought like warriors to keep the world champions at bay. Just as had been the case throughout the tournament, Hugo Lloris was exceptional in goal. In front of the skipper, Lyon's 22-year-old centre-back Samuel Umtiti – in only his second international appearance – looked commanding alongside Laurent Koscielny.

This was a night for courage, strength and determination, and nobody epitomised those characteristics more than Moussa Sissoko, the maligned Newcastle midfielder, who had surprisingly cemented his place on France's right wing. In many ways, Sissoko, with his fearless attitude and relentless running, became a symbol for Deschamps's tough, hard-working team; France, after all, had many individuals more talented than him, yet the coach knew Sissoko would show the tactical discipline, selfless attitude and physicality that he needed.

At the end of a first half that had been dominated by Germany, Bastian Schweinsteiger inexplicably handled inside the box, gifting France a penalty, which Griezmann emphatically converted. From that moment, the passionate crowd stirred up an extraordinary noise, roaring every time a blue shirt won a tackle and injecting energy into the home side. The confidence shifted to the French as *Les Bleus* appeared to grow in strength. On seventy-two minutes, as France hounded Germany's defenders inside their own box, Joshua Kimmich lost possession. Pogba crossed and Manuel Neuer, under pressure from Giroud, punched the ball into the path of Griezmann, who rifled home.

As the ball hit the net, Giroud did not move. He simply thrust his arms aloft, staring up into the Mediterranean sky. For the striker who had grown up supporting Olympique de Marseille, this was his greatest moment so far. 'The atmosphere in Marseille was just extraordinary,' the ex-Montpellier man says, smiling at the memory of a night that saw France announce their return to highest level. 'We were carried by that incredible crowd. It was such a tough game. We were a bit lucky to open the scoring, then after that we defended like mad.'

Giroud scored three goals overall at Euro 2016 and had a hand in several more, but his combative, never-say-die attitude was equally important to France's progress. 'At this level, the most important thing is the strength of your team, not your individuals,' Giroud stresses. 'You have to have that collective ingredient which means you can count on each other during the difficult times. That's something the coach has brought us. As a forward you can always help the team by running back and winning the ball. Against Germany, Antoine [Griezmann] and I ran so hard. I don't know how many kilometres we covered that night, but we gave absolutely everything we had. The whole team battled. Everyone together. It was a little taste of what was to come in 2018.'

For players like Sissoko, Matuidi and Giroud, scrapping is part of their nature. But seeing somebody like Griezmann – a wonderfully silky footballer with brilliant close ball skills, technique, game intelligence and vision – also fighting for every ball as if his life depended on it sent out an important message: nobody was too big, or too good, to do the dirty work. Griezmann bought into the team ethos that had been preached by Diego Simeone at Atlético Madrid, and he had no qualms about rolling his sleeves up for Deschamps either.

Ultimately, the 25-year-old paid a price for his tireless running against Germany. Like many of his colleagues, Griezmann struggled to hit his stride in the final against Portugal just three days later. France had been brilliant against the best team in the world inside the red-hot cauldron of the Stade Vélodrome. But stirring themselves again to defeat a far more prosaic, defensive Portuguese team in the colder surrounds of the Stade de France proved too difficult. 'We might have won the final had we played it in Marseille,' Giroud reflects. 'It's impossible to know, but the atmosphere in Paris wasn't the same.' Meanwhile, Stéphan admits, 'We played our final three days too early.'

In truth, *Les Bleus* should really have claimed their third European title. Portugal, who had mustered just one victory inside ninety minutes during their entire stuttering campaign, lost their talisman Ronaldo to injury on twenty-five minutes and did not threaten until the eightieth minute when Lloris clawed away Nani's miscued cross. Griezmann and Giroud both squandered good chances, Rui Patrício performed miracles in the Portugal goal, and André-Pierre Gignac struck the post at the end of normal time.

But with French legs tiring, and with Ronaldo frantically instructing his teammates from the sidelines, Portugal gained the ascendancy. Eder's precise low shot in the 109th minute clinched an historic success for Fernando Santos's team.

The disappointment inside the France dressing room was considerable. But it was not all bad news. Despite coming up short, Deschamps's honest, hard-working and distinctly likeable side had succeeded in lifting the nation from the doldrums. The tournament that much of France had been dreading ended up being an unmitigated success.

With six goals, Griezmann was the Euro 2016 top scorer. He was also voted as the tournament's best player. But it was his attitude as much as his ability that pleased his coaches. 'When you have a player like Antoine, it's a dream,' Guy Stéphan states. 'As well as being a brilliant footballer, he's a competitor. Even if defending isn't the best part of his game, when he's out on the pitch he gives everything to help the team win. It's extremely unusual to have a player of Antoine's calibre who is also prepared to work like crazy. There aren't many like him in the world. And, of course, when the others see how hard Antoine is working, they follow his example.'

Griezmann became the talisman of this deeply refreshing team. *La Génération Griezmann*, as they became known, were a carefree bunch. Above all, this new wave of talent looked happy to be playing for France. In contrast with the moody, misbehaving teams of France's past, this side – packed with cool young cats like Pogba, Kanté, Umtiti and Coman – were easy to like.

Griezmann, of course, was at the heart of it all. His 'telephone call' celebration – which he later explained was a tribute to the American rapper Drake – became an instant hit on playgrounds around the country. Some may have mocked *Les Bleus* for unashamedly stealing Iceland's wonderful 'thunderclap' celebration after their semi-final win, but it created one of the strongest moments France's players had shared with their supporters in a long while. It was hardly surprising to see a grinning Griezmann at the centre of the festivities, gathering the troops in the corner of the Stade Vélodrome to orchestrate the Scandinavian ritual. 'Antoine is always happy when he's with us,' Stéphan says, sounding ever-so-slightly like a proud father. 'He's just a kid who loves football, and he loves making people happy.'

With Deschamps running a tight ship and Griezmann helping transform both the team's image and results, *Les Bleus* looked ready to hit the heights again. Some experts even believed that with the addition of a young, fast, clinical striker, they could on go on to achieve great things.

CHAPTER 18

MBAPPÉ, LE RECORDMAN

Kylian Mbappé commenced the 2016/17 campaign with his motivation levels and ambition sky high. After winning youth tournaments with both AS Monaco and France that summer, he delivered on a promise that he had made to his parents: he passed his *Baccalauréat*. Mbappé did not enjoy studying, that much was clear, but the qualification he secured in 'management of sciences and technologies' served as proof of the intellectual capabilities his teachers knew he had in him.

It also showed that Mbappé gets what he wants when he puts his mind to something. Even before his playing career had taken off, the boy who seemed to have it all mapped out was safeguarding his future. 'I need this diploma for when I've finished playing,' he told *Le Parisien* in January 2017. 'I'd like to be a coach. My dad and uncle have shown me the way, and it's a profession that's always fascinated me.'

Now with the academic side sorted, he could focus his efforts entirely on the life he knew he was destined for: scoring goals, winning trophies and setting records. Mbappé was raring to go. Again, however, nothing would be easy. More obstacles were placed in front of the impatient teenager, and had he been a less forceful, less determined, less talented individual, that season would surely have passed him by.

Monaco boss Leonardo Jardim offered Mbappé an early

boost by starting him alongside Guido Carrillo in the opening fixture against EA Guingamp at the Stade Louis II. But with the hosts trailing 2–0 before half-time, the teenager clashed heads with Guingamp defender Christophe Kerbrat. He was forced off; another young talent, Bernardo Silva, came on in his place, and Monaco rescued a draw. Mbappé, however, suffered bad concussion and had to stay in hospital overnight.

The enforced three-week lay-off that followed frustrated him, but he fully expected to return to the side in September. Jardim, though, had other ideas. During Mbappé's absence, the Portuguese coach struck on a winning formula and places were suddenly hard to come by in his ultra-effective 4–4–2 formation.

With Fabinho making a successful conversion from right-back to central midfield, the Brazilian offered Jardim's team a muscular and athletic core alongside Tiemoué Bakayoko. Thomas Lemar and Bernardo were technical, pacy operators on the flanks, and their penchant for cutting inside opened up space for the full-backs Djibril Sidibé and Benjamin Mendy to roar into. Up front, Jardim had the option of pairing either Valère Germain or Carrillo with Radamel Falcao, or of playing the experienced Portuguese schemer João Moutinho just behind the club captain. The principality outfit stringed together impressive wins against FC Nantes, Paris Saint-Germain, Lille and Rennes, and surged to the top of the table in September.

Most kids would have accepted the situation, trained hard and waited for their opportunity. But Mbappé is not most kids. He was furious at being left out of Monaco's squad entirely for the trip to Wembley to play Tottenham in the Champions League. Mbappé knew he had a chance to beat Karim Benzema's record as the youngest Frenchman to score in the competition, and he does not like missing chances. According to L'Équipe, his disappointment was so great he refused to play in the UEFA Youth League that same day.

The nine minutes that Jardim offered Mbappé at the end of a

league game at FC Metz on 1 October – during which time he set up his side's seventh goal for Gabriel Boschilia – were hardly going to placate the hungry attacker.

Wilfrid Mbappé met Monaco's vice-president Vadim Vasily-ev to express the family's concern, but his son remained on the fringes. Kylian's father decided that some kind of action needed to be taken. So he issued a warning to the club via an interview with *L'Équipe*. 'The current situation is creating frustration and Kylian isn't happy,' Wilfrid declared. 'Some people say he's only seventeen and needs to be patient, but this is not a question of impatience because he was promised by the club he would play. He needs to be playing at his age. We'll have to think things over during the January transfer window.'

It was another example of how Kylian's parents were intent on fighting for their son's success. If Wilfrid's main concern was ensuring his son's career stayed on track, Fayza looked after every other aspect of his upbringing. In *La Chaîne L'Équipe*'s documentary *Kylian Mbappé, Hors Normes* (*Kylian Mbappe, Out of the Ordinary*) the former headteacher of Kylian's prima-ry school Yannick Saint-Aubert tells the story of Fayza erupt-ing when, in 2016, she discovered that her boy was getting his boots cleaned by a Monaco employee. 'Do you realise who this person cleaning your boots is? Never again,' she reportedly said according to Saint-Aubert. 'I forbid you from having somebody else clean your boots. You come from the north of Bondy, from a working-class neighbourhood with strong human values. Don't you start getting into habits like that.'

In November 2016, after his father's public comments, Kylian found himself banished to the Monaco reserves. To his credit, he did not sulk on the away trip to the minnows of Le Pontet. Quite the opposite. He scored two goals and made another, pinging the ball firmly back into the court of Monaco's manage-ment. Jardim handed Mbappé a reprieve, selecting him from the start against Montpellier HSC, and the teenager delivered an emphatic response. Lining up alongside Falcao for the first time, he was devastating. Mbappé won a penalty after burning Ellyes Skhiri for pace, then nodded in Bernardo's searching cross. He later set up Germain to score as Jardim's stylish team romped to a 6–2 triumph.

Jardim was coming under pressure to play the boy every week at this point, but he remained wary of exposing Mbappé too often too soon. 'He's very young,' the coach argued. 'There will be positive periods during which I will play him, but also more difficult times when I'll protect him.' The Portuguese is an expert at nurturing young talent and his 'slowly, slowly' approach worked wonders with the likes of Fabinho, Lemar and Bernardo.

But Mbappé was in a hurry and desperately wanted to play every week. In an interview with Canal Plus in 2018, he revealed just how much it annoyed him when his tender age was offered as a reason for him not playing. 'I've never tolerated people referring to my age,' he said. 'If you're good you play, if you're not good you don't play. Don't talk to me about age. Talk to me about football and [about my] level.'

Invariably when he came off the Monaco bench, he showed the coach what he was missing. During a twenty-seven-minute cameo against AS Nancy, Mbappé scored one and set up another. Then on a rare start before Christmas he registered his first senior hat-trick – three wonderfully clean, clinically taken goals – against Rennes in the Coupe de la Ligue. Watching his first strike that night, it was impossible not to have flashbacks to a young Thierry Henry. Starting from a position on the left, he suddenly darted in behind the defenders and left them for dead as he eased smoothly through the gears, appearing to glide across the turf. Then, in one swift movement, Mbappé opened up his body and placed a shot inside the far post with the inside of his right boot. Twenty years previously, Henry was scoring identical goals on that exact same pitch.

The similarities are uncanny, and they are not restricted to the pitch. Like Henry, Mbappé grew up in the Paris suburbs and learned his trade at Clairefontaine and then Monaco. Both are unfathomably quick, have silky skills and an eye for goal. Just as importantly, both possess strong characters and a fierce determination to succeed. When Henry visited Monaco's training ground that season, and met his protégé for the first time, Mbappé suddenly got all shy. Face to face with one of his role models, the cool swagger disappeared and for once he looked his age. 'It was a special moment,' a chuffed Mbappé told the Monaco TV journalist afterwards. 'He's a childhood idol of mine.'

Ever since France's 1998 exploits, the French media has tried hard to find successors to the individuals that made up that World Cup-winning squad. Mourad Meghni, Yoann Gourcuff, Samir Nasri and Marvin Martin were all billed as the next Zinédine Zidane, only to come up very short. Philippe Cristanval was supposed to be the next Laurent Blanc, and Kurt Zouma got billed as 'the new Marcel Desailly' after joining Chelsea. Ex-French youth international Ricardo Faty, who now represents Senegal, was flattered by the comparisons he drew with Patrick Vieira after signing for AS Roma at nineteen. But they almost certainly did not help him. 'I didn't realise at the time, but I think it does put extra pressure on you,' Faty states pensively. 'People wanted me to be the new Vieira – they maybe even expected me to be the new Vieira. I could sense that, and I ended up disappointing them.'

Mbappé does not seem at all fazed by the Henry comparisons. He looks well equipped to emulate and possibly even surpass France's all-time record goal scorer. But those who played with Henry are not yet totally convinced. 'I hope Mbappé can do as well as Thierry did, I really do, but I have some concerns,' Henry's former Arsenal teammate Emmanuel Petit tells me. 'His strength right now is his spontaneity, his freshness and his pace. But I don't know if he has the technique that will allow him to continue producing these performances over the long term.' Robert Pirès does not need any prompting on the matter. He puts the comparison on the table himself, but claims Henry may have been superior as a boy. 'I had the pleasure of playing with Titi and I can tell you he was doing the same things [as Mbappé] at the age of nineteen,' says Henry's World Cup-winning colleague. 'They're the same players. Titi was probably even better. But I'm not worried about Mbappé. He's going to keep on improving and he'll have a great career.'

Henry was nineteen when he clinched the league title at the Stade Louis II. Mbappé did it a year earlier. By the end of 2016, Monaco were the most prolific side not just in France but in the whole continent, and Jardim's players had all fallen for Mbappé's charm. 'Kylian's already brilliant, and he works hard too,' Bernardo told *L'Équipe*. 'I'm sure he'll reach a very high level.' Benjamin Mendy – who had joined from Marseille the previous summer – was as struck by Mbappé's mentality as much as his ability. 'People told me he's a respectful boy with his head on his shoulders, and that's definitely true,' said the left-back, also in *L'Équipe*. 'When you add in his talent, you get something immense. He's fast, he penetrates, and he can finish. We just try to give him the freedom he needs on the pitch.'

Jardim did his best to keep a lid on expectations but Monaco's secret was now out. In France, at least. On 11 February 2017, Mbappé became the second youngest player to score a Ligue 1 hat-trick, rattling three past FC Metz in the space of forty-two minutes. The media hailed the arrival of a new star, but Mbappé laughed off the superlatives used to describe him. 'I'm not a phenomenon yet,' he told reporters. 'Messi, Ronaldo, Neymar – they're phenomena. I'm still a long way away. It makes me smile when I hear people talking like that.'

He knew he still had so much more to give. The French press were already drooling over him, but Mbappé wanted the world to sit up and take notice. On a windy February night at the Etihad Stadium, he got the chance to show off his skills to a wider public. Mbappé had been used sparingly in the Champions League until then, playing just twenty-five minutes in the group stage, but Jardim sensed the time was right to unleash his eighteen-year-old speedster, picking him from the start against Pep Guardiola's star-studded Manchester City.

What followed was compelling viewing. Nobody had expected Mbappé to start. City's centre-backs John Stones and Nicolás Otamendi certainly looked unprepared as this raw, unknown forward set about making his mark. During an incredible first half, Mbappé sprinted into the channels, flicked passes wide to Lemar and Bernardo, exchanged one-twos with Falcao, and generally frightened the life out of the City defence.

He did everything at breakneck speed, so much so that the television director at the Etihad nearly missed the Frenchman's opening Champions League goal. As TV viewers watched a replay, Mbappé was surging on to a long pass through the middle. The picture switched just in time for the world to see Monaco's number twenty-nine pulling away from Otamendi and crashing an unstoppable shot past Willy Caballero and high into the net to put the visitors 2–1 ahead. The emphatic nature of the finish evoked memories of David Trezeguet, who, at the age of twenty, had struck a similar blow for Monaco just six kilometres up the road at Old Trafford to account for Manchester United.

Mbappé was not as effective in the second half and nor were Monaco. Falcao missed a penalty, then goalkeeper Danijel Subašić gifted City an equaliser by allowing Sergio Agüero's tame shot to pass through his legs. The English side had been let off the hook and they took advantage of Monaco's naivety to run out 5–3 winners in one of the most memorable first legs the Champions League has ever produced. To lose after dominating the contest for so long, Monaco felt downhearted. Yet there was also a sense that with Mbappé in that kind of form they could do remarkable things in the final third of the season.

And so it proved. In the second leg, despite the fact City now knew about Mbappé, they could do little to stop him. Caballero made a superb reflex save to deny the striker on seven minutes at the Stade Louis II, but he was only delaying the inevitable. Seconds later, Mbappé met Bernardo's near-post cross to halve the deficit. Monaco passed the ball quickly and precisely, using the full width of the pitch and pinning City back. Fabinho converted Mendy's cutback, and though Leroy Sané pulled one back, the hosts deservedly went through on away goals after Bakayoko's header made it 6–6 on aggregate.

Mbappé had been brilliant again, and Guardiola took it upon himself to establish some initial friendly contact with the wonderkid after the final whistle. But rather than admiring his own performance, Mbappé watched the game back again with a critical eye, trying to work out what he could have done better. He later said he had been guilty of 'going missing' for long periods during that game. 'When you watch me against Manchester City, you think "Where has Kylian gone?" I'm looking for people in the stands. I'm dreaming, I'm smiling at family and friends,' he told *France Football* magazine. 'I don't do that any more. I'm much more awake and focused.'

The press was far more indulgent. '*Le Magicien*' screamed the front page of *L'Équipe* on 6 March 2017, accompanied by a photo of Mbappé's acrobatic goal against Nantes. But his own demanding attitude was allowing him to push back the boundaries. The youngest player to score in both legs of a Champions League knockout tie, he grabbed two more away to Borussia Dortmund in the quarter-finals. In the return leg, he netted for a fourth consecutive knockout game, becoming the youngest player to reach five Champions League goals, as Monaco ran out emphatic 6–3 victors. Then, at eighteen years, four months and twenty days old, he became the youngest man to find the net in a semi-final, slotting past Gianluigi Buffon at the Juventus Stadium.

Later that year, as the records kept on tumbling, Mbappé offered a fascinating insight into his insatiable attitude to football. 'I just want to give my all for the team every day and enjoy myself out on the pitch, because first and foremost football is a pleasure,' he told Canal Plus. 'Beating records is what animates me, so I'm very happy at the moment. I always assume that someone else will come along one day and do even better than me. So you have to aim as high as possible because there'll always be someone else.'

Monaco were knocked out by the Italian side despite Mbappé's goal in Turin, but nothing could stand in the way of their eighth domestic league triumph and the first in seventeen years. They roared to the title by finishing with twelve consecutive victories, thanks in no small part to Mbappé's brilliance. Despite his struggles in the early months, he finished the campaign with twenty-six goals, fifteen of them in Ligue 1. Factoring in his eight league assists, he was involved in a goal every sixty-five minutes on average, a statistic that only Lionel Messi could better in Europe's top five leagues.

'But this boy is so much more impressive than any statistic,' wrote *L'Équipe* the day after Monaco won the league title. There was a sense that you had to see him to believe him. I had the pleasure of commentating on Monaco's title-clinching victory over Saint-Étienne for the global television audience. Besides the incredible goal he scored that night – tearing onto Falcao's through-pass, accelerating clear and dribbling around Stéphane Ruffier, all at lightning pace, before slotting the ball home – Mbappé stood out through his calmness and composure. At the full-time whistle, as the likes of Mendy, Bernardo and Bakayoko cavorted wildly about the Stade Louis II pitch, the eighteen-year-old just walked around contentedly, waving to friends and soaking everything up. When a reporter asked him if he intended to celebrate in the nightclubs of Monte Carlo, he replied with a serious edge: 'No, we still have a game to play against Rennes this weekend. We need to recuperate.' Mendy – who quite possibly had other plans – confirmed on social media that Kylian was having an early night. 'He's got school tomorrow,' the defender cheekily tweeted.

There would be no tweeting from Kylian that evening. Indeed, when the players gathered on a stage that had been rapidly installed on the pitch for the official trophy ceremony, he was the only Monaco player not carrying a mobile phone. 'Everyone has his own way,' Mbappé later said on TF1. 'I just wanted to take everything in. The club staged an amazing party with fireworks. I didn't see the point in having my phone.'

Mbappé spoke and acted in a way that belied his tender age. Deschamps had no qualms about calling him up to France's senior squad in March 2017, despite the fact he was only eighteen and had not yet featured for the under-21s. Olivier Giroud remembers the first time he met his future attacking partner at Clairefontaine. 'I could see he was very mature for a kid of his age,' Giroud recalls. 'He was cool and expressed himself very easily with the other guys. He has this self-confidence and that is a real asset.'

The debutant nearly scored with his first touch after coming on against Luxembourg, but the goalkeeper Jonathan Joubert pulled off a fine save. 'Zizou scored in his first game, but I didn't manage it,' Mbappé noted afterwards with genuine frustration. He did, though, look totally at ease on the international stage. In his second start, against England in June, Mbappé – along with fellow youngster Ousmane Dembélé – repeatedly cut swathes through the Three Lions, despite Gareth Southgate opting for three centre-backs. 'Southgate had Phil Jones, John Stones and Gary Cahill in central defence but they all suffered against the speed and directness of Mbappé and Dembélé,' noted Daniel Taylor in *The Guardian*.

Mbappé hit the crossbar and was denied his first France goal by some fine saves from Tom Heaton in the first half and Jack Butland in the second. *Les Bleus* played with ten men for most of the second period, after Varane was sent off, but still dominated and Mbappé was rewarded for his hard work when he set up Démbélé to seal a 3–2 friendly victory.

The English press watched on with envy as the depth of French talent became apparent. 'England lost to ten-man opposition because they simply could not cope with the speed and ability of two rising superstars in Kylian Mbappé and Ousmane Dembélé,' Jason Burt wrote in the *Telegraph*. 'The youthful forwards ripped through the heart of Southgate's side. It was, at times, awesome, and almost unstoppable... Dembélé, Mbappé, Lemar, Kanté, Mendy, Sidibé and Pogba – woof – looked like they were playing a different sport at times.' The newspaper's chief sports writer Paul Hayward looked at the bigger picture, tweeting: 'France provided seventy-five players in this season's Champions League (number one supplier). Amazing production line, as we saw in that England game.' 'France, to put it bluntly, were a cut above,' concluded Daniel Taylor.

It was obvious that Didier Deschamps had a glittering array of talent to choose from, and that the 2018 World Cup squad would be his strongest yet. Managing those kids, however, could prove a challenge. They were brilliant with a ball at their feet, but they could also be impatient and impetuous. 'Kylian and Ousmane are part of this exciting new generation,' Deschamps's assistant Guy Stéphan says. 'We also have guys like Anthony Martial and Jonathan Ikoné. In France, we say that they are from "Generation Z". These are kids who are connected, confident and unafraid. They're very creative, but they also have a tendency to switch off. You have to keep your team talks short or you lose them. What I like is their confidence. They have fantastic dribbling skills and they don't worry if they mess something up. They just try again and again.'

• • •

Mbappé's emergence in the 2016/17 campaign would both directly and indirectly transform the Ligue 1 landscape. Until then, PSG had been dominating the domestic scene with consummate ease. The previous year they clinched their fourth straight league title by finishing thirty-one points clear of second-placed Lyon. But Jardim's wonderfully balanced, technical and quick side were worthy champions. Furthermore, Monaco had not only shown PSG up at home, they had outdone them in Europe too.

When the Qatar Sports Investments group purchased the capital club in 2011, their stated aim was to win the Champions League within five years. But despite spending close to €1 billion on established talents like Zlatan Ibrahimović, Thiago Silva, Edinson Cavani and Thiago Motta, they were yet to get past the quarter-final stage. That Monaco had just reached the last four of the competition – and had done so with a Paris-born teenage dynamo at the forefront of the team – did not go down well in Doha.

PSG's European failures were now recurrent and increasingly spectacular. One particularly humbling night at the Camp Nou sent shockwaves across the Mediterranean and Arabian Seas all the way to Qatar. On 8 March 2017, PSG were dumped out at the last-sixteen stage in the most implausible, humiliating circumstances by Barcelona. Unai Emery's side had won the first leg 4–0 at the Parc des Princes, and were still 5–3 up on aggregate in the eighty-eighth minute of the second leg. Then the sky fell in. They conceded three late goals and crashed out. 'This is a nightmare for us,' PSG's shell-shocked president Nasser Al-Khelaifi told reporters. 'I still can't believe it.'

This was not the scenario Qatar's royal family had envisaged. Not by a long shot. The oil- and gas-rich nation had injected huge sums into the club with the aim of turning an underachieving team into a superpower that enjoys regular Champions League success and generates a glamorous, unanimously positive image for Qatar. 'Why did Qatar buy PSG? What are they looking for?' mused geopolitical expert Pascal Boniface in an interview with French daily *Les Echos*. 'They are looking for visibility, they want to protect themselves. Instead of investing in weapons, they are investing in sport. It's a long-term strategy.'

PSG's capitulation in Barcelona was the kind of visibility Qatar could have done without. They had embarrassed themselves in front of an enormous global audience. 'The PSG brand has become synonymous with failure,' the journalist Vincent Duluc wrote in *L'Équipe*. 'There was no point rising this high merely to sink so very low. The entire Qatari project is under threat.' It possibly already was. The year before, Manchester City accounted for the French club in the Champions League, this time in the quarter-finals, and the experience was just as chastening for PSG's head honcho, the Emir of Qatar Sheikh Tamim bin Hamad Al Thani. City are owned by Qatar's neighbour Abu Dhabi, and if there is one opponent Al Thani did not want to lose to it was the English side.

The City defeat cost Qatar credibility, but for Al Thani the now infamous *remontada* (comeback) in Barcelona proved the tipping point. It was one public humiliation too many and would have far-reaching consequences. Exactly one month after the Barcelona defeat, the Emir himself paid a surprise visit to PSG's training ground. His message to PSG's top brass was clear: plan A isn't working so let's move on to plan B, and let's get it right this time. According to an unnamed former PSG director quoted in *Le Monde* newspaper, Al Thani was fuming and told his close friend Al-Khelaifi that there was no more room for error. 'The Emir said: "I don't care about these [UEFA Financial Fair Play] regulations. Find a way around them. We have to break the bank. We need something to lift Qatar, to show Qatar in a positive light."'

Qatar's image suffered a further blow in June 2017 after this small but powerful nation of 2.6 million inhabitants was plunged into a diplomatic crisis and cut off from its Arab neighbours. This grave situation merely strengthened Al Thani's resolve to shift the world's media spotlight towards matters far more pleasant: namely by splashing an astonishing and unprecedented sum of more than €400 million on two football players.

PSG effectively set their sights on the two individuals who had been most central to their problems. Neymar – Barcelona's freakishly skilled Brazilian superstar – arrived first. 'The transfer of the century,' as *Le Parisien* called it, had the desired impact, creating a wave of excitement in France and stunning the world of football. What better way to gain revenge for the Camp Nou drubbing than by poaching the chief instigator that night from under the noses of the Catalans?

The €222 million that PSG paid to secure the 25-year-old forward – tipped at the time by most experts to become football's next megastar after Lionel Messi and Cristiano Ronaldo – raised many eyebrows. PSG, after all, had been fined €60 million by UEFA in 2014 for failing to comply with Financial Fair Play Regulations, and European football's governing body warned them that their annual operating deficit would not be allowed to exceed €30 million a year.

The Neymar fee more than doubled the previous world record – set by Manchester United when they bought Paul Pogba in 2016 – and had Europe's traditional powers Barcelona, Bayern Munich, Real Madrid and Juventus up in arms. The Spanish League even refused to accept PSG's money, insisting that they were breaching UEFA rules. This merely delayed the Brazilian's debut by a week, *Le Monde* explaining that a solution was found after the sum was eventually transferred to Barcelona by Neymar's entourage.

Yet incredibly, while the rest of Europe complained, PSG were working busily behind the scenes to secure a second almighty coup.

Kylian Mbappé had no intention of leaving Monaco in 2017 having so far enjoyed only six months as a first-choice player. When PSG's freshly appointed sporting director Antero Henrique met Mbappé's father in Bondy on his first day in the role on 2 June, he was told that the striker was staying in the Côte d'Azur for another year at least. 'If Kylian changes his mind, PSG will still be there,' Henrique told Wilfrid, according to *Le Parisien*.

In Mbappé's mind, one full season at Monaco, where he felt happy and settled in a pressure-free environment, was the best possible way to prepare for the 2018 World Cup. Monaco, apparently, felt the same way. 'Today we're capable of refusing a €130 million offer for Kylian because the project has changed since 2014 and our financial position is no longer the same,' vowed Vasilyev. 'We'll have a calm discussion with the family, but the idea is that he stays and that's what we're working towards.'

Those comments did not deter Europe's biggest clubs. City boss Pep Guardiola, Liverpool manager Jürgen Klopp and Arsenal's Arsène Wenger all expressed their interest and reportedly held talks with Wilfrid. Real Madrid coach Zinédine Zidane even spoke directly to Kylian on the phone. Inevitably the striker, who worships Zidane and grew up dreaming of playing for Real Madrid, was deeply flattered. But Arnaud Hermant revealed in his book *Mbappé: Le Phénomène* that Zidane inadvertently planted seeds of doubt in Mbappé's mind by suggesting that he would have to bide his time to win his place in a side that already included Ronaldo, Benzema and Gareth Bale.

PSG remained in close contact. They had a trump card in the form of Marc Westerloppe, who was now PSG's head of youth recruitment. Westerloppe knew Wilfrid well. When he worked for RC Lens, he had come close to bringing Kylian to the northern club before he joined Clairefontaine back in 2011. With Westerloppe's help, another meeting was arranged for 7 July, this time in the Mbappé family home. Unai Emery was present, along with Henrique, and the Spanish coach assured Kylian that he would be a first-choice player at the Parc des Princes. Henrique, meanwhile, divulged that both Dani Alves and Neymar would also be Paris-bound that summer. When Alves completed a switch from Juventus just days later, the Mbappé family were impressed.

But as pre-season commenced, Kylian was committed to having another season at Monaco. Little did he know that Monaco's stance was changing. The club's Russian billionaire owner Dmitry Rybolovlev, who had suffered an extremely costly divorce in 2015, was seemingly ready to cash in on the prodigy. A fee of €180 million had even been agreed with Real Madrid without the Mbappés' knowledge, and Leonardo Jardim was charged with the task of informing Kylian that he would be allowed to leave. According to *L'Équipe* journalist Hermant, the youngster was dumbfounded when his coach broke the news to him on 16 July during a training camp in the Swiss Alps. He had not seen Monaco's U-turn coming and he felt let down by Jardim. Above all, he was not prepared to allow somebody else to make such a big decision for him.

The succeeding weeks would be tense. Mbappé was now intent on leaving Monaco, a desire that was only strengthened by the subsequent sales of Bernardo, Bakayoko and one of Kylian's closest friends, Benjamin Mendy. But he did not want to join Real Madrid. Not yet anyway. At the very least, he wanted to have a full season in Ligue 1 first. When Neymar signed for PSG and started sending Mbappé text messages urging the Frenchman to join him, the idea of returning to his hometown became more appealing.

Monaco were extremely reluctant to sell to PSG and thus strengthen their domestic rival, but with the player determined to leave, and to choose his own destination, they had a weak hand. Mbappé was picked for the first game of Monaco's title defence, a 3–2 win over Toulouse, but after that the directors instructed Jardim not to play the restless attacker. The sums of money being discussed were far too great to risk an injury.

Nasser Al-Khelaifi made several trips to Monaco, and it is believed that a breakthrough in negotiations was achieved on 24 August when PSG's president was in the principality for the Champions League draw. Crucially, Monaco had agreed to an initial season-long loan of Mbappé to PSG with an (unofficial) obligation to buy for €135 million plus €45 million in bonuses the following summer. That way the transfer fee could be included in PSG's accounts for the 2018/19 season, offering them a more realistic chance of complying with Financial Fair Play Regulations in 2017/18.

The five-year contract, which was masterfully negotiated by Mbappé's parents without interference from agents or lawyers, made Kylian the richest eighteen-year-old in sport. His annual salary, estimated to be just over €20 million a year, was superior to Paul Pogba's at Manchester United. Indeed, Antoine Griezmann, who had recently extended his contract with Atlético Madrid, was now the only Frenchman earning more than the new PSG man.

The French club's second eye-watering transfer of the summer was confirmed on 31 August during the final hours of the window. Mbappé celebrated the news by scoring his first goal in a France shirt later that evening, coming off the bench to seal a superb 4–0 victory over the Netherlands. Asked by reporters at the Stade de France if it had been a dream day, a relaxed Mbappé said: 'I'm not sure what a dream day is, but this has certainly been a good one. It's got close.' He was taking everything in his stride.

Six days later, his remarkable poise in front of the cameras and his warm, natural smile charmed the hordes of journalists, supporters and tourists who had gathered at the Parc des Princes for his glitzy presentation. 'It's a great pleasure for me to be joining one of the best clubs in the world,' started Mbappé, looking the part in a slim-fitting suit and black tie. 'This is an ambitious club that's putting together a plan to become the very best. That's what seduced me. It was also important for me to stay in France after playing for just six months at the top level. I wanted to come back home, to the town I grew up in. With hard work and humility, we'll be able to achieve our goal of winning lots of trophies, including the club's ultimate dream: the Champions League.'

Al-Khelaifi hailed the capture as great news for Ligue 1. But with Monaco losing so many fine players and PSG acquiring two of the best around, many observers worried about the competitiveness of the league. PSG were already top of the table by the end of August having won all four games, scoring fourteen goals in the process. When Mbappé made his debut away to FC Metz in September, lining up alongside seasoned internationals in Neymar, Edinson Cavani and Julian Draxler, the one-sided nature of the contest confirmed those fears. Mbappé scored and the visitors won 5-1 at a canter.

PSG's formidable front-three of Mbappé, Cavani and Neymar, or 'the MCN' as they became known, were irresistible. Mbappé was positioned on the right flank, with Cavani providing power, movement and a constant goal threat through the middle, and Neymar drifting in from the left flank, often to devastating effect. Indeed, the Brazilian's first steps in the French league were majestic. He scored three and made three more in his first two outings, leaving opponents in awe. 'I didn't realise he was that good,' Guingamp midfielder Lucas Deaux enthused after Neymar's debut. '€222 million seems like a bargain to me.'

Mbappé looked energised when he was around Neymar, a player he had admired from a distance over a number of years. He was happy to play second fiddle to the former Santos man that season, invariably looking up and seeking out his teammate as soon as he got the ball. 'It's true that I have a great understanding with Neymar, both on and off the pitch,' said Mbappé in an interview with *France Football* magazine. 'When I first arrived in Paris, there was no debate. He was the superstar and I had come to support him, to help him.'

With Neymar leading the charge, PSG blew their opponents away both at home and in Europe. They set a new Champions League record by scoring twenty-five goals in the group stage, with 'the MCN' contributing sixteen of them. Mbappé set more records, establishing himself as PSG's youngest Champions League scorer and becoming the youngest man ever to hit ten goals in the competition. Frustratingly for the fans, they came up short again in the last sixteen, this time losing to the eventual winners Real Madrid. But domestically PSG were untouchable. Emery's charges won the treble, registering an unbelievable total of 171 goals in all competitions.

Mbappé had enjoyed a fine season overall, and his medal collection was already mightily impressive. But by his own lofty standards, his statistics were not so great. The Frenchman's thirteen league goals were only good enough to secure thirteenth position in the scoring charts, and his overall tally of twenty-one strikes in all competitions was dwarfed by Cavani's forty and Neymar's twenty-eight.

The fact that he had to adapt to a new position and a new team almost certainly slowed him down. But Mbappé believes there was a psychological aspect too. 'When you are seventeen or eighteen, you don't quite dare to finish off all your actions because you haven't shown anything yet. You haven't yet earned that right,' he remarked to *France Football* magazine. 'It's important to respect a certain form of hierarchy, and that means giving the ball to the strongest players.' As a result of this altruism, he had to settle for the prize of 'Best Young Player' in Ligue 1 and the 'Golden Boy' award in Europe. Mbappé finished seventh in the 2017 Ballon d'Or rankings, becoming the youngest man ever to make the top ten. But there was still room for improvement – and in 2018 he had every intention of upping the ante.

CHAPTER 19

CHAMPIONS DU MONDE...
ENCORE!

18 JUNE 2018

It is Monday morning and the France players are looking pleased with themselves as they file into the video room at the team's World Cup base camp in Istra, a small town situated 70km north-west of Moscow. *Les Bleus* have just got their World Cup campaign off to a winning start, edging past Australia 2–1 in a tight encounter in Kazan. Jokes are being told and life inside the France camp for once feels rosy.

Then Didier Deschamps stands up, puts on his glasses and starts to talk. 'I hope you all slept well,' the manager says sternly. 'We're going to look back at our last game, starting with the negatives and moving on to the positives. You won't be surprised to hear that the first part is going to be much longer than the second.'

Over the next few minutes, Deschamps delivers a brutal assessment of the team's performance. In the pictures captured by TF1's documentary *Les Bleus 2018: Au Cœur de L'Epopée Russe* (*The Blues: At the Heart of the Russian Adventure*) it is obvious the players are hanging on his every word. 'Let's start with the stats,' Deschamps begins as a concerned silence descends on the room. 'Total distance run by Australia's players: just over 111km. Distance run by us: 102km. So, it was like they had an extra man. Five Australians ran more than ten kilometres in the game. We had just one player do that, and it's no surprise who,' Deschamps says, nodding towards N'Golo Kanté.

France's 1998 World Cup-winning captain is just warming up. His next offensive is aimed at his most junior player, the new golden boy of French football: 'Let's look at the number of sprints made at over 20km/h, also known as "high-intensity sprints". They did twice as many as us and they ran twice as far. In our team, Kylian is the player who did the fewest: 3 per cent. And I thought speed was your strength?' Deschamps quips, glaring at Mbappé, who, unflinchingly, returns the look.

Mbappé had actually started the game brightly, forcing Maty Ryan into a save after just ninety-three seconds. But the youngest Frenchman ever to appear in a World Cup at nineteen years and six months old gradually disappeared without trace, along with fellow attackers Ousmane Dembélé and Antoine Griezmann.

By dropping Olivier Giroud, and opting for a faster, younger, more mobile front-three, Deschamps had picked the team that most supporters and the media were clamouring for. The tactic had worked well on the few occasions that he had tried it in the past. Against England, in 2017, Mbappé flourished when playing through the middle with Giroud. Then, in March 2018, Deschamps picked the teenager as his main centre-forward for the first time away to Russia. Mbappé was superb, scoring twice in the 3–1 win.

At Monaco, he had excelled in a central role alongside Radamel Falcao, but Mbappé was employed mainly on the right wing by Unai Emery at Paris Saint-Germain. Responding to Deschamps's assertion that he can be effective in a variety of positions, Mbappé stated before the World Cup that he would prefer to have a more clearly defined role. 'For now I can fill in

wherever, but at some point I'll need to specialise in one position,' he told Canal Plus.

Yet it was his change in behaviour since joining PSG that
was more concerning than his change in position. There was
a feeling that the big-money move to the capital had gone to
his head, and what's more, his admiration for Neymar, and his
desire to try to emulate the Brazilian on the pitch, was detract-
ing from his game. 'He spends every day playing and training
with Neymar and this worries me,' Emmanuel Petit says with a
furrowed brow when I speak to him in Paris. 'There are things
I've noticed that I've not liked. It looks like he wants to play
like Neymar, but that's not his game. When he gets the ball, he
always wants to do something fancy – a flick or a backheel. But
that's Neymar, it's not Mbappé. Kylian's game is about speed and
finishing. He needs to focus on that.'

Against Australia, Mbappé started on the right, with Dembélé wide left, and Griezmann playing as a false nine. He was
given a licence to roam, though, and spent much of the game in
a central area. The trouble is, so did Dembélé and Griezmann.
Les Bleus had no width, and with the Socceroos sitting deep,
the French forwards were denied space. They posed virtually no threat to the side that were ranked thirty-sixth in the
world. 'The movement and body language of the front three
was abject,' observed the match report in *L'Équipe*. 'The paucity
of the performance was inversely proportional to the level of
their talent.'

When Mbappé is denied space, he can get frustrated and
the flaws in his game rise to the surface. The longer the contest
went on, the more uninterested he appeared and his reluctance
to track back and fight for the team became increasingly apparent. Hugo Lloris was the busier of the keepers in the first
half, but France got the break they needed when Griezmann
was adjudged to have been fouled by Josh Risdon following the
first-ever use of VAR at a World Cup. Yet even after Griezmann

converted, a careless handball from Samuel Umtiti gifted Australia a penalty and an equaliser.

The intensity of France's play changed when Blaise Matuidi and Giroud came on in the latter stages. At last, they had some drive in midfield and a focal point in attack. Unsurprisingly, Giroud was involved in the winning goal, exchanging passes with Pogba whose shot looped up off Aziz Behich, struck the underside of the bar and bounced fractionally over the goal-line.

It was a win, but France had been underwhelming and unimpressive. Deschamps knew his side would not go far playing in such a pedestrian manner, and he set about drilling the message home inside the video room in Istra. His strong words were greeted mainly with silence, although Pogba did speak up when the manager accused his players of 'strolling' about. 'In the first half we didn't know when we were supposed to press,' the Manchester United midfielder complained. Deschamps raised his eyebrows and responded curtly. 'We didn't do it. We didn't do enough of it. I can spend the next hour showing you if you like, Paul, but I don't want to see one person laughing.'

For many years, the French national team lacked a figure of authority. Young, talented millionaire footballers did not respect Raymond Domenech, a manager who had won nothing at the highest level. Laurent Blanc had the aura, and the playing record, but his laid-back attitude ultimately offered the players too much leeway. Deschamps was different. From the moment he arrived and stated in his first press conference that only 'exemplary behaviour' would be accepted from his players, the boundaries had been clear. Mbappé could have reacted badly to Deschamps's criticism. Being singled out like that in front of your teammates cannot have been pleasant. But Mbappé respects Deschamps. He may not have been born when the France legend lifted the World Cup – and was not even a glint in his parents' eyes when Deschamps clinched the Champions League as Olympique de Marseille skipper in 1993 – but the

PSG star knows his football. He knows it is impossible to be as successful as Deschamps, to play at the highest level in France, Italy, England and Spain for nearly two decades, without possessing special qualities. He sees how the likes of Pogba and Griezmann listen when Deschamps talks, and he too is open to the coach's advice.

'The coach put his finger on what wasn't right,' Mbappé says in the TF1 documentary. 'The team hadn't done what he'd asked for and expected, so his reaction was normal. The whole of France saw the game. We hadn't represented the country well. We didn't give everything we had. We're capable of playing better than that, so we had to ask questions of ourselves straight away and do better.'

Deschamps's assistant Guy Stéphan is convinced that the post-Australia team meeting played a key part in France's success. They had won but the players were not allowed to sit back and relax – and Mbappé, in particular, seemed to heed Deschamps's advice.

'Kylian needs to be brought into line sometimes because he's very young,' Stéphan tells me when we meet in Paris in December 2019. 'People forget how quickly he's risen. He started at sixteen and he's won trophies everywhere he's been. It's a fantastic story but he needs to digest all of that. He has a lot of qualities, but also points to work on like his heading and his left foot. He needs to be made aware of certain things and Didier helped him in that respect. There's a close relationship between the two of them. Kylian is very respectful towards Didier. He listens to him.'

The fact is these days the France players know that if they do not toe the party line they will simply not be picked. It does not matter how good an individual is, how many trophies he has won with his club and how much money he earns, if he does not put the team first at all times, Deschamps will ignore him. During Deschamps's playing days, Aimé Jacquet dispensed with Éric Cantona and David Ginola, and France still won the World Cup.

Now in the role of team selector, Deschamps shares those same collective values as Jacquet. 'Didier's philosophy is clear: the star is the team,' Stéphan stresses. 'He always picks very, very good players – that much is given – but it is true to say they don't have to be the best players. You need to find players who can live together for a month and who'll always act for the good of the team.' When I suggest that Deschamps shies away from working with difficult, characterful individuals, Stéphan disagrees. 'We have strong characters,' he counters. 'Paul Pogba is a strong character. So long as the player respects the team, respects the rules of the team, it's not a problem for Didier. Even if he has a strong personality.'

When Deschamps named his World Cup squad, he ignored an extraordinary array of elite talent. In the attacking sector alone, Karim Benzema (Real Madrid), Alexandre Lacazette (Arsenal), Anthony Martial (Manchester United) and Kingsley Coman (Bayern Munich) all missed out. Nobody had expected the coach to offer Benzema a reprieve in the aftermath of the sex-tape scandal, but when the Real Madrid striker won the Champions League again in May 2018, certain critics raised their voices once more. Christophe Dugarry, the ex-France attacker, was the most outspoken, accusing his former team-mate of 'taking the France team hostage' by continuing to hold a grudge. 'We have a centre-forward who's won four Champions League trophies, but he doesn't play because he spoke badly of Deschamps,' Dugarry said incredulously on RMC radio. 'He says it's in the best interests of the France team. Well I think it's in Deschamps's best interests, not the team's, to leave Benzema out.'

Coman's injury problems went some way to explaining his absence, but Lacazette and Martial were fighting fit and were left feeling hard done by. In his last game under Deschamps,

Lacazette had scored both France's goals in a 2–2 draw away to world champions Germany. But evidently the coach had seen something he did not like. Had Lacazette shown a poor attitude in training or complained about spending time sitting on the bench? Deschamps would not say, but it seemed obvious that Lacazette's attitude was a primary factor.

In Deschamps's eyes, Lyon's softly spoken captain Nabil Fekir and Marseille's well-liked winger Florian Thauvin were far less likely to rock the boat than Lacazette or Martial if they had to remain on the substitutes' bench. The coach desperately wanted a happy camp in Russia, and the inclusion of Marseille stopper Adil Rami – an extremely funny, popular, larger-than-life character – showed just how far he was prepared to go in the name of team spirit. Rami was nowhere near as quick, mobile or dependable as Manchester City's Aymeric Laporte, but with Raphaël Varane, Umtiti and PSG's Presnel Kimpembe all ahead of him in the pecking order, he was unlikely to play anyway. Rami's primary value would be his presence in the dressing room rather than on the pitch.

Likewise few considered Steven N'Zonzi to be a more gifted central midfielder than Adrien Rabiot. Deschamps, however, had grown tired of the PSG player's complaints and did not believe his France displays matched those with his club. When Rabiot turned in a poor performance after coming off the bench in Bulgaria, he disappointed Deschamps with his excuses. 'It was quite hard because it was cold and I wasn't warm,' he said. 'I was scared of injuring myself.' In the past, Rabiot had complained about being used as a holding midfielder for PSG. Deschamps decided former Blackburn Rovers and Stoke City man N'Zonzi would be the safer option as back-up for Kanté.

Rabiot was nevertheless included on a list of eleven standby players. Those players were allowed to go on holiday but were asked to keep in shape in case there was an injury. Rabiot decided that such a role was beneath him. He sent an email to the FFF informing Deschamps he would not be adhering to the request. 'Since my first call-up, I've played eighty-eight matches for PSG, a big European club, including thirteen in the Champions League,' he later posted on Instagram. 'I've scored nine goals and won seven trophies ... There is no sporting logic behind the coach's choice.' Laporte was among those to support Rabiot's stance, posting an emoji applauding the statement. Deschamps probably felt that his choices were vindicated.

This fresh controversy could have cast a shadow over France's preparations. When President Emmanuel Macron commented on Rabiot's position, and television shows began debating his decision to exclude himself, it felt like a return to the dark old days. But Deschamps acted quickly and decisively. On the first day of France's World Cup training camp at Clairefontaine, he delivered a withering verdict. 'I can understand his immense disappointment but not his actions,' Deschamps said. 'This is a 23-year-old with a few caps who has decided to exclude himself. He's made an enormous error. Hopefully it will help him grow up and think. When you play at the highest level, you can't allow emotions to take over.' The message was unequivocal, and it ended the discussion.

For a professional footballer, playing in a World Cup is *the* pinnacle. That Rabiot had sabotaged even a slender chance of fulfilling that ambition incensed Deschamps. It was impossible for him to comprehend.

Later that evening, the coach switched the players' attentions away from Rabiot and towards a far more unfortunate absentee. As they took their places at the dinner table, they each found a copy of a letter on their plates. It had been written by Laurent Koscielny, the Arsenal centre-back whose ankle injury had cruelly cost him his place in Russia. 'Take the time to read it,' Deschamps said soberly. 'There are important messages in there about team spirit.' Koscielny's words touched the players deeply and served as a timely reminder of how fortunate they were to be representing their country.

Deschamps was moulding the mentality of his players. The teams of France's recent past had unquestionably been hampered by individualistic mindsets. But the current cohort appeared to understand that the collective had to come first. Mbappé confirmed as much in an interview with *Le Parisien* in May 2018. 'When I was younger, I desperately wanted to win the Ballon d'Or,' he said. 'But my priority has switched to collective prizes. There is nothing better than sharing a trophy with your teammates. Would I swap a Ballon d'Or for the World Cup? Oh yes, of course! I'd happily give the Ballon d'Or away for a World Cup or a Champions League trophy.'

Deschamps wanted his players to be more acutely aware of the weight of responsibility that comes with pulling on the blue shirt. Back in the Domenech era, they were in a bubble and totally cut off from the public. In 2018, it was different. Open training sessions were held at Clairefontaine, and in Nice and Lyon where *Les Bleus* played their final warm-up games, which were concluded by lengthy autograph sessions with fans.

The day after they arrived at their base camp in Russia, twenty-three travelling France fans were invited to the hotel to spend time with the twenty-three players. The squad's accommodation in Istra contrasted sharply with the luxurious, isolated palaces of past tournaments. This four-star hotel was comparatively basic, but the rooms were comfortable and the staff friendly. The team was greeted by some traditional Russian dancing when they arrived. The bedroom doors had a portrait of each player painted on them, and they were presented with personalised Russian dolls. It may sound trivial, but this would be their home for five weeks. 'You need to find the right balance,' Stéphan explains. 'You need the place to be calm, but you don't want it to be cold and lonely. The hotel in Istra was a warm, happy place. When we played a game in Kazan or Moscow, the guys were all really happy to be going back. They felt good there, they felt they belonged. The staff were amazingly friendly, and the day we left they all cried.'

France's growing unity was evident in their second game against Peru. Deschamps reinstated Matuidi and Giroud – two players renowned for their battling qualities – and altered the shape to a 4–2–3–1. Matuidi's industry on the left flank offered balance and allowed Pogba more possibilities to make forward raids from his starting position alongside Kanté in central midfield. Griezmann and Mbappé linked up effectively with the ever-available Giroud, and *Les Bleus* dominated in the first half.

They were rewarded on thirty-four minutes when Pogba won possession high up the pitch and threaded a pass through for Giroud. His shot deflected over the goalkeeper and may have been going in, but Mbappé made sure, gratefully side-footing home from one metre out. It was a big moment for the nineteen-year-old. Not only had he become France's youngest goal scorer at a major tournament, he had also provided a positive response to his demanding manager.

Deschamps had been on Mbappé's case ever since the Australia game, reminding him repeatedly of his defensive responsibilities during training sessions and bellowing a steady flow of instructions at him during that first half against Peru in Yekaterinburg. Mbappé was intelligent enough to realise that Deschamps's ranting was for his own good. 'We were five metres away from each other, so I was the one he shouted at,' Mbappé later told *France Football* magazine. 'I was on the receiving end during every game, and in the debriefs afterwards. But he knows he can lay into me. I take it well. I understood that it was for my good and for the good of the team. If him shouting at me for the whole ninety minutes means the other guys are left in peace, then that's not a problem.'

Les Bleus were under the cosh in the second half. Peru, cheered on by their 25,000 enthusiastic fans, had to score to avoid elimination and they threw everything they had at Deschamps's team. Pedro Aquino struck the woodwork with a blistering strike on fifty minutes, but after that scare France rolled their sleeves up and resisted admirably. The 1–0 triumph represented another slender success, and again it had not been pretty, but this performance had been far more intense and cohesive than the first.

Just like in 1998, France had sealed early qualification to the knockout stages, and as twenty years previously they were able to rotate the line-up against Denmark. But if Jacquet's charges had defeated the Scandinavians 2–1 in an entertaining encounter thanks to goals from Youri Djorkaeff and Emmanuel Petit, Deschamps's men played out a stiflingly dull goalless draw in Moscow. The result did secure them first place, but the large following of French fans were furious with the flat, uninspiring nature of the display. They roundly booed their own players at the end of the game, and the debate with regards to Deschamps's conservative managerial style reappeared.

In truth, it had never been far from the surface. France had qualified for Russia by limping through a relatively straightforward group. After losing in Sweden and, most shockingly of all, drawing 0–0 at home to Luxembourg, they ground out single-goal victories over Bulgaria and Belarus to book their place at the World Cup. The critics asked how a nation blessed with so many sparkling attacking players could produce such a prosaic team. When, two weeks before the World Cup started, Zinédine Zidane stunned everybody by resigning as Real Madrid manager, most of France thought he would be replacing Deschamps after the tournament.

France's round of sixteen tie against Argentina was make or break. Deschamps appeared tenser than usual during his pre-match press conference in Kazan. As the coach and his captain Hugo Lloris offered a series of dry, uninteresting responses to the world's media, the UK journalist sitting next to me stifled a yawn. 'There's only one thing more boring than a France match,' he said. 'And that's a France press conference.'

It is fair to say that Deschamps's reputation outside France is not especially glamourous. The English struggle to understand how players like Moussa Sissoko and Giroud get picked consistently while Laporte and Lacazette are ignored. The Spanish are convinced he has a personal issue with Benzema. The rest just find his defensive approach tedious.

But ask his players what they think and the responses are unanimous. Giroud even looks slightly annoyed when I suggest Deschamps is not held in the highest esteem on the English side of the Channel. 'I'm not on social media so I don't know what people are saying, but sometimes my mates tell me about stuff,' he begins, frustrated by the suggestion that Deschamps could still have critics. 'For me, the most important thing is what happens on the pitch. The best way to respond to all those people who like to comment, to all of these pseudo-experts, is to win football matches. Maybe our style doesn't seduce the specialists, but we've shown other virtues: solidarity and cohesion. These virtues are indispensable if you want to win a major tournament.'

Glancing out of the window, perhaps to check his manager Frank Lampard is not walking past, the Chelsea forward suggests the foreign criticism of Deschamps's side might be fuelled by envy. 'England and Belgium have apparently had golden generations,' the striker says. 'But what have they won? England were eliminated from Euro 2016 by Iceland. The day those countries win something we can give them recognition. Didier has detractors because of certain choices he made, but who can legitimately criticise him today? Only three people have won the World Cup as a player and a coach: Mário Zagallo, Franz Beckenbauer and Didier Deschamps. I just think there are just a lot of jealous people. But the facts are there. There's nothing else to say.'

Mbappé is just as demonstrative in his praise, insisting that Deschamps got his World Cup selection 100 per cent right. 'The coach pieced together a great squad,' he told *France*

Football magazine. 'He's a very intelligent person and he analysed everything. He knew which players could be valuable on the pitch, which could be valuable off the pitch, and which could contribute to both aspects. The make-up of the squad was excellent, faultless. Having super players isn't enough on its own to win a tournament. To go all the way you need a healthy atmosphere. If you don't have that, it's no secret, you'll never make the effort for your friend.' In another interview with TF1, Mbappé said he was 'prepared to die on the pitch' for Didier Deschamps.

Les Bleus possessed that sense of togetherness, but they also had individual leaders. Lloris has worn the captain's armband since 2012, and he is hugely respected within the group. But the naturally calm, quiet Tottenham Hotspur goalkeeper is not the most vocal in the dressing room. As the tournament progressed, Pogba's presence grew and he was invariably the one to deliver the motivational talks.

Before running out at the Kazan Arena to face Argentina, Pogba made a rousing speech that quite clearly came from the heart and captured the feeling within the squad. 'I want to see warriors out there today,' he started. 'I don't want to go back home tonight. I'm *not* going home tonight! Tomorrow, I'm staying on at the hotel. We're going to eat more of that fucking fried pasta! I want you to give everything you've got. You must be ready to give your lives out there. We're warriors, mates, soldiers. Today we're going to kill those Argentines! Messi, no Messi, I couldn't care less!'

This was a very different Pogba to the one that frustrated Manchester United fans with his apparent lack of commitment. This was a Pogba who felt totally invested. The scene was recorded in the documentary *Les Bleus 2018: Au Cœur de L'Epopée Russe* and it illustrated just how fired up the midfielder was and how influential he had become for France. He backed the words up with a marauding performance against Argentina.

Les Bleus needed Pogba at his best to overcome the 2014 finalists. Mbappé's electric seventy-metre run through the heart of the Argentinian side had enabled Griezmann to open the scoring from the penalty spot. Yet the team failed to capitalise on their first-half superiority. Ángel Di María levelled with a majestic long-range shot before Gabriel Mercado put the *Albiceleste* ahead on forty-eight minutes.

France were trailing for nine minutes. It was the only time they would be behind during the entire tournament. But when Benjamin Pavard, the unheralded Stuttgart right-back, swerved a stunning right-footed shot into the top corner to equalise with the goal of the tournament, it was obvious something special was happening.

The strike vindicated Deschamps's left-field selections of Pavard and Lucas Hernández. The Atlético Madrid full-back surged up the left and his cross set up Pavard. Both were twenty-two and barely known to the French public, yet they both possessed the kind of gritty determination that Deschamps demands of his players. Hernández, who had flourished at Atlético under Diego Simeone, a similarly pragmatic, demanding coach to Deschamps, enjoyed an exceptional World Cup, rendering the concerns about Benjamin Mendy's injury problems irrelevant.

The final thirty minutes in Kazan conjured the kind of euphoria France fans had not felt in more than a decade. As Jorge Sampaoli's team tried to regain the initiative, they left gaping holes in their defence and Mbappé exploited them in the most devastating fashion.

If his first goal showed off his close ball skills, awareness and deadly finishing, the second provided a perfect example of what Deschamps's team was all about. Kanté collected the ball in a deep position. His slick pass up to halfway was exquisitely flicked on first-time by Griezmann into the path of Matuidi on the left. The left-footer injected pace into the move with his first touch, then slipped a probing ball into Giroud's path with his second. The big striker, aware that Mbappé was bombing on outside him, knocked it in behind the defence with his first touch. Mbappé's speed and his composure in front of goal did the rest. In the space of nine seconds, four precise passes and six touches of the ball, France had carved Argentina wide open.

This was nothing like Spain's *tiki-taka*. *Les Bleus* had no intention of keeping the ball for the sake of it. Indeed, they were happy to sit back and defend for long periods, allowing the opposition the lion's share of the ball. But when they decided to hurt their opponents, they were able to do so in a quick, cold-blooded manner. 'Football is constantly evolving,' the former France coach Gérard Houllier tells me in his Paris office. 'Spain had a philosophy that worked. In 2014, Germany took the best out of the Spanish possession game, and they added in their own physical, powerful qualities. France added speed. Back when Spain dominated, we thought you needed 70 per cent of the possession to win, but France showed you can be dangerous with only 30 per cent. The ability to combine speed and technique has become a big weapon in the modern game.'

Agüero's late goal did not take the gloss off France's sensational 4–3 win and the scenes of collective joy on the pitch at full time suggested that the players knew this was the start of something special.

When Deschamps gave his triumphant troops the chance to let off some steam in Moscow later that evening, they gleefully accepted. But upon returning to their Istra hotel in the early hours of the morning, the high-spirited players continued to fool around. Rami had retired to his bedroom and, in his own words, was 'naked and playing Fortnite' when his excited teammates tried to come in and ransack the place.

To defend his territory, the Marseille man grabbed a fire extinguisher and began to spray his teammates with foam. To his shock, his actions triggered a fire alarm throughout the hotel and a vapour was released from holes in the walls. 'I was so scared,' Rami told TF1. 'There was smoke everywhere. Then the security people arrived and said: "It's toxic, everybody get out."' Above all, Rami feared that his World Cup was over. 'Everybody went outside, including Didier Deschamps in his pyjamas. When I saw him coming towards us, I said to myself, "Oh shit." Then when I saw the security staff, police and firemen coming, I thought "I'm dead."'

Deschamps was not pleased about being woken up at 4 a.m. and he was ready to give his players a monumental rollicking. Then something happened. He was struck by a rare moment of mellowness. He observed his players, saw the way that they were remaining united, even at this awkward moment, and decided that, in fact, it was not the end of the world. 'They were about a 100 metres from me,' the coach told *La Provence* newspaper. 'I heard them saying, "Let's stick together. This is nobody's fault; it was all twenty-three of us." As I walked towards them, I asked myself if anything like this had happened in my playing career. I looked at them and decided not to say anything.'

An extremely united, unbreakable unit had formed. France never looked like they would lose in the quarter-finals against a Uruguay team shorn of injured striker Edinson Cavani. Griezmann had been having a relatively quiet tournament in front of goal, but France's playmaker proved to be decisive in Nizhny Novgorod.

The opening goal on forty minutes arrived thanks largely to a piece of insider knowledge, as Guy Stéphan explains: 'Antoine played with [Diego] Godín and [José] Giménez at Atlético, and he knew that when they defend a free-kick, they like to take a step back just as the ball is delivered. So he started his run-up and then stopped at the last moment, knowing they'd run backwards. That enabled Varane to gain a yard of space so that when Antoine did play it in, he got there first. At this level it's the tiny details like that which make the difference.'

Hugo Lloris's brilliance was another such detail, the France captain producing an extraordinary save on the stroke of half-time, diving low to his right and clawing Martín Cáceres's close-range header off his line with a strong right hand. The save evoked memories of Gordon Banks against Pelé in 1970 and strengthened the impression that Uruguay would never find a way through. When Lloris's opposite number Fernando Muslera allowed Griezmann's speculative long-range strike to slip through his grasp, the game was up.

If Uruguay were swatted aside with minimal fuss, Belgium were a far tougher proposition. Roberto Martínez's team had been the tournament's most entertaining side, staging a dramatic comeback to beat Japan before knocking out Brazil in another thrilling, breathless match. In Kevin De Bruyne and Eden Hazard, Beligum possessed two of the world's finest creative talents and many were tipping them to go all the way and lift the trophy. But they met their match in Saint Petersburg in the form of Deschamps's ultra-disciplined team.

On one of the few occasions that Hazard escaped the attentions of Pavard, Varane darted across to close down the space and deflect the winger's vicious centre over the crossbar. Whenever De Bruyne found space to shoot, Kanté, Pogba or Matuidi would appear from nowhere to block. Again, the breakthrough came from a set piece, and again it was a defender who provided the finish, Umtiti nipping ahead of Marouane Fellaini to meet Griezmann's corner at the near post on fifty-one minutes. The final half-hour saw Belgium attack relentlessly but there was no way through. 'I sensed my team was so strong, so solid that day,' Deschamps told *L'Équipe*. 'We could have played for a long time and the Belgians wouldn't have scored. That day, we took pleasure from imposing our collective strength.'

At times, France resembled the defensive Portugal side that won Euro 2016, or even the Greek team that was so difficult to break down in 2004. But just occasionally they treated the world to glimpses of their mouth-watering ability. In the fifty-fourth minute, Hernández broke up the left and played a pass inside to Matuidi. He flicked it on first-time to Mbappé with the outside of his left boot. France's number ten then produced a moment of magic that brought memories of Zidane flooding back. With two extraordinary, quick-fire touches of the football – one with the instep of his right boot and the other with his left – the nineteen-year-old, back to goal, split the entire Belgian defence in half with a delicately caressed drag-back. For a second, Giroud had just Thibaut Courtois to beat, but the striker did not get his shot away quickly enough and Mousa Dembélé's lunge denied France what would have been another contender for goal of the tournament.

Deschamps's team was capable of offering so much more. Yet they deliberately chose to play within themselves in order to prioritise their defence, a tactic that infuriated the beaten Belgians. 'Honestly, I'd rather lose with Belgium than win with France,' claimed Hazard. 'We play better football.' Goalkeeper Courtois was even more damning. 'We lost to a team that doesn't play, a team that defends,' the goalkeeper complained. 'It's a shame for football that Belgium didn't win.'

France did not care less. By now the country had worked itself into a frenzy and millions of French people, young and old, began making plans for an almighty party on 15 July.

One player was being hailed more than any other, and one song was being sung in the bars and on the Paris metro more than any other. Pogba and Griezmann had been exceptional throughout, two of the team's most talented individuals leading by example by fighting hard and adhering to Deschamps's tactics to the letter. Varane and Lloris had both been colossal until then, enjoying faultless, inspirational campaigns. Meanwhile, Mbappé's dynamic, carefree performances had reinvigorated an entire country. Yet the player who was getting the most love in the lead-up to the final was N'Golo Kanté.

This small, shy midfielder from the Paris suburb of Suresnes became the symbol of France's 2018 side. He was the epitome of the team player. Kanté never stopped running, never stopped fighting and, unlike so many modern-day stars, he never sought the limelight. He was quiet, kind and extremely likeable – unless of course you were playing against him. The way Kanté expertly nullified the threat of Messi in that pulsating round of sixteen tie was an example of his extraordinary intelligence as much as his speed, strength and stamina. Against Uruguay and Belgium, the Chelsea man was equally immense, and Kanté's signature song – sung to the tune of the 1969 hit *'Les Champs-Élysées'* by Joe Dassin – became France's unofficial anthem. 'N'Golo Kanté, pala palalala! N'Golo Kanté, pala palalala! He is small, he is kind, he's eaten up Leo Messi,' chanted the French fans in adulation of their new, impossibly simple and modest hero.

Tellingly, France's squad also adopted Kanté as their favourite. He is the only player who does not speak in TF1's World Cup documentary, yet he still finds himself at the heart of many of the strongest shared moments. In the dressing room after the Belgium game, Varane and Pogba mischievously approach Kanté in the corner, touch his brow and look at each other in mock disbelief. 'He hasn't even broken sweat,' Pogba exclaims before the pair explode with laughter.

On the bus back to Istra, the players repeatedly sang the Kanté song, adapting the words to include the line 'We all know he's a cheat' in the chorus. Samuel Umtiti had earlier told the press that Kanté sometimes cheats in card games, and the idea that this ideal human being did actually have a fault created great amusement. All the while, Kanté, the team mascot, said nothing, while sporting an enormous, endearing grin.

France's midfield metronome unexpectedly struggled in the final. Facing a dynamic Croatian side that boasted arguably the best central trio of the World Cup in Luka Modrić, Ivan Rakitić and Ivan Perišić, Kanté's timing was uncharacteristically out of kilter. He got booked on twenty-seven minutes and was at fault for Croatia's first goal. Deschamps replaced him with N'Zonzi early in the second half. But otherwise everything else went swimmingly for *Les Bleus* on a magnificent night in Moscow's Luzhniki Stadium.

The coach had learned from the experience of Euro 2016, when the euphoria of beating Germany in the semi-finals had impacted on their preparations for the showpiece. This time, Deschamps ensured his players were sufficiently rested and utterly focused. As they enjoyed their final evening together, sitting around a campfire that overlooked the lake adjacent to their hotel, there was a distinct sense of calm assurance in the ranks. A feeling that nothing could stand in their way. 'Three words are important,' Deschamps told the press on the eve of the game. 'Serenity, confidence and concentration. To prepare well, we need the right dose of those three things.'

France's nerve would indeed be severely tested by England's semi-final tormentors. As the claps of thunder rumbled menacingly overhead, Croatia whipped up a storm on the pitch. Zlatko Dalić's team attacked in waves, but France stubbornly stood firm. Deschamps's men chose their moments, and delivered a series of sucker-punches to become the first side to score four in a World Cup final since Brazil in 1970.

Was this another case of Deschamps getting the rub of the green? Ever since *Les Bleus* defeated Germany at Euro 2016, French people have cultivated this myth about their national team coach being one of the luckiest men in football. Germany, after all, had been missing several key men that night (most notably Mats Hummels, Sami Khedira and Mario Gomez) and the hosts got all the breaks going in Marseille.

It is fair to say that Deschamps's lucky star was shining again in the stormy Moscow sky during a frenetic first half. *Les Bleus* opened the scoring against the run of play when Mario Mandžukić headed Griezmann's free-kick past his own goalkeeper.

But as Perišić evaded Kanté to rifle home a brilliant and de-served equaliser on twenty-eight minutes, France looked to be rocking. The match-defining moment arrived before the break as VAR intervened for the first time in a World Cup final, judg-ing that Perišić, positioned just behind Matuidi at the near post, had handled Griezmann's corner. His arm was close to his side, there was no intent, but by the letter of the new law the decision was valid.

Griezmann scored to put France 2–1 up and leave Croatia crestfallen. Their energy levels dropped in the second half and France started to turn the screw. When Pogba plunged a dagger into Croatian hearts on fifty-nine minutes by placing a beautifully curled shot beyond Danijel Subašić the game was almost up. 'What efficiency! What efficiency!' screamed the commentator Grégoire Margotton on French television – an underwhelming description for an outstanding goal, but one that perfectly summed up Deschamps's France.

This team was cold-blooded. They were not always great to watch but they were ruthless and incredibly effective. Above all, they were winners. This was a team built in the image of its coach, the most decorated Frenchman in football history. Luck can occasionally play a part. But when you are a serial winner the reasons lie elsewhere.

Deschamps later said he had not doubted the outcome of the final for a minute. Having witnessed his side's unity and resil-ience against Belgium, he knew they would go all the way. Of course things might have been different had VAR not awarded a penalty, but there was by this point an unwavering belief inside the France camp. 'I wouldn't say we felt invincible because you can always lose a match if you don't put in all of the ingredients,' Giroud tells me. 'But there was real confidence. We had devel-oped such a strong collective spirit. We knew that if we all did our bit, we'd be very hard to beat.'

With Croatia 3–1 down and chasing the game, Mbappé came

into his own. He was not distracted by the four ladies dressed as police officers – later identified as members of the 'Pussy Riot' punk collective – who came running on to the pitch campaigning for the release of political prisoners in Russia. The France forward calmly high-fived one of the invaders before reverting his focus back to the small matter of winning the World Cup.

In the sixty-fifth minute, the kid whose speed, brilliance and refreshing attitude had captured the world's imagination, stamped his name on the tournament once and for all. Collecting a pass from Hernández, he took one touch to control the ball and swept a precise shot into the bottom corner from twenty metres out. Mbappé looked like he was playing in his back garden, or rather on one of those sandy pitches in Bondy, such was the cool, simple, almost easy nature of the strike.

A star had been born and Deschamps's tyros had become the youngest World Cup winners since Brazil forty-eight years previously. Lloris's late blunder that gifted Mandžukić a goal mattered little. The match finished 4–2 and, as the heavens opened over the Luzhniki Stadium, France were on top of the world again.

CHAPTER 20

UN FUTUR GLORIEUX?

Hundreds of thousands of joyous people are gathered in and around the Avenue des Champs-Élysées to greet the newly crowned world champions whose flight back from Moscow has been delayed. It is hot and some of those who cannot get close enough decide to cool off with a swim in the River Seine. Many partied through the night and have not yet been to bed. The crowds are awash with *Tricolore* flags, the mood is euphoric, and repeated renditions of *La Marseillaise* are helping to pass the time.

But as France's open-top bus finally reaches the immense roundabout underneath the Arc de Triomphe and prepares to turn right up the street known as '*La Plus Belle Avenue du Monde*' (The Most Beautiful Avenue in the World), Kylian Mbappé is not really in the mood for crazy celebrations. He is tired, keen to rest, and wondering if all this fuss is really necessary. 'Kylian didn't want to go down the Champs-Élysées,' the president of the FFF Noël Le Graët, who was sitting next to him on the bus, recounts in the M6 documentary *Kylian Mbappé: Les Secrets d'un Surdoué* (*Kylian Mbappé: The Secrets of a Gifted Man*). 'He was asking himself if it wasn't a bit too much. He likes to show his talent on the pitch, but he didn't really fancy this.'

Just like when he won the league at AS Monaco, Mbappé did not see the point in partying for days. He was already looking forward to his next challenge. 'He was happy, he savoured the moment,' France winger Florian Thauvin told M6, 'but Kylian has objectives in his mind and he wants to relax so that he can perform as well as possible. He's set himself a clear course.' Mbappé confirmed as much later that day. 'Winning the World Cup is a unique feeling and one that I want to experience again,' he said on TF1. 'Top players don't content themselves with what they've already done. They always want to do more. So there you go. The aim now is to win more and more.'

Those words provide a telling glimpse into the mindset of a nineteen-year-old who, just twenty-four hours earlier, was scoring in, and winning a World Cup final. He was probably relieved that the bus drove controversially quickly down the Champs-Élysées, completing the 1.3km parade in only twelve minutes before the players were rushed off to the Élysée Palace for a reception with President Emmanuel Macron.

Mbappé could have shown his teammates around the magnificent eighteenth-century building if he had wanted to. The teenager had already visited Macron's home in February 2018 after being invited to attend a lunch with Didier Drogba and another great striker of the past, George Weah – now the President of Liberia – to discuss the role of sport in Africa. When asked by Macron to offer his thoughts, Mbappé said to Weah: 'Listen, I'm very proud to be here, and I'm flattered to meet you, but I do not have the qualities necessary to advise you on the topics discussed. However, if I can be of help, I am available.' Again, Mbappé had surprised and impressed his audience with the maturity of his words.

Five months later, in a very different atmosphere, Mbappé's level-headedness stood out once more. The likes of Adil Rami and Benjamin Mendy had not contributed nearly as much as Mbappé to France's victory, yet the young forward was happy to stay in the background as his more extroverted teammates whipped the palace guests into a frenzy. Macron had invited 1,300 young footballers from the Paris region to attend the ceremony, but he probably did not expect Paul Pogba to take the microphone and start up an impromptu singalong with the kids in the palace gardens.

As Macron stood next to Pogba trying hard not to look concerned by this surprising turn of events, the midfielder turned DJ asked his friend Mendy to kick matters off with a rendition of the *Les Bleus'* unofficial anthem '*Ramenez la Coupe à la Maison*' by Vegedream. Pogba then took matters into his own hands, getting everybody to join in with the now famous N'Golo Kanté ditty. While the players, children, Didier Deschamps and even the country's President sang along, Mbappé was in the corner quietly signing autographs.

Macron, like his predecessor Jacques Chirac in 1998, jumped at the opportunity to associate himself with the World Cup winners. The youngest President in France's history spent time with the team at Clairefontaine before the tournament and attended both the semi-final in Saint Petersburg and the final in Moscow. But unlike Chirac, the forty-year-old pulled off the role of supporter quite convincingly. 'Chirac knew nothing about football and tried to look the part by wearing a France shirt,' notes the journalist Joachim Barbier. 'Macron wore a suit and tie, but he didn't look out of place. We know he is a Marseille fan and when he was in Russia he celebrated like a fan.'

Macron understood that Deschamps's team portrayed a positive image of modern-day France. It also mirrored the youthful, brave, dynamic image he was trying to cultivate for himself. When he leaped up onto a desk in the presidential stand at the Luzhniki Stadium and began punching the air in delight and screaming exuberantly after France's opening goal against Croatia, some questioned his sincerity. But the reactions looked spontaneous and as the game progressed, Macron's joy merely intensified.

In the dressing room after the game, there seemed to be a genuine connection between this fresh-faced head of state and the France players, some of whom are not that much younger than him. Macron joined in with the singing and dancing, and happily obliged when Manchester City defender Mendy asked him to 'dab' for a selfie.

The relaxed, friendly attitude displayed by the France players in front of Macron contrasted with the more distant, courteous behaviour that the 1998 side adopted with Chirac. These Generation Z youngsters do not seem afraid of anything or anyone, and they will not cower in the face of authority. 'They aren't intimidated by power,' Barbier states. 'They don't think twice about dabbing with the President and spraying champagne over Vladimir Putin. This was their party and they weren't going to let anybody change that. At the Élysée Palace, Pogba took the microphone, they sang their N'Golo Kanté song, they invited friends and family up to sing with them. Kanté's sister was wearing a hijab but nobody was going to make a fuss about it. This was their moment and they were going to enjoy it on their terms.'

The wearing of hijabs in public areas – and in particular full-face veils – continues to fuel debate in French society, yet interestingly, and refreshingly, there was no racial, ethnic or religious discussion surrounding the 2018 team. Unlike twenty years previously, when the origins of Aimé Jacquet's players was a hot topic and the term *black-blanc-beur* emerged to highlight the diversity of *Les Bleus*, nobody in France was describing Kanté as a Malian immigrant or Pogba as a descendant of Guinea.

These guys were French, their cultural diversity was recognised and accepted as part of modern society, and the media did not even think to evoke their backgrounds. 'There was not a single article in *L'Équipe* or any of the mainstream papers that referred to the origins or skin colour of our players,' highlights author and journalist Joachim Barbier. 'The players are now second- or third-generation immigrants. They are considered French first and foremost.'

It was a different story outside of France, however. In the United States, the South African-born comedian and presenter of *The Daily Show* Trevor Noah said that Africa, not France, deserved credit for winning the World Cup. 'Yes, I'm so excited! Africa won the World Cup! Africa won the World Cup!' he chanted to rapturous applause and laughter from the audience. 'I mean look, I get it, they have to say it's the French team. But look at those guys, look at those guys,' implored Noah as a photo of *Les Bleus* appeared behind him. 'You don't get that tan by hanging out in the south of France, my friends.'

The President of Venezuela, Nicolás Maduro, expressed a similar view. 'France's team looked like an African team,' he declared. 'The reality is Africa won the World Cup, with immigrants who arrived [in France] from Africa. Stop racism against Africa in Europe!'

Others were happy to embrace the phenomenon. In a speech delivered in honour of the late Nelson Mandela, Barack Obama cited *Les Bleus* as an example of what can be achieved when discrimination is set aside. 'Look at the French football team,' the former US President said. 'Not all of those folks look like Gauls to me. But they're all French. They are all French!' Obama seemed to understand what was gnawing away at the American subconscious: Deschamps's squad – seventeen of whom were non-white – did not match the traditional image that many of his countrymen have of the French.

Yet the France players felt very sure of their own identity. Three days before the final, Pogba again assumed the role of leader, taking it upon himself to speak on behalf of the group when the question of ethnicity was raised by a foreign journalist in a press conference. 'This is what France is,' Pogba shrugged. 'There are many origins represented here. That's what makes France beautiful. Today France has many colours. We all feel

French. I'm very happy to have grown up in France and to have the French culture. France is beautiful like this, this is the way we love it and will always love it.'

In the aftermath of the World Cup, Mendy reacted to a post on social media that was gaining traction. The tweet in question listed the twenty-three members of France's squad accompanied by a national flag that corresponded to each player's origin. The young left-back replied with a tweet of his own that showed the same list accompanied by twenty-three *Tricolore* flags. 'Mentalities in France have changed over the last twenty years,' the historian and specialist in immigration Yvan Gastaut explains. 'Back in 1998, the victory raised awareness in France on matters of immigration, integration and racism. But the country has moved forward since then. These days, every France player knows he is French. It's something that is taken as given. It's natural. The 2018 victory just brought people closer together. It strengthened the feeling that a multicultural France can be a happy country.'

As if to highlight the point, after defeating the Netherlands in their first home match as world champions, *Les Bleus* partied on the Stade de France pitch, with two famous performers of Ivorian origins, Magic System and Vegedream, providing the music. The 80,000 fans had the time of their lives and nobody questioned the choice of the musicians. 'I'm not sure any other European country would celebrate a national triumph with two African performers,' says Barbier. 'But this is modern France and the fact that this was seen as being perfectly normal shows how much progress has been made.'

There were differences between 1998 and 2018, but there were similarities too. From the moment *Les Bleus* defeated Argentina, the infectious feel-good factor that was so present in 1998 swept through France again. 'The country was quite calm during the group stage,' Barbier recalls. 'People thought the team was boring and they weren't happy at all after the terrible game with Denmark. But the first knockout game changed everything. The fact that we beat a big football nation, and we did it so dramatically with this great kid Mbappé exploding, everybody in France got World Cup fever.'

France fans, generally speaking, do not offer the same kind of unconditional support to the national team as other major nations like England, Italy or Argentina. But when *Les Bleus* start winning the country comes alive. 'We do not have the sporting culture that you have in England,' *L'Équipe*'s chief football writer Vincent Duluc explains. 'In France, the whole society, including the politicians, became interested in football at the same time: in 1998. But we have confused sporting culture with winning culture. Sometimes in France it feels like we have to win otherwise people are not interested.'

However, there was interest aplenty during the knockout phase as supporters poured into the 230 fan zones that had been set up around France. On the day of the final, the Champs de Mars – the scene of the biggest fan zone situated in front of the Eiffel Tower – had to be closed off three hours before kick-off because its capacity of 90,000 had been reached. Soon after Mbappé had rifled in the fourth goal, an estimated 2 million people took to the streets of Paris and headed towards the Champs-Élysées to celebrate.

If 1998 was a milestone for multicultural France, 2018 was a celebration of France's youth. Besides the fact Deschamps's team was packed with exciting young footballers, the second World Cup presented the nation's under-25s with an opportunity to enjoy their own party, having heard so much about that inaugural win from their parents and grandparents. Those from Generation Y (Millennials) and Generation Z could easily relate to this team.

Seconds after the final whistle had blown in Moscow, TF1 commentator Grégoire Margotton thanked the entire squad for bringing so much happiness to the country. Tellingly he referred to each player by his first name. Likewise when each World Cup winner had his face beamed onto the front of the Arc de Triomphe later that evening, the image was accompanied by the player's first name and the town from which he hails.

These players were like your mates. It was easy to imagine sharing a drink with Adil Rami and Benjamin Mendy, playing cards with N'Golo Kanté and Thomas Lemar, or enjoying a kickabout with Antoine Griezmann and Blaise Matuidi. As much as the disgraced bunch from 2010 were seen as spoilt and out of touch, the 2018 group – which included two survivors from that squad in goalkeepers Hugo Lloris and Steve Mandanda – came across as being kind, fun and refreshingly down to earth.

For the Class of 1998, it must have felt strange to now have to share the nation's love. Yet Marcel Desailly, who was working as a pundit in Russia during the tournament, showed no signs of jealousy when he bear-hugged his great mate Deschamps and high-fived the triumphant players inside the dressing room before recording a series of hysterical videos on his phone.

When we meet a year later, Desailly's admiration for the 2018 team remains intact. 'I was so happy because they're great players and great guys who deserve success,' he tells me. 'Twenty years on, they have provided France with another good example of integration. Football has changed since my time. The guys are all very rich now. But when you see Pogba and Mbappé, players who are serious and haven't been involved in any off-field scandals, it's a great example for society. Kylian has shut a lot of people up. Here is a balanced kid from an immigrant background who is well educated, who works hard and who wins. It will help people to like immigrants a bit more.'

•   •   •

The four goals that *Les Bleus* scored against Croatia are getting played on a loop in the reception at the FFF headquarters, a discreet building in Paris's fifteenth *arrondissement*. In recent years, this place had become synonymous with crisis meetings; television cameramen would camp outside to catch footage of Raymond Domenech arriving for crunch talks or Patrice Évra attending a disciplinary hearing.

Winning a World Cup can have a transformative effect, though, and on this bright November morning the mood feels far lighter. Ex-Olympique Lyonnais coach Hubert Fournier is the man calling the shots from a football point of view at the FFF these days. The position of technical director – previously filled by Gérard Houllier and Aimé Jacquet – remains crucial in France. Fournier must define the country's youth development strategy, and he is convinced that this particular sector is now in rude health. 'Today, France provides a huge number of young footballers and the work we carry out at our *Pôles Espoirs* [early development centres] is one of the reasons for that,' he states.

In France, there are now fifteen *Pôles Espoirs* for kids aged between twelve and fifteen, including the most famous one in Clairefontaine. From the 2018 squad, three players – Alphonse Areola, Blaise Matuidi and Kylian Mbappé – attended the Clairefontaine academy, but in all seven came through one of the *Pôles Espoirs*. 'Our aim is to gain development time so that when the kids later join a club academy they are ready for the challenges they'll face,' Fournier explains. 'This is why we have so many precocious footballers. The fact that France won the World Cup with the youngest side since 1970 shows that our players are ready for the highest level from a young age.'

One of the consequences of France's meticulous development process is that French players are being lured abroad earlier. A glance at the World Cup squad confirms the trend: Antoine Griezmann moved to Spain at fourteen, Paul Pogba quit Le Havre for Manchester United at sixteen, Raphaël Varane left RC Lens for Real Madrid aged eighteen, Ousmane Dembélé was eighteen when he traded Rennes for Borussia Dortmund, and Benjamin Pavard moved from Lille to Stuttgart at the age of twenty.

'In France we have a big pool of players and the French system is still good at providing the raw materials,' states the journalist and author Daniel Riolo. 'We ensure the player is well prepared physically. But the finishing touches, notably the mental side of competing at the highest level, are now being developed abroad. Griezmann didn't learn to be a competitor in France. Pogba learned top-level football at United and at Juventus. Varane wouldn't be the player he is today had he not joined Real Madrid.'

That may be true, but nobody can claim that Mbappé received his football education abroad. The man who is likely to be the talisman for the national team for years to come is a pure product of the French system. 'That's what people will say,' Vincent Duluc of L'Équipe counters, 'but are Clairefontaine and Monaco really responsible for Mbappé? If you ask me the person who taught Mbappé how to play football was his father.'

Regardless, French football will gladly take responsibility for Mbappé, and given the way that the FFF's image has suffered of late, who can blame them? 'Kylian's emergence has boosted everybody here,' Fournier tells me. 'It's brought a new dynamic. What's great about Kylian – and the whole World Cup squad – is they give off a good image. Since 2010, the FFF has worked hard to improve the image of Les Bleus. It's been one of the key strategies. For us it's very positive that the team is made up of well-rounded individuals who are fully aware of the responsibilities they have when they wear the France shirt.'

By choosing to at least launch his career in Ligue 1, Mbappé has boosted France's club game as well as the national team. He is an example for aspiring footballers, and a flagbearer for les banlieues. 'Kylian makes kids dream,' Fournier says. 'These days every young boy in France wants to be the next Mbappé. That kind of example has no price. Kids from immigrant backgrounds and kids in precarious situations are inspired by him. Football is one way to climb the social ladder. It's not the only way, but football is a good example. Our job is to make the youth of France dream and Kylian is helping us do that.'

Judging by the feedback I get from my children who attend a school in the Paris suburbs, Fournier is right. Mbappé's famous cross-armed celebration is all the rage on the playground there (it has definitely overtaken the Pogba dab and the Griezmann Drake celebration) and even teachers are using the PSG striker's notoriety to help them in the classroom. Indeed, the freshly coined 'Mbappé rule' helps children to understand that in the French language, the letter 'm', and not 'n', is used before a 'b' or 'p'. 'Mbappé' and 'champion' are the words chosen to illustrate the rule. Unsurprisingly, in 2019 Mbappé was voted France's favourite personality for children aged between seven and fourteen in a poll conducted by Ipsos for the kids' magazine *Journal de Mickey*.

But French children are not the only ones looking up to Mbappé. In the 2019/20 season, some of the Premier League's brightest young stars began copying the PSG forward's celebration. England full-back Trent Alexander-Arnold posed proudly in front of the travelling fans with his arms crossed and his hands tucked into his armpits after scoring Liverpool's fourth at Leicester. Arsenal's Brazilian forward Gabriel Martinelli did the same when playing away to Chelsea.

Mbappé's global fame began to skyrocket during the World Cup year. He was setting records for precocity off the pitch as well as on it, with the Musée Grevin – the Paris equivalent to Madame Tussauds – making him the youngest person to have his own waxwork model. In Bulgaria, one the country's most famous rappers Fyre composed a song named 'Kylian Mbappé' as a tribute to the Frenchman. 'We wanted to link his success to ours,' the artist told *So Foot* magazine. 'He's a great example to our generation. Just look at him: he's a teenager but he's already a superstar.'

International brands are now fighting to associate themselves with the footballer. The Indian fashion designer Manish Arora started a trend by presenting a new range of clothes at Paris Fashion Week that featured Mbappé's name and face on the front. The Japanese men's skin care company Bulk Homme have signed a commercial deal with the striker – as have Good Goût, the French organic food manufacturer who wanted Mbappé to help them break into the global market.

In October 2018, the Swiss luxury watch manufacturer Hublot made Mbappé one of their ambassadors, putting him in the company of a host of exceptional sports personalities, including José Mourinho, Pelé, former Australia cricket captain Michael Clarke and the world's fastest man Usain Bolt.

By 2019, Mbappé was listed as the seventh-wealthiest footballer on the planet by Forbes with estimated annual earnings of $30.6 million (including a salary of $26.6 million and $4 million in endorsements). He was just behind Pogba, and way off the leading trio of Lionel Messi, Cristiano Ronaldo and Neymar, all of whom earned more than $100 million. Yet Mbappé's financial worth is set to explode in the coming years. The clothing range he has launched with Nike – who sponsor his boots as well as PSG's kit – will help bridge the gap. Bondy Dreams, as the collection is called, reflects Mbappé's hometown both in name and allure; every item has the *département* Seine-Saint-Denis and its corresponding number ninety-three printed on it, and the dominant colour of green used for the range is a nod to Bondy's rural past.

That such a wide variety of brands have already secured commercial deals with the wonderkid shows just how universal his charms are. 'He appeals to teenagers just as much as he does more mature people,' states Hublot's marketing director Philippe Tardivel in the book *Mbappé: Le Phénomène* by Arnaud Hermant. 'He's comfortable in society. He's an icon. Even before he became an ambassador, when we talked about him with our clients around the world, their eyes would sparkle.'

UN FUTUR GLORIEUX?

Thanks to Hublot, Mbappé got the chance to meet Pelé in April 2019. The Brazil legend had already expressed his admiration for the PSG hitman on social media, and the three-time World Cup-winner seemed genuinely excited to cross paths with the man he considers his heir apparent in Paris. 'Kylian embodies the new generation of footballers and espouses the values of a sport that inspires and unites the world,' Pelé enthused. 'I am happy that he symbolises hope: the hope that anything is possible regardless of our origins or our social status. For me, the key to success can be captured in two words: humility and perseverance. Kylian has perfectly understood this.'

Mbappé continues to display his human side by showing extreme generosity when it comes to worthy causes. In November 2018, after a building collapsed in Marseille, he gave up time to meet with a young fan who had lost his mother in the tragedy. Two months later, when the plane carrying Cardiff City striker Emiliano Sala and his pilot David Ibbotson disappeared over the Channel, Mbappé donated $30,000 to help fund a private search party for the late Argentine forward. A similar appeal was later launched to find Ibbotson's body, and Mbappé pledged an identical sum, although this time he used a different name in a bid to avoid publicity.

More recently, in January 2020, Mbappé launched his own association called Inspired by KM. In a nod to his year of birth, ninety-eight children, aged nine to sixteen, have been selected from the Seine-Saint-Denis *département*. Mbappé explained that through this organisation he will accompany the children throughout their education during the coming years with the aim of helping them to realise their dreams. He remains an ambassador for Premiers de Cordée, the charity to which he donated his World Cup bonus that assists disabled and hospitalised children through the realm of sport. When the coronavirus pandemic struck in March, the Fondation Abbé-Pierre – a charity that helps homeless people in France

– released a statement thanking Mbappé for his 'very large donation'.

If Mbappé is extremely active away from the pitch, his strong, supportive and totally trustworthy entourage – led by his ever-present parents – ensure the striker's focus does not waver. As a result, his football career is continuing to flourish.

Following his World Cup exploits, PSG's new coach Thomas Tuchel wanted to ease France's hero back into the action slowly. But with the champions trailing away to modest EA Guingamp in just the second week of the season, Tuchel felt obliged to send him on at half-time. Despite only having a short break, the summer had clearly done Mbappé good. He looked more confident than ever. Indeed there was an untouchable aura about the forward as he scored two superb goals to inspire a 3–1 victory.

Unlike during his first season at the Parc des Princes, Mbappé no longer felt more junior than his attacking partners Neymar and Edinson Cavani. He underlined his status by scoring four times in the space of thirteen exhilarating minutes against PSG's supposed title rivals Olympique Lyonnais. Tuchel was clearly taking a hard-line approach with the youngster, sensing that he needed to be challenged on a regular basis. After PSG's 5–0 win over Lyon in October, the German was asked to comment on him becoming the youngest man to score a Ligue 1 quadruple. 'He got four but considering the chances he had he probably should've scored seven or eight,' was the coach's reply.

Three weeks later, Tuchel shocked everybody, Mbappé included, by leaving the World Cup-winner on the bench for the biggest game of the season so far: Le Classique against Olympique de Marseille. It was punishment for turning up late to a team meeting and the decision infuriated him. But Mbappé produced the ideal reaction: sent on in the sixty-second minute, he surged through the heart of the Marseille defence to score the game's opening goal with one of his first touches of the ball. It was breathtaking. It was brilliant.

Overall, in the 2018/19 campaign Mbappé enjoyed a sensational run. Operating mainly as a central striker alongside Cavani, with Tuchel offering Neymar a free role just behind, he scored thirty-three league goals in twenty-four starts and five substitute appearances, helping the capital club storm to yet another title. At times, he was unplayable.

But despite all of this, his image in France was no longer 100 per cent positive. Mbappé had failed to end PSG's habit of embarrassing themselves in the Champions League. In the absence of both Neymar and Cavani, he had impressed as the sole centre-forward against Manchester United at Old Trafford, scoring once and terrorising the English club's defence with his speed. After the 2–0 first-leg win, the player accused the French media of stirring up negativity, suggesting they should have more faith in French teams. 'People need to stop selling fear and stop being afraid,' he declared.

Yet PSG and Mbappé then produced a second-leg performance that terrified observers more than ever. They crashed out at the last-sixteen stage for a third season running as a United team missing ten regulars triumphed 3–1 in the capital. Gianluigi Buffon and Thilo Kehrer both committed awful mistakes that led to goals, and nobody performed particularly well for the home side, but Mbappé, who squandered his one chance of the night by slipping as he bore down on goal, received more criticism than anyone.

The self-assured attitude that had served him so well until now – and had generally been applauded in the media – was suddenly getting cited as an example of big-headedness. 'The press showed Mbappé some indulgence during his early years,' reflects *L'Équipe*'s chief football writer Vincent Duluc. 'But as soon as he turned twenty, it felt like that indulgence stopped. We thought: "It's OK now, he's a big boy."' Mbappé handed the media more ammunition by lunging in on Rennes defender Damien Da Silva and getting himself sent off in the dying seconds of the

2019 Coupe de France final. He had to watch PSG lose the penalty shootout on a television in the dressing room.

Ten months on from his Russian heroics, Mbappé seemed unhappy and reports claimed he was considering leaving PSG. That sentiment grew when he stepped up to accept his 2018/19 Ligue 1 Player of the Season award and delivered a speech that left his audience open-mouthed. 'This is a very important moment for me,' Mbappé began. 'I've arrived at a first or second turning point of my career. I feel now is maybe the time to have more responsibility. I hope this will maybe be at Paris Saint-Germain, that would be with great pleasure, or maybe [I will go] somewhere else for a new project.'

The timing of Mbappé's comments was poorly chosen and he later admitted it had been a mistake. This was a night of celebration and every other award winner had taken the time to thank teammates, coaches and rivals. Mbappé mentioned only the PSG president Nasser Al-Khelaifi. But the message was nevertheless extremely powerful: this twenty-year-old forward was telling the bosses of one of the richest clubs in world football that the team needed strengthening and that he should be the main man.

For many in the media, the outburst was further evidence of his growing egotism. 'Mbappé's image has evolved,' noted *Le Monde* newspaper on 10 June 2019. 'The honeymoon period is over. His words, which previously drew praise for their maturity, and are now being interpreted as arrogance.'

Two days previously, Mbappé had disappointed along with the rest of the France team in a Euro 2020 qualifier away to Turkey. *Les Bleus* succumbed to a 2–0 defeat and Mbappé lost the ball an alarming twenty-two times, one record that he would have preferred to avoid. Although Deschamps's side recovered from that setback to win their qualifying group, Mbappé's performances for his country were all too often marred by poor decision-making and increasing shows of individualism.

The great strength of France in 2018 had been their collective spirit, but with Mbappé's notoriety rising by the day there are concerns that the inner harmony could be broken. 'The other players have a lukewarm, mixed relationship with Mbappé,' claims Duluc. 'On the one hand they are happy he's there, they recognise his talent, but on the other hand he upsets the balance because he is disrupting the hierarchy of leadership.'

The *L'Équipe* journalist has witnessed many a battle of egos in France dressing rooms through the years, and he believes Mbappé may become a source of tension. 'Euro 2016 was all about the Griezmann generation,' Duluc explains. 'But Griezmann isn't the one people are talking about now. In France, he still has the status of a leader. It's 50/50 with Mbappé. But abroad, Mbappé has crushed Griezmann in terms of perception. Mbappé has become a world phenomenon while Griezmann has remained simply a good player.'

The fact is Mbappé has earned his status on the pitch. In 2019, he scored forty-one goals and was rewarded by *France Football* magazine with the French Player of the Year gong for the second time in a row. Upon receiving the prize, he gave an interview to the magazine in which he was persistently asked about his changing attitude and growing obsession with personal statistics. 'People think Kylian has changed,' Mbappé said. 'But that's false. He plays to be decisive and important for his team.'

Referring to himself in the third person suggested that perhaps he had changed, yet the 21-year-old insisted that only the way people look at him has evolved: 'I've understood that I cannot control the way people perceive me,' he said. 'I try to be as sincere as possible, but if people interpret that differently, what can I do? At Monaco, I was the little kid playing for a team that everybody really liked. In joining PSG, the team that is apparently distorting [the fairness of] the league and the team that everybody likes to have a pop at, it's inevitable that my popularity and my image change.'

What is totally clear is that Kylian Mbappé wants to write his name in football history. He has already broken dozens of records through his precocity, yet in his eyes this is only the beginning. Mbappé fully intends to follow in the footsteps of modern-day legends Lionel Messi and Cristiano Ronaldo and, if possible, go even further than the pair who collected eleven of the twelve Ballon d'Or awards between 2008 and 2019.

The early signs are promising to say the least. By the age of twenty-one, Mbappé had scored 126 goals in 200 games for club and country, including nineteen strikes in the Champions League. At the same stage, Messi had scored fewer than half of Mbappé's tally, netting fifty-one times in 138 appearances, with eight Champions League goals. Ronaldo had found the net thirty-five times in 176 games, but scored only once in the Champions League and that was in a qualifying playoff.

In terms of trophies, Mbappé has accumulated more do-mestic titles than Messi and Ronaldo put together at the same age; and while the Argentine had already lifted the Champions League before turning twenty-one, the Frenchman can trump him with a World Cup.

What Mbappé is doing is totally unprecedented in the world game, but every trophy he wins merely whets his appetite further. His career plan is hugely ambitious and will almost certainly involve one or more spells abroad. The groundwork is already being laid. In his spare time, while his peers are play-ing FIFA, Mbappé has private English and Spanish lessons. In January 2020, he showed off his progress by charming the English-speaking world with an interview he gave to the BBC.

Thanks to his relationship with Zinédine Zidane, who, like Pelé, is a huge fan of the striker – and thanks to his well-documented love for Real Madrid – Mbappé already has the Spanish public eating out of his hands. In an interview with the Italian newspaper *La Gazzetta dello Sport*, Mbappé hinted he will represent several clubs and play in several countries during his career, much like Juventus star Ronaldo. 'It's too late for me to carve out a career like Messi's. I would've had to stay at Monaco,' he said. 'Without taking anything away from Messi, now I have to draw on Cristiano's career for inspiration.'

Ligue 1 might not hold on to Mbappé much longer, but France's ability to unearth and nurture exceptional young footballers is so strong the next generation is already arriving and looks every bit as exciting. In fact, Mbappé's records for precociousness may even be under threat. On 4 January 2020, Rayan Cherki became the youngest man to score for Lyon when he struck against Bourg-en-Bresse in the Coupe de France aged sixteen and 289 days. Two weeks later, the technically assured forward produced an even more astonishing display, scoring twice against top-flight club FC Nantes in the next round.

Cherki, a small, quick and perfectly balanced number ten, might even have scored a hat-trick; he won a penalty for Lyon midway through the second period, and immediately grabbed the ball, indicating that he wanted to take it. Already, at just sixteen, that extreme confidence was there. The youth-team graduate was overruled by Lyon striker Moussa Dembélé, who took the ball off him and then duly missed the spot kick. As if to prove he did not hold a grudge, Cherki set up a goal for Dembélé just moments later. He even registered a second assist for Martin Terrier, as Lyon pipped Nantes 4–3. Cherki's exploits were instantly recognised by a certain Mbappé, who tweeted: 'Don't talk to him about age!'

The great thing about Ligue 1 is that youngsters will get the playing time if they are good enough, regardless of their age. Cherki, like Mbappé before him, looks sure to become a first-team regular by the age of seventeen, and should his development continue as expected, he will soon be on the path to greatness. With another seventeen-year-old, Eduardo Camavinga, emerging as Rennes' best midfielder in 2019/20, and dozens of teenage starlets strutting their stuff on Ligue 1 pitches week in, week out, the future for *Les Bleus* looks every bit as exciting as its present.

The heroes of France's past are unanimously enthusiastic about the present. Both Emmanuel Petit and Robert Pirès are convinced that the 2018 world champions can go on to win more major tournaments and create their own legacy. 'I believe they can follow up the World Cup success by winning the Euros, just like we did twenty years ago,' Petit says. 'We have a great generation of players who've been together since the 2014 World Cup. That's crucial. Didier has a really strong spine that he can count on.'

For Pirès, that formidable backbone of Lloris, Varane, Pogba, Kanté, Griezmann and Mbappé gives *Les Bleus* a real advantage over their opponents in Europe. 'Of course we can win the next Euros. We'll be one of the favourites. But be careful,' Pirès warns, raising his index finger. 'The Euros are even harder to win than the World Cup. Spain, Germany, the Netherlands and even England have strong teams. But the advantage we have is our core. The guys know each other well and they could all be around for another five, six, seven years. I don't want to be chauvinistic,' smiles the proud Frenchman, 'but the French way remains very strong. We develop great young players who can play at the highest level very young.'

As ever with France, the key will be to avoid over-confidence. That was the problem back in 2002 when the world and European champions flunked woefully in South Korea. But you get the feeling that with Deschamps at the helm, the players will remain grounded this time around. Deschamps's assistant Guy Stéphan was Roger Lemerre's second in command, two decades ago, and he insists lessons have been learned: 'I'll certainly try to use that experience,' Stéphan says. 'Back in 2002, we were too comfortable and we didn't prepare properly. But by the time we realised, it was too late. Getting to the summit is great, but the hardest part is staying there. You have to keep the team fresh, make sure the motivation levels remain high, and keep on improving and improving.'

Complacency cost the French game dearly during the 2000s. In order to avoid another slump, Gérard Houllier insists the football development teams at Clairefontaine need to remain active. 'When things are going well there's a danger of thinking, "This is great, we don't need to change anything. Let's stick with the winning formula." But now is exactly the time that you need to change,' Houllier stresses. 'Above all, you need a strong technical director. He's the one who has to analyse the trends, predict how football will evolve, and adapt the programme accordingly. And of course he has to get that prediction right.'

Houllier's days as technical director of the FFF are over, but his passion remains and inevitably he has a clear idea of where he believes the game is heading. 'Football will continue to get faster and even more physical,' Houllier predicts. 'So France need to develop more Mbappés. But they mustn't only develop Mbappés,' he adds quickly. 'They must develop some Desaillys, Petits and Zidanes as well.'

The quality of the work being carried out by the current technical director, Hubert Fournier, will only become apparent in future years. For now, the onus is on Deschamps to keep his world champions on track and to try to create a lasting legacy. He has the necessary tools at his disposal, and in Kylian Mbappé France possess the most exhilarating talent in world football and a forward who is determined to make his mark on the history of the game.

• • •

Following *Les Bleus* over the past two decades has been a truly fascinating experience. Whether watching the brilliance of Zidane, Henry, Ribéry or Griezmann out on the pitch, or reporting on the latest meltdown off it, there has literally not been a dull moment. What has become clear is that the French national football team represents a deeply cherished institution in France. It carries an extraordinary power over the nation that brings great responsibility: when *Les Bleus* are winning France feels like a happy, united place. When they are not the image of an angry, fragmented society emerges.

Just as the 1998 win did not eradicate the many problems embedded in society, the 2018 triumph has not eradicated discrimination, crime and unemployment. Yet those victories brought pride and happiness to millions of souls; and with the likes of Mbappé, Pogba and Kanté – all brilliant black footballers from *les banlieues* – leading the charge in the current team, *Les Bleus* are doing more good to the image of France's immigrant youth and stigmatised suburbs than any politician ever could.

These are unquestionably exciting times for France fans. The dark, miserable days of player strikes, infighting and sex-tape scandals now appear to be a long way away. However, with *Les Bleus*, as we have discovered during the past twenty years of extraordinary highs and desperate lows, it is very difficult to predict what might be around the corner.

ACKNOWLEDGEMENTS

The first person I should thank for inspiring this book is Kylian Mbappé. Watching, reporting on and commentating on French football has been my passion for the last two decades, but only after witnessing Kylian against Argentina in Kazan did I feel the need to get this story down on paper. In 2018, this kid changed the entire rhetoric surrounding French football. The fact that my two little girls took such a shine to him – just like the majority of kids in France – may well have influenced me too.

I'm very grateful to my beautiful wife Éva. If we hadn't met in 2002, I probably wouldn't have stayed in France, let alone written a book about football here. The first time we met, she told me all about how she used to go to the Vélodrome to watch Jean-Pierre Papin and Chris Waddle during her childhood in Marseille. Straight away something told me I'd met someone special. Éva, as ever, has been fantastic over the past months, keeping me sane as I worked day and night to get this written in time for Euro 2020 (doh!). I owe so much, of course, to my wonderful parents, who, besides giving me love and support, encouraged me to pursue my passions for both French ladies and football.

My literary agent, Melanie Michael-Greer, has been fantastic.

Melanie was convinced the UK market needed a book on French football (she's surely right!), and I'm so pleased and flattered she wanted me to write it. Biteback Publishing have advised, encouraged and supported me throughout. Their enthusiasm and the confidence they expressed in me from the start was a constant source of strength. Special thanks to my editor James Lilford for all his positive feedback and helpful pointers. James would often tell me the copy I sent over was 'very clean', but this, in fact, was largely thanks to Chris Burke, one of my oldest and most loyal Paris friends, who proofread everything and spotted the many mistakes. Your help was invaluable, Chris!

I wanted this story to be told by the people who experienced it. So thank you so much to all the former and current players and managers who gave up their time to speak to me. Robert Pirès, in particular, was extremely helpful. If there is a nicer World Cup winner around than Super Bob himself, I'm yet to meet him! To have a foreword written by Arsène Wenger, a man I have admired for so long, is a true honour. Thanks to Darren Tulett and Sultane Icboyun for helping to smooth certain relations, and to Lionel Gauthier who eventually succumbed to my pestering and agreed to set up a meeting for me with Lilian Thuram, who, as I'd expected, proved to be compelling company.

Other journalists and authors have helped hugely. The book-writing machine that is Jonathan Wilson offered me the benefit of his wisdom (although in return I had to listen to him recount his latest cricket exploits in every minute detail). Amy Lawrence spoke so eloquently about Zinédine Zidane that I suggested she write the book for me. Luckily, she declined. Thanks to the fountain of knowledge that is Vincent Duluc, my good friend Joachim Barbier, Arnaud Ramsay, who I discovered is my neighbour, Ilyes Ramdani, Yvan Gastaut and the always forthright Daniel Riolo. I thought I already knew everything about French football, but your anecdotes proved otherwise and have given this book a level of depth and insight I could not have achieved without you.

Merci beaucoup, les amis!